MINOR TROUBLES

MINOR TROUBLES

RACIAL FIGURATIONS OF YOUTH SEXUALITY AND CHILDHOOD'S QUEERNESS

Erin J. Rand

THE OHIO STATE UNIVERSITY PRESS
COLUMBUS

Copyright © 2025 by The Ohio State University.
All rights reserved.

Library of Congress Cataloging-in-Publication Data
Names: Rand, Erin J., 1974– author.
Title: Minor troubles : racial figurations of youth sexuality and childhood's queerness / Erin J. Rand.
Description: Columbus : The Ohio State University Press, [2025] | Includes bibliographical references and index. | Summary: "Examines a series of public controversies regarding young people and queer sexuality in the US—adult concerns about teen sexting, the bullying and suicides of queer kids, trans youths' access to gender-segregated bathrooms at school, and sex education—to show that actions geared toward protecting the idea of childhood innocence come at the expense of real youth of color and queer, trans, and gender-nonconforming youth"—Provided by publisher.
Identifiers: LCCN 2024040462 | ISBN 9780814215814 (hardback) | ISBN 0814215815 (hardback) | ISBN 9780814284001 (ebook) | ISBN 0814284000 (ebook)
Subjects: LCSH: Youth—Sexual behavior—United States. | Sexual minority youth—Sexual behavior—United States. | Teenagers—Sexual behavior—United States. | Gender-nonconforming youth—United States. | Rhetoric—Social aspects.
Classification: LCC HQ27 .R36 2025 | DDC 306.7083/0973—dc23/eng/20241125
LC record available at https://lccn.loc.gov/2024040462

Other identifiers: ISBN 9780814259351 (paperback) | ISBN 0814259359 (paperback)

Cover design by Ashley Muehlbauer
Text composition by Stuart Rodriguez
Type set in Minion Pro

CONTENTS

Acknowledgments   vii

INTRODUCTION	Childhood's Queer Troubles	1
CHAPTER 1	Illegal Desires: The Sexting Panic and the Criminalization of Queer Black Girls	33
CHAPTER 2	Wounded White Boys: Figuring Queer Vulnerability to Bullying and Suicide	67
CHAPTER 3	Too Much to Tolerate: School Bathrooms, Trans Temporality, and Black Excess	106
CHAPTER 4	From Reticence to Abundance: Talking Back to the History of Sex Education	154
CONCLUSION	Refiguring Futures: Youth Innovations in Agency and Vulnerability	193

Bibliography   209

Index   231

ACKNOWLEDGMENTS

Although acknowledgments typically recognize the public contexts and professional colleagues that support and inspire our work, this is a project that began at home and remained, in many ways, very personal. I started writing this book in the midst of the simultaneous emergencies of the beginning of the COVID-19 pandemic and the un/expected news that my previous breast cancer had recurred and would require immediate and more aggressive intervention. Ongoing cancer care and complications (not to mention the long-term effects of the pandemic) would thwart my progress for the next four years, derailing my plans and my deadlines with relentless regularity. Through it all, my wife, Courtney LaMere, has been a steadfast advocate and essential source of fortitude. She miraculously acquired surgery recovery supplies during lockdown (nothing shows love like an entire case of graham crackers!), listened as I fretted endlessly about ideas, issued regular reminders that writing is sometimes nonlinear, and sustained me in so many other ways through the darkest moments of health and work. Put simply, neither this book nor I would be complete without her.

This project has been bolstered and enriched by so many others too. Jen Clary-Lemon and Rachel Hall both read early versions of every chapter and offered incredible feedback. As editors, critics, helpers, mentors, and friends, Angela Aguayo, Jonathan Alexander, Vanessa Beasley, Barbara Biesecker, Dan Brouwer, Rafael Cervantes, Emerson Cram, Rachel Dubrofsky, Suzanne Enck,

Leslie Hahner, Ashley Hall, Leslie Harris, Jo Hsu, Claire Sisco King, Jeffrey McCune, Timothy Oleksiak, Kendall Phillips, KJ Rawson, Stacey Sowards, Mary Stuckey, and especially Lisa Flores have offered encouragement, advice, and important critical insights throughout this process. Kats Mendoza and Cat Fribley have cared for me from afar. Jess Sims might be surprised to find herself mentioned here, but her affirmations hung on my wall and got me through some of the toughest bits.

I am especially grateful for the generosity of Kimberly Huggins, Brittany Brathwaite, and Antjuanece Brown, who took the time to talk with me and trusted me with their stories. The stunning image on the cover of this book is T. J. Brown's art, which he so kindly allowed me to use to represent the splendid excess and trouble of queerness. My ongoing connections with all of these folks have been one of the unanticipated delights of this project. As a small way of showing my appreciation for their contributions, I plan to donate any royalties from this book to the Q Center, a Syracuse, New York, organization serving LGBTQ+ youth.

I received financial support for this project through the National Communication Association's 2016 Karl R. Wallace Memorial Award and the 2021 NCA Mid-Career Scholars' Writing Retreat; additionally, the College of Visual and Performing Arts at Syracuse University provided a vital research leave and a Faculty Enrichment Grant. An early version of a piece of chapter 4 appeared as "'Black Women Deserve Great Sex': The Queer Generosity of KIMBRITIVE" in *QED: A Journal of GLBTQ Worldmaking* 8, no. 3 (2021): 169–76; a portion of chapter 3 was published as "'The Rosa Parks of the Trans Bathroom Debate': Gavin Grimm and the Racialization of Transgender Civil Rights" in *Quarterly Journal of Speech* 110, no. 1 (2024): 51–73. I appreciate those opportunities to advance my thinking with the help of excellent feedback from reviewers and editors.

Many years ago, I pitched a very different project to Tara Cyphers, and I am so glad she remained enthusiastic about the book that eventually emerged. It's been a circuitous path, and I appreciate her guidance as well as her patience through it all. Many thanks to everyone at The Ohio State University Press, including Kristen Ebert-Wagner, Ashley Muehlbauer, Samara Rafert, Stuart Rodriguez, Olivia Sergent, Meghan Tarney, and Elizabeth Zaleski; to my indexer, Holly Day; and to the three reviewers of this manuscript, for their labor and care with my words.

INTRODUCTION

Childhood's Queer Troubles

Arkansas Attorney General Leslie Rutledge faced a difficult task when she attempted to convince Jon Stewart that her state's ban on gender-affirming medical care for transgender youth—the first statewide ban of its kind—was a valid way to protect children. In her interview with Stewart on the October 6, 2022, episode of his show *The Problem with Jon Stewart*, she argued that some legitimate medical professionals have significant concerns about the benefits of gender-affirming care for trans youth.[1] He asked her repeatedly to name the source for her allegation, noting that the American Medical Association, the American Association of Pediatrics, and the Endocrine Society, among others, all offer guidelines for gender-affirming care as an empirically verified means of improving mental health outcomes for trans young people. When Rutledge could not produce the name of the organization that recommended against such care, nor explain why Arkansas legislators would contradict medical experts' advice, she instead resolutely asserted that the state's first priority is "to protect the children in Arkansas." Denying trans young people access to

---

1. I use the term *trans* throughout this book, following the lead of scholars like GPat Patterson and Leland G. Spencer, who contend that *trans* is "an intentional move to hold space for a range of gender expansive people—who may identify as trans, transgender, and/or transsexual, and who move through the world as men, women, nonbinary people, agender people, and other non/gendered positionalities." Patterson and Spencer, "Toward Trans Rhetorical Agency." In certain contexts, I also add "gender-nonconforming" in order to include other young people whose gender presentations exceed the expectations of the heteronormative and binary model.

potentially lifesaving care for gender dysphoria, in Rutledge's view, is a crucial way to preserve the innocence of youth—"Allow a child to be a child," she insisted.[2]

The reality is that gender-affirming care (including counseling, hormone blockers, hormone replacement therapies, and rarely for minors, gender-confirmation surgeries) is recognized by every major medical association in the United States as a medically necessary treatment for gender dysphoria. In addition to the mental health benefits that Stewart mentioned (which include decreased anxiety, depression, suicidal behavior, and psychological distress, and increased quality of life), gender-affirming care also offers trans youth social and legal benefits, such as more confidently navigating school and peer relationships, and being able to update the gender marker on their driver's licenses, school records, and other identity documents.[3] Not only is gender-affirming care obviously beneficial to trans youth, then, but the proliferating anti-trans discourse provoked by gender-affirming care bans and other anti-trans legislation has devastating effects on the mental health of LGBTQ+ youth, even when the proposed bills are not signed into law. A recent study found that trans and nonbinary youth report the greatest harms from such public debate, with 86 percent saying that they experienced a negative impact on their mental health, including feelings of fear and alienation, more experiences of bullying, and a diminished sense of safety in healthcare settings.[4] Truly caring for LGBTQ+ youth, in other words, must also mean allowing a child to be a trans child.

Rutledge's commitment to protecting children, therefore, is patently false: not only would her state's ban on gender-affirming care deprive Arkansas trans youth of potentially lifesaving medical and therapeutic interventions, but it also contributes to a hostile political climate that imperils all LGBTQ+ young people. As I write, the ban in Arkansas has been blocked by a federal judge who ruled it unconstitutional, but the state is appealing this decision and has also passed another law aimed at limiting access to gender-affirming care by criminalizing medical providers; meanwhile, twenty-one other states also ban or restrict gender-affirming care for trans minors.[5]

Thus, I open with this example not because it is uniquely injurious but because it is representative of the current public discourse about trans and queer young people in the United States and because it neatly illuminates two

---

2. "War over Gender."
3. "Outlawing Trans Youth."
4. Rummler, "State Laws Restricting Rights."
5. MAP, "Healthcare Laws and Policies."

of the animating problems of this book. First, Rutledge's claim to "protect the children" not only is a ruse for promoting legislative action that will cause harm to queer and trans kids but also provides cover for the racialized distribution of those harms. For instance, LGBTQ+ youth of color report higher rates of suicidal thoughts and suicide attempts than their white peers, making the interventions of gender-affirming medical care even more urgent for their survival.[6] Yet trans youth of color in states with gender-affirming care bans are less likely to have the resources to navigate complicated and constantly changing policies or to travel out of state to other providers. Black trans and gender-nonconforming youth, in particular, already experience more stigma in healthcare settings and more barriers to care than white young people; additional obstacles to gender-affirming care will only increase Black trans youths' disparities in mental health, social integration, and legal safeguards.[7]

Second, Rutledge's sleight of hand regarding the protection of children posits the limitation of rights as the means for security. Her assertion of childhood's essential vulnerability (where trans young people require the paternalism of the state to keep them safe from their own private medical decisions) forecloses childhood's potential agency (where trans young people express their knowledge of their own genders and seek, with their guardians' assistance, the medical care to which they are entitled). By substituting childhood vulnerability for childhood agency, Rutledge specifically and intentionally excludes trans youth from the protection she claims to offer. In other words, trans youth are sacrificed—their rights to private medical decisions violated, their ability to claim their own gender identities denied, the preciousness of their lives squandered—in the interest of maintaining the category of childhood's defining features of innocence and vulnerability.

This tension between agency and vulnerability will reappear throughout *Minor Troubles*, as young people's own characteristics—their gender nonconformity, their queerness, their Blackness, their sexual agency—cause trouble for adults' investment in the innocence of the category of childhood. As I will suggest, the racialized rhetorical figuration of the child, when it is instrumentalized in public deliberation, brings cultural ideas about the qualities of childhood into contact with the lives of real children, producing material consequences that are disproportionately harmful to youth of color and queer, trans, and gender-nonconforming youth.

---

6. Trevor Project, "2022 National Survey."
7. Goldenberg et al., "Stigma, Gender Affirmation."

Of course, while Stewart's interview with Rutledge provides a brief look at some of the central themes I explore, I could have begun with any number of other contemporary examples that also illustrate conservative unease with racial, gendered, and sexual difference in contexts involving children: legislation that prohibits discussions of LGBTQ+ histories and lives in schools, bans on books that feature anti-racist or queer-inclusive messages, prohibitions on education about systemic racism and critical race theory, accusations of "grooming" leveled at adults who teach sex education to minors, worries about drag queen story hours, and unfortunately many more. These controversies get their grip in the public imagination precisely because they target children, but also because race, gender, and sexuality are all flashpoints for cultural unease—especially when young people are involved. As Ian Barnard asserts, threats to the purity and sanctity of children "summon up apparently limitless reserves of unreflective fear, panic, anger, and hysteria," and those feelings constrain the possibilities for genuine debate.[8] To invoke hypothetically endangered children, then, is to make a virtually irrefutable argument that fallaciously but nonetheless efficaciously substitutes an emotional petition for rational deliberation. Whether or not the children in question are actually imperiled—by learning an accurate history of slavery, by using a classmate's proper pronouns, by reading a book with a queer protagonist—their imagined distress is instrumentalized as a call for adults to act.

In other words, the idea of the endangered child is a potent rhetorical tool—"a figure to be used, sometimes as a weapon," as Susan Jarratt puts it—that can be deployed strategically to justify policies that limit the freedoms of both young people and adults.[9] The controversies that we are witnessing today about race, gender identity, and sexuality are remarkable for the transparency with which the figure of the child is weaponized. However, this instrumentalization of childhood is far from unprecedented; rather, it emerges from the sedimentation of youthful vulnerability as a racialized characteristic, the construction of childhood as a repository of adult anxieties, and the mobilization of childhood as a means of maintaining systemic privileges and inequalities that have been decades and even centuries in the making.

Rather than lingering in the present moment, therefore, *Minor Troubles* moves into the recent past, engaging with a series of case studies from the early twenty-first century that produce the rhetorical possibilities of the present. In the following chapters I examine recognizable public controversies—adult

---

8. Barnard, "Rhetorical Commonsense," 4–5.
9. Jarratt, "Editor's Message," 1.

concerns about teen sexting; the bullying and suicides of queer kids; trans youths' access to gender-segregated bathrooms at school; and sex education—in order to trace how vulnerability and agency emerge through the racialized, sexualized, and gendered figurations of childhood (re)produced in each debate. For instance, the first chapter's discussion of the perceived technological menace of teen sexting in the 2000s demonstrates the disproportionate criminalization of youth of color and queer youth, and how the exclusion of Blackness inaugurates the vulnerability of childhood. In chapter 2's analysis of the media attention to the bullying and suicides of queer youth in 2010 and beyond, vulnerability is tethered to whiteness, masculinity, and queerness, and these assumptions of inherent vulnerability shape government policy and school programs. Chapter 3's close scrutiny of one community's debate about gender-segregated bathrooms in 2014 reveals the way childhood is figured according to normative temporalities of development and racialized understandings of transness, and how agency emerges in the disavowal of histories of anti-Black racism. And finally, in chapter 4 the racist and heteronormative aims of American sex education programs are resisted by a contemporary innovative program founded in 2014 that provides comprehensive sexual-wellness education for marginalized youth and presents an alternate version of vulnerability that enables rather than replaces youthful agency.

Reading across these cases, I examine the rhetorical figurations of youth that emerge. Drawing on queer and trans of color critiques of the whiteness of the figural child, I notice how the imagined qualities of childhood often obscure the material realities of actual living young people—especially youth of color and queer, trans, and gender-nonconforming youth. The whiteness of the figural child is crucial to its rhetorical clout, so I use the phrase *racial figurations of childhood* to foreground the fundamental role of racialization in childhood's instrumentalization. Racial figurations of childhood, I suggest, create strategic vulnerabilities, enable and limit agency, and generate material precarities for real young people through (often covert) racialized logics. The central argument of *Minor Troubles* is that when racial figurations of childhood are deployed in political discourse, the relationship between the figural and the material is rhetorical: the irresistible image of innocent white childhood depends upon the dehumanization of racialized youth, and through the process of rhetorical figuration, produces vulnerability and agency for real young people as its effects. That is, through the rhetorical process of figuration, cultural *ideas* about childhood and its characteristics come to justify policies, discipline behaviors, regulate identities, control knowledges, and determine interventions that shape the *realities* of the lives, bodies, and experiences of actual children.

Some Children Are Never the Future: The (White) Figural Child of Queer Studies

Queer scholarship on childhood takes the cultural taboo on children and sexuality—and especially children and queerness—not as a stifling constraint but as an impetus for provocative engagement. As Hannah Dyer suggests, childhood can be a "locus of anxiety" and a "dense site of meaning" that animates questions of queer sociality, alienation, and futurity, and sometimes serves metaphorically to understand the development of queer studies itself and as a resource for its growth.[10] Indeed, the figural child has occupied a foundational role in queer scholarship at least since the field's origin in the early 1990s, when, as Mary Zaborskis puts it, Eve Kosofsky Sedgwick's work in the inaugural issue of the journal *GLQ: A Journal in Lesbian and Gay Studies* invoked the child as "an enduring figure for the field to generate its theories and worry over its futures."[11] The sacralization of the child's purity imbues this figure with emotional capital that is both heavy with affect and unequally distributed.[12] To make queer contact with the figural child, then, is to dare to acknowledge queerness's abiding associations with various perversions related to childhood; it is to confront what Juana María Rodríguez calls the "discursive demons" that "haunt LGBT politics of respectability," to turn the threat of ignominy into critical vantage point.[13]

My claims about the racial figuration of childhood in *Minor Troubles* are situated generally within queer scholars' observations about the constraining political role of the figural child, but they respond more specifically to queer and trans of color critiques that the innocence and vulnerability so crucial to the figural child's cultural value are inextricably bound up with whiteness. The qualities of childhood that are said to warrant the concern and protection of adults, that is, cling only to particular kinds of young bodies because whiteness is the attribute through which childhood is defined. In this section I trace some of the foundational work on the figural child and the racial critiques it generated, and then turn to the central role of Blackness in defining childhood's boundaries. I end by positing childhood's troublesome queerness as its promise for the future. The racial figuration of childhood that I forward here is an attempt to put the (white) figural child invoked in public and political discourse in contact with the material realities of the racialized, queer, trans, and otherwise precarious children that it erases.

---

10. Dyer, "Queer Futurity and Childhood Innocence," 291.
11. Zaborskis, "Eve Sedgwick's Queer Children," 29.
12. Robinson and Davies, "History of Constructions," 8.
13. Rodríguez, *Sexual Futures*, 17.

One of queer scholars' most significant insights about childhood has been to notice how the child is mobilized in cultural discourse as queerness's limit: the child is a vulnerable figure innocent of sexuality and imperiled by queerness, thus pressed into use to justify anti-queer politics and policy. This perspective coheres around Lee Edelman's critique of "reproductive futurism," which structures not just the content of various political discourses but the very contours of the political itself. Reproductive futurism refers to the seemingly self-evident need to privilege the protection of a fantasy of the Child. The Child—capitalized to indicate that it refers to the image or figure of the Child, not to the experiences of any actual children—is imagined to be "immured in an innocence seen as continuously under siege" and requires the sacrifice of the queer and the reinforcement of heteronormativity to maintain its purity and vulnerability.[14] The Child, Edelman argues, regulates the political by requiring political discourse to invest in a collective future held out for the good of the Child, the ideal citizen and "fantasmatic beneficiary of every political intervention." When the terrain of politics is thus constrained by the terms of "fighting for the children," it becomes impossible to articulate an oppositional position.[15]

To refuse this mandate to value above all the imagined freedom of the figural Child is to pose a threat to the social order, and according to Edelman, is precisely what queerness can do to resist the constraints of reproductive futurism. The "real strategic value" of queerness, then, is in its resistance to what the Child figures: an unquestioned faith in the reproduction of a future envisioned for the Child, a future that must exclude queers.[16] Thus, Edelman's self-described polemical engagement offers the provocation that "*queerness* names the side of those *not* 'fighting for the children,' the side outside the consensus by which all politics confirms the absolute value of reproductive futurism."[17] He offers the intensely polarizing directive that acceding to rather than denying queerness's destruction of the social order is the only way to disrupt the endlessly heteronormative reproduction of the past in the future.[18]

While Edelman's figure of the Child and its role in sustaining reproductive futurism has generated a great deal of subsequent queer scholarship (a kind of future-oriented reproduction of its own), it is the queer of color critiques of his work that speak most urgently to the struggles and crises of childhood today and that activate my claims here. Queer and trans scholars of color have

---

14. Edelman, *No Future*, 21.
15. Edelman, *No Future*, 2–3.
16. Edelman, *No Future*, 18, 30.
17. Edelman, *No Future*, 3.
18. Edelman, *No Future*, 3.

objected stridently that the future Edelman envisions does not only exclude queers but has never been available to Black, Brown, and Indigenous people, poor people, people with disabilities, and so on. José Esteban Muñoz makes this point directly, noting the disavowal of Blackness in Edelman's work. He argues, "The future is only the stuff of some kids. Racialized kids, queer kids, are not the sovereign princes of futurity," and "all children are not the privileged white babies to whom contemporary society caters."[19] The problem is not that Edelman neglects actual children of color but that he does not recognize how the political dominance of reproductive futurism is also a reflection of the dominance of whiteness. Muñoz acknowledges Edelman's distinction between the futurity of the figural Child and the futures of actual children but contends that Edelman's "framing nonetheless accepts and reproduces this monolithic figure of the child that is indeed always already white." In other words, Edelman's figural Child restages whiteness as the universal norm and "hand[s] over futurity to normative white reproductive futurity."[20] As Tavia Nyong'o reminds us, the vision of the future that Edelman describes is a specifically white national narrative that attempts to pass itself off as a shared investment in the Child. Edelman's figural Child cannot account for what Nyong'o describes as the ambivalence and skepticism with which Black culture tempers its sentimentality about the Child, recognizing that the Black child is more likely to serve "as a kind of foil, always already streetwise, tough, precociously independent," to the purity of the (white) Child.[21] The figural Child also colonizes other nonwhite understandings of the cultural role of children. For example, Lester-Irabinna Rigney describes Indigenous views of children not as ideal, vulnerable citizens to be protected but rather as agents who act intergenerationally as "custodians of ancient and contemporary Indigenous knowledges" and "co-constructors of knowledge with their elders, families and community."[22] Even if the political deployments of the Child can appear in a variety of skin tones, then, the relationship Edelman presumes between childhood and futurity is characterized by whiteness.

Thus, the figural (white) child that structures national politics generally and controversies about young people and sexuality specifically does not reflect—and indeed, often actively obscures—the particularities of the marginalized children who are exempted from its protections. As Kathryn Bond Stockton explains, "it is a privilege to need to be protected—and to be sheltered—and thus to have a childhood." Racial and class privilege signal

---

19. Muñoz, *Cruising Utopia*, 94–95.
20. Muñoz, *Cruising Utopia*, 94–95.
21. Nyong'o, "Have You Seen His Childhood?," 52.
22. Rigney, "Aboriginal Child as Knowledge Producer," 580.

weakness and innocence, and are therefore central features of the "idea" of the child.[23] Therefore, it is not merely that children of color and queer, trans, and gender-nonconforming youth are excluded from the category of childhood, but in fact that their exclusion is precisely what defines the boundaries of the category. Their identities and bodies mark—and are marked by, often detrimentally, sometimes fatally—the margins of childhood, rendering its innocent vulnerability intelligible, lovable, and anodyne.

Building on and amplifying trans and queer of color critiques of queer scholarship on the figural child, then, I want to emphasize that any instrumentalization of the emotional capital of the (white) figural child is also a strategic manipulation of race. *Rhetorical* figurations of childhood, as I explain later in this introduction, are also always *racial* figurations of childhood. In other words, it is not just that race is one intersectional consideration of understanding childhood but that race is integral to childhood's rhetorical figuration. In the next section, I demonstrate that the whiteness of the figural child emerges specifically through its constructed relationships to Blackness. This is not, of course, to suggest that race is best thought in a Black/white binary or that other histories and practices of racialization on the bodies of children (such as the placement of Indigenous children in residential schools or the separation of Mexican children from their parents at the border) are not also key to the contemporary operations of the racial figuration of childhood. Rather, it is to note that the idea of childhood in the United States has been constructed historically in tandem with anti-Blackness. Due in part to the intimate and material relationships forged through practices of enslavement, colonization, and their legacies, Blackness thus occupies a central role in defining and troubling the boundaries of the category of childhood.

Ambivalent Blackness: Exiled from Childhood, Disqualified from Adulthood

The quality of innocence, understood as a lack of familiarity with the world and a perceived emotional and cognitive incapacity to deal with certain kinds of information or experiences, is a primary signifier of contemporary Western notions of childhood. Often treated as "a natural, inevitable, and universal aspect" of childhood, the association between childhood and innocence is, in fact, rhetorically and historically produced in the service of white supremacy.[24]

---

23. Stockton, *Queer Child*, 31.
24. Robinson and Davies, "History of Constructions," 7–8.

Meanwhile, the assignation to or exclusion from childhood has been a means of justifying the enslavement and dehumanization of Black people.

Black scholars and writers have long pointed out the devastating ways in which Black children are not perceived to embody the innocence associated with youthfulness and therefore are not granted the grace, compassion, and protection typically extended to children. These claims cut across scholarly and popular discourse, as well as a variety of institutional and historical contexts. For instance, Kristen Henning draws on her experience as a juvenile defender to describe the disproportionate criminalization of Black youth, who commit typical teenage offenses at the same rates as white youth, but for whom normal adolescent mischief is distorted into crime and deviance.[25] Likewise, Dorothy Roberts argues that the child welfare system produces a "thin line between dependency and delinquency" when it comes to Black children; rather than being treated as "innocent victims in need of protection," Black youth are considered "delinquents in need of discipline" and pushed deeper into entanglements with the state and systems of criminal punishment.[26] Therefore, institutions like the juvenile justice system and the child welfare system—both ostensibly designed to recognize the unique dependencies of children and shelter them from undue harm—do not merely safeguard youthful innocence but produce it along racialized lines. They strip the supposedly universal childlike qualities of innocence and vulnerability from Black youth, leaving them even more exposed to a range of violences, including those perpetrated by the state.

Recognizing that Black children are often denied the benevolent protection typically associated with childhood has led other scholars and writers to understand the involuntary sacrifice of innocence as the price Black youth pay for survival. That is, they describe Black children as having to give up the simplicity and naivete of childhood in exchange for an adultlike knowledge of the workings of white supremacy. As Audre Lorde puts it, Black children are "never allowed to be children," because learning to survive in an anti-Black world demands the surrender of innocence.[27] This sacrifice is even more stark for what Elizabeth Alexander calls "the Trayvon Generation"—those Black young people who have grown up witnessing the relentless repetition and mediation of the deaths of Black adults and youths. Such awareness of violence takes a toll on both Black children and their caregivers, who live with the truth that they cannot sufficiently protect Black youth, while recognizing that their own anxiety may contribute to stifling childhood's joy and exuberance. The

---

25. Henning, *Rage of Innocence*, 13, 241.
26. Roberts, *Torn Apart*, 251–52.
27. Lorde, *Sister Outsider*, 171.

Trayvon Generation, in other words, steeped in stories of "fear and futility" and the vulnerability and violence of Black life, has never had the privilege of childlike innocence.[28]

The impossibility of childhood innocence for the Trayvon Generation—and for the Black youth who populate this book—may be particular to the mediated spectacles of today's anti-Black violence, but its persistence is due in part to its deep historical roots, in which racism and capitalism entwine. That is, according to the property relations of the institution of US chattel slavery, Black youth acquired status as commodities rather than as children. As Saidiya Hartman contends, Black children were rendered "by-product[s] of the relations of production," dispossessed and conscripted to enslavement even before birth.[29] For Hortense Spillers, the treatment of enslaved children as property results in a disruption to kinship systems, whereby "'kinship' loses meaning, since it can be invaded at any given and arbitrary moment by the property relations," and where the familial status of the child is thus uncertain. The humanity of the child, she suggests, is instantiated through recognition by the mother; to detach the child from such kinship relations, then, produces calculated ambiguity regarding the Black child's status as human subject or as commodity object.[30]

Black youths' disconnection from innocence and humanity—from the idea of childhood itself—has been further normalized and popularized in the nineteenth-century figure of the "pickaninny," which served to maintain the dominance of whiteness after the abolition of slavery. This depiction of Black youth often included exaggerated features, partial nudity or raggedy clothing, and crucially, always exhibited immunity to pain or serious injury.[31] Robin Bernstein describes the pickaninny as a reaction, in part, to the efforts of abolitionists who had experienced some success in highlighting the physical and emotional suffering of enslaved people as a means of establishing their humanity. The falsehood of Black insensateness, when no longer tenable with respect to Black adults, was simply relocated to the bodies of Black children.[32] The repetition of representations of violence against Black children (through the ubiquitous insensate pickaninny in film, advertisements, plays, and children's books and toys) normalized the acts of violence, the Black child's apparent indifference to pain or distress, and the lack of consequences

---

28. Alexander, *Trayvon Generation*, 8–9; 68–69. I am indebted to Janae Kea's insights on Alexander's work.
29. Hartman, "Belly of the World," 166–68.
30. Spillers, "Mama's Baby, Papa's Maybe," 74–76.
31. Bernstein, *Racial Innocence*, 34–35.
32. Bernstein, *Racial Innocence*, 51.

for the perpetrator. When Black juveniles were understood to be invulnerable and to not suffer, then, it was impossible to see them as victims, or even as children at all.

But defining Blackness out of childhood would not have been complete without a corresponding positive association between childhood and whiteness; the racial figuration of childhood, that is, developed as a tool for defining and enforcing dichotomous racial categories. For Bernstein, whiteness is the hinge that links the characteristics of innocence and vulnerability to new understandings of childhood that emerged in the mid-nineteenth century. The association of (white) childhood with innocence coincides with the shift away from the Calvinist doctrine of original sin in the late eighteenth and early nineteenth centuries in the United States. Whereas children previously had been viewed as inherently sinful and in need of Christian salvation, by the early nineteenth century the notion of "romantic childhood," with its understanding of children as natural, uncorrupted blank slates, had taken hold.[33] This new vision of childhood, as Mary Niall Mitchell argues, imagined the innocence of white children largely in opposition to the "devilishness" of Black children, who were rendered as "tricksters of untamed and immoral stripe."[34] As sexual innocence and vulnerability came to be synonymous with white childhood, then, Black children's perceived strength and resilience did not merit the status nor protections of childhood. Girls and girlhood were central to this version of racialized childhood because while white girls were increasingly viewed as innocent, tender, and in need of protection, perceptions of Black girls emphasized their sexuality, maturity, and toughness; Black girls, in other words, were the foil against which the whiteness of childhood innocence was established. Thus, by the beginning of the twentieth century, the innocence of childhood—and humanity itself—became exclusively associated with the vulnerability of the white child.[35] This polarization of childhood and Blackness also helped make legible a Black/white racial binarism that further erased non-Black children of color.

However, although the denial of the qualities of childhood to Black children goes far to explain the whiteness of the category of childhood's need for protection, the dehumanization of Blackness can also be witnessed in a direct inversion of this logic. That is, Black people are also subject to violence and disenfranchisement insofar as they are consigned to the status of perpetual children and therefore disqualified from the rights of adults. As Toby Rollo explains, the idea of the subhuman child underlies both the principles of racialization and the structure of chattel slavery; this figuration does

---

33. Bernstein, *Racial Innocence*, 36–42.
34. Mitchell, *Raising Freedom's Child*, 68.
35. Bernstein, *Racial Innocence*, 36, 68.

not highlight the innocent and vulnerable characteristics of the figure of the child but rather its savage, uncivilized, and irrational qualities. Rollo asserts, "where Black peoples are situated as objects of violence, it is often precisely because Blackness is identified with a state of childhood and because the child is already understood as a perennial archetype of naturalized violence, servitude, and criminality."[36] For Rollo, then, being a child or being categorized as a child is certainly not a means of protection—it is a means for excluding certain subjects from full political and economic agency.

The association of Blackness with childhood is nowhere more explicit than in the scientific racism of the nineteenth and early twentieth centuries, which cast racial distinctions in terms of human development and family roles and justified both the colonization and enslavement of Black peoples. Understood as one of the "child races" within this racial hierarchy, Blackness thus came to represent the willfulness, the disobedience, the feralness of childhood, which required the paternalistic power of the colonizer to introduce civilizing order and discipline. Franz Fanon captures this violent guardianship of the white colonizer in terms of a maternal authority seeking to save a colonized population from "barbarism, degradation, and bestiality." This mother figure is not imagined to protect her "child" from external dangers but rather from its own perversity and "malevolent instincts," "from its ego, its physiology, its biology, and its ontological misfortune."[37] When the racialized other is understood as perpetually childlike, the enslaved or colonized subject is presumed to not possess the maturity and rationality to handle the responsibility of the full rights of adulthood. And unlike actual (white) children, who are designated as such by virtue of their age and who will eventually become adults, Black adults identified as children by virtue of their race have no hope of eventually claiming the rights of adulthood. Instead, the Black subject is understood to be perpetually childlike, ontologically disqualified from equal standing and self-possession.

Thus, whether Blackness is figured as a form of permanent childhood or always already precluded from it, the manipulation of the category of childhood serves to freeze Black children and adults within apparently fixed states of being, denying the possibilities for growth, development, learning, and temporal movement that characterize human agency. Blackness is suspended in an impossible temporality where Black youth are deprived of the safeguards and beneficence typically offered to children, while Black adults are confined to the subservience and dependency of childhood.[38]

---

36. Rollo, "Color of Childhood," 310.
37. Fanon, *Wretched of the Earth*, 149.
38. Breslow, "Adolescent Citizenship," 474.

At the end of the day, these seemingly contradictory positions regarding the racialization of childhood vulnerability—Black youth do not qualify for the privileges of childhood innocence but Black adults are denied the responsibilities of maturity—are rhetorical contrivances, or racial figurations, if you will, that serve white supremacy and colonialism. Both figurations have less to do with defining childhood and the boundaries of the category itself, and more to do with rhetorical dehumanization that justifies historical and contemporary anti-Black violence, leaving Black and other youth of color increasingly precarious. That is, anti-Black logics position Black people as either never children or always children, and childhood itself as a status that merits either protection or control; both can be equally and even simultaneously true, depending on their expedience. Thus, Black children can stand in for the wickedness and eroticism that is denied in innocent white children, while Black adults can be refused autonomy on the pretense of civilizing protectionism.

If Edelman's figural (white) Child is a symbol of the hope for the future that undergirds contemporary politics, then, it is on the backs of real Black children that such a future can be materially wrought. Indeed, not only are Black, Brown, and Indigenous children not incorporated into the vision of the future, but their physical removal, incarceration, erasure, and assimilation are often perceived as crucial steps in securing the desired (white) future of the nation. Children of color are subject to violent policies and treatment on the basis of race because childhood itself is a site at which colonial and national projects of subjugation are carried out. Blackness is thus pressed into service, playing a crucial and crushing role as whiteness's rhetorical ballast. My naming of the racial figuration of childhood throughout this book is one means for remembering that the child (and its corollary, the human) has been defined in opposition to Blackness, even as anti-Black rationalities ask us to forget this construction.

Childhood's Queer Desires

Up to this point I have been focusing on how the figural child represents queerness's limit—a figure rooted in anti-Blackness to be mobilized strategically on behalf of heteronormativity and white supremacy. But the figural child might also be understood to represent queerness's hope: embodying an inchoate eroticism that preexists sexual and gender socialization, the child's queerness exceeds and evades (with willful refusal or blithe disregard) cis- and heteronormativity's demands. The possibilities of childhood's queer desires become evident in the incongruity between the figural child (who is necessarily white, cisgender, and fundamentally but not yet heterosexual) and the actual lives of youth of color and queer, trans, and gender-nonconforming young people, whose embodiments, identities, and longings haunt the figural child's margins. That is, the racial figuration of childhood that excludes youth of color and queer and trans youth certainly limits their options for thriving within hostile or indifferent institutional contexts, but it does not and cannot fully determine their possibilities of existence. Ricky Gutierrez-Maldonado refers to this productive excess of Black and Brown, queer, trans, and gender-nonconforming youth as "too muchness"—that which escapes rhetorical capture because existing language cannot fully account for the multiplicity and vitality of their lives. Much like my own understanding of queerness, which I have elaborated elsewhere as an undecidability or indeterminacy that enables agency, Gutierrez-Maldonado posits queerness as a form of unintelligibility, "an unstructured flow that pushes and exceeds the discursive boundaries of sexuality."[39] Thus, while the overarching claims and the majority of the case studies in this book point to the ways that the figure of the child is deployed to the detriment of actual children—to constrain the possibilities of public deliberation, to reinforce white supremacy and cis- and heteronormativity, to restrict the agency of youth—the queerness of children is not so easily squelched.

To keep childhood's queerness humming through the following pages, I offer the neologism "hetero(non)sexuality" to point to the impossibility of "normal" childhood sexuality—impossible for all young people, but especially for youth of color and queer, trans, and gender-nonconforming youth. Hetero(non)sexuality refers to the contradictory demands identified by Steven Bruhm and Natasha Hurley that children should remain innocent of sexual desire and intentions (their own and others'), while also being tacitly and incipiently heterosexual.[40] Children are proto-heterosexuals, embodying the promise of future heterosexual normativity (as when adults refer to small children's mixed-gender friendships in romantic terms, stage photos of them in kissing poses, or adoringly accuse babies of being "flirts" or "heartbreakers"), but are expected to be fully ignorant of their desire and desirability until an "appropriate" age. Hetero(non)sexuality marks this unattainable dual mandate for children to be, as Stockton puts it, "not-yet-straight": delaying sexuality while simultaneously incubating a specific and narrowly defined version of sexuality.[41] My use of this term additionally asserts that adults ascribe the quality of hetero(non)sexuality to young people in order

---

39. Rand, *Reclaiming Queer*; and Gutierrez-Maldonado, "Lawrence 'Larry' King," 64.
40. Bruhm and Hurley, *Curiouser*, ix.
41. Stockton, *Queer Child*, 7.

to disavow children's but buttress their own agency, and that they do so by defining hetero(non)sexuality against the perception of the sexual precocity of youth of color and queer, trans, and gender-nonconforming youth. In other words, it is not just that queer, trans, and racialized youth seem to deviate from cis- and heteronormativity's prescribed path, but that those deviations are the condition of possibility for hetero(non)sexuality's production, as well as the perceived threat that creates its continued exigence.

Consequently, throughout this book runs an undercurrent of childhood's wonderous and sometimes odd queerness, which may take the form of any number of libidinous desires or embodied practices that cannot be accounted for within the limited taxonomy of adult sexual identities. I thus join those scholars who seek to read queerness in, rather than out of, childhood, who contend, like Bruhm and Hurley, that children are "*curiouser* than they've been given credit for" in our cultural stories that seek to contain them.[42] The queerness of childhood constantly troubles the coherence of the figuration of the hetero(non)sexual child, lurking just beneath its innocent surface; as Stockton puts it, "if you scratch a child, you will find a queer."[43] Indeed, childhood's queer desires might be said to be the condition of possibility for any coherent sense of sexuality (as heterosexual, asexual, bisexual, lesbian, gay, queer, or otherwise) to develop, whether in childhood or adulthood. In other words, the queerness of childhood is not opposed to heterosexuality but rather to the lack of desire (and desirability) upon which the figure of the child is premised; it emphasizes the strange yearnings and appetites of childhood, not necessarily coded as sexual but still sensuous and embodied and potentially erotic.

But I am also attentive to the fact that when children do not behave as adults anticipate, their queerness, their curiousness, their racialized excessiveness tends to be subject to discipline. When young people's gendered and sexual agency conflicts with adults' insistence on the innocence, nonsexuality, and vulnerability of white childhood, in other words, kids get in trouble. For Sara Ahmed, the "troublemaker" is one who gets in the way of the happiness of others or "who violates the fragile conditions of peace"; the troublemaker refuses to keep the peace because they will not acquiesce to the violence of the restrictive role to which they are assigned. In Ahmed's formulation, troublemakers are associated with desire, will, imagination, curiosity, and the promise of the unfamiliar; trouble, in other words, might be understood as a trace of queerness, a marker of when young people find themselves at odds with

---

42. Bruhm and Hurley, *Curiouser*, xiv.
43. Stockton, *Queer Child*, 1.

adult expectations and cultural demands for their naivete and incognizance.[44] Youth of color and queer, trans, and gender-nonconforming youth form what Steven Angelides calls the "troublesome shadow" of adult figurations of childhood, getting in the way of adults' faith in a childhood that is defined in terms of whiteness, purity, and hetero(non)sexuality.[45] The young people in *Minor Troubles* thus are often perceived to be endangered and in need of correction, but paradoxically also tend to embody the trouble in which they find themselves.

Importantly, the troubling and curious queerness of childhood in this book does not appear in literary or filmic representations or in fictional devices but rather in the actual bodies and lives of racially marked queer, trans, and gender-nonconforming youth. Childhood's queerness, in other words, emerges in part from the dissonance between the rhetorical figuration of the white and hetero(non)sexual child and the materiality of the Blackness, queerness, and transness of the young people who populate these pages. To locate queerness's promise in childhood's queer substance and desires is to reject the violence of the present or a white reproductive nationalist future as the only options; it is to hold out hope, alongside Muñoz and others, for "a 'not-yet' where queer youths of color actually get to grow up," a queer way of being in the world that sacrifices neither critique nor utopian political imagination.[46]

Malleable Meanings: Instrumentalizing Childhood Vulnerability and Agency

As the previous section demonstrated, the qualities of innocence and vulnerability—and indeed, the category of childhood itself—are anything but natural; instead, they are rhetorical constructs that convey cultural values regarding race and sexuality. The flexibility of the figuration of childhood enables it to be reformulated across various historical and political contexts, to change in response to the material circumstances of children, and to appear at the heart of a wide variety of cultural conflicts and anxieties.[47] Childhood, in other words, is a contingent designation whose rhetorical force emerges from its malleability. While the affective potency of the category of childhood may remain relatively constant over time, it is available to a variety of meanings

---

44. Ahmed, *Promise of Happiness*, 60–62.
45. Angelides, *Fear of Child Sexuality*, xiii.
46. Muñoz, *Cruising Utopia*, 96.
47. Duane, *Suffering Childhood*, 4.

and can be instrumentalized across a wide range of contexts. To imagine childhood in terms of future potentiality is, as Emerson Cram suggests, to understand children as the "matter" in an extractive regime to cultivate energy for the settler state. Cram's argument, which focuses on Canadian residential schools, highlights how "subpopulations" such as Native youth are viewed "as matter to extract and fuel settler futures," and points to how racialized, heteronormative, eugenic logics of civilization depend upon children as the raw material of nation-building.[48]

The malleability of childhood and its subsequent value as a cultural resource is partly due to the biological and psychological realities of childhood as a transitory stage of life: by definition, children are able to—indeed, expected to—grow and transform over time, becoming something other than they are currently. For Claudia Castañeda, the child's capacity as a "becoming rather than a being" or "an entity in the making" is exactly why it works differently from other categories of identity. Unlike the contrasting category of "adult," which is presumed to be more static, the child not only changes on its own (for instance, physiologically) but is also trained and disciplined into particular kinds of culturally mandated changes (through parenting, schooling, religious training, and so on) that are supposed to occur on a normative timeline. Therefore, the child is never complete or whole in itself, and as Castañeda argues, "it is precisely this incompleteness and its accompanying instability that makes the child so apparently available: it is not yet fully formed, and so open to re-formation."[49] If its incompleteness renders the child particularly open to redeployment, it also creates the possibility for multiple kinds of failures (not reaching certain benchmarks for physical and social growth and enculturation) and justifies myriad policies, programs, theories, and laws that seek to shape appropriate development.[50]

The malleability of childhood thus enables the strategic and inconsistent ascriptions of vulnerability that emerge across the case studies in this book. I suggest that differential assignments of vulnerability to young people is a crucial component of the (re)production of racial figurations of childhood, insofar as vulnerability is naturalized for the most privileged youth but disavowed in those who are the most materially precarious. Therefore, practices meant to shelter children from harm tend to consolidate the privileges of vulnerability in the bodies of white children, leaving queer youth and youth of color with neither the safeties promised to childhood nor the rights permitted to

---

48. Cram, *Violent Inheritance*, 101–5.
49. Castañeda, *Figurations*, 1–3.
50. Castañeda, *Figurations*, 4.

adulthood.⁵¹ The racialized privileges of weakness and vulnerability are thus built into the figural child, and they also take material form through a variety of protections, written into law, policy, and curricula, that shape the physical, economic, educational, and social contexts of childhood. Racial figurations of childhood, that is to say, exploit childhood's malleability, both depending upon and cultivating whiteness's exclusive claims to vulnerability.

Childhood's (white) vulnerability is most frequently and persuasively mobilized in public discourse when it is imagined to be at risk from an external agent of corruption, producing the figure of the dangerous, predatory adult as antagonist to the figure of the vulnerable child. Numerous scholars have argued persuasively that the imagined adult predator functions as a stimulus for asserting conservative values that recuperate the heteronormativity of the nuclear family as well as for securitization policies in which some bodies are constructed as always potentially criminal, and others as always potentially victimized.⁵² But even though the threat of the dangerous adult remains a perennial justification for adults to monitor young people's innocence (the current panics over drag queens and "groomers" are excellent examples), in this book's case studies the real source of adult anxiety about children and sex—though it is aggressively disavowed—is the myriad forms of racialized queerness *within* childhood. That is, I am interested in the way vulnerability is manipulated as a characteristic of childhood when adult demands for innocence bump up against young people's own articulations of their gendered and/or sexual selves or their own sexual expression or actions—what I have described in the previous section as childhood's troublesome queerness.

I treat the malleable category of childhood, therefore, as a site at which tensions between interdependency and independence, between relationality and individuality, between vulnerability and agency are negotiated. The rhetorical production of vulnerability, in other words, is entangled with agency—the agency of young people themselves, but also quite frequently in public discourse about children, the agency of adults. To manipulate the perceived vulnerability of the category of childhood, with all its affective authority and material implications, powerfully enables adults' capacity to act, regardless of the extent to which those actions are in the best interests of real children.

---

51. Stockton, *Queer Child*, 65.
52. Barnard, "Rhetorical Commonsense," 19; and Rodríguez, *Sexual Futures, Queer Gestures*, 32–33. See also: Fischel, "Transcendent Homosexuals," 296; Durber, "Paedophile and 'I'"; and Ohi, "Molestation 101," 196. As I have argued elsewhere, the criminalization of certain forms of sexual expression is often less effective at genuinely protecting children than at reasserting conventional sexual morality in the face of cultural and technological transformations. See Rand, "PROTECTing the Figure of Innocence," 251–72.

The tensions between vulnerability and agency that emerge from the racial figuration of childhood are evident in a variety of contexts where institutions deploy childhood vulnerability as justification for their actions. Wendy S. Hesford's work on humanitarian rhetorics and children's human rights illustrates one way in which the nation's international strength depends upon representations of childhood vulnerability. Hesford examines how governments produce and exploit the figure of the "child-in-peril" as a means to articulate humanitarianism's "moral ethos," as "a humanitarian proxy for and performance of political sovereignty," and as "a humanitarian cover for political violence."[53] Hesford argues that the "child-in-peril" is an effect of humanitarian rhetorics that confer a state of emergency and vulnerability based on certain children's perceived entitlement to qualities such as innocence and futurity—an entitlement that varies, of course, depending on race, class, gender, sexuality, disability, and citizenship. Much like Castañeda's characterization of childhood in terms of becoming or incompleteness, Hesford refers to the child-in-peril as a liminal subject which exists in a temporary state of ambiguous transition or transformation: between identities, between temporalities, between homes, or between life and death. The child's liminality, Hesford suggests, "operationalizes the humanitarian threshold as a site of political and moral struggle," therefore determining not only which children move international audiences to action, but also promoting the nation's humanitarian efforts as exceptional while obscuring their role in the systemic and historical production of the crisis.[54]

National and international rhetorics invoking childhood illuminate the way children function doubly as both objects and forces of socialization. Karen Sánchez-Eppler describes this dual role in terms of the relationship between *childhood* as a discourse, or "a rhetoric for the articulation of social norms," and *children* as actual persons who are impacted or even harmed by those norms.[55] These roles are often in conflict, producing a "disjunction between the rhetorical power of childhood and its lived precariousness." As an example of this fraught relationship, Sánchez-Eppler points to the American tendency to cynically make political claims supposedly in the name of the child while "consistently fail[ing] to support the daily needs of children, underfunding schools, dismantling welfare programs, refusing to grant children's voices an assured role in the institutions that most directly impact their lives, and generally disregarding the rampant juvenilization of poverty."[56]

---

53. Hesford, *Violent Exceptions*, 48, 199, 44.
54. Hesford, *Violent Exceptions*, 172, 44–45, 64.
55. Sánchez-Eppler, *Dependent States*, xxiii.
56. Sánchez-Eppler, *Dependent States*, xv.

Thus, the mobilization of childhood vulnerability can ignore—or even be used as a tool to actively obscure—the material precarities of actual young people.

This doubling of the role of childhood has implications for children's agency as it is manifest in legal rights, as well as for the boundaries of personhood and human agency more generally. For some, childhood is defined legally and institutionally primarily in terms of its restrictions on young people's freedom. For instance, Gill-Peterson suggests that minors are "subject to a specifically *infantilizing* form of governance" that deprives them of the ability to make decisions for themselves and limits their ability to act.[57] Likewise, Paul Amar contends that childhood involves a pernicious infantilizing refusal of agency that renders children as "spectacles of compelling innocence," "objects of emergency protection," and "hubs of 'securitization'" within specific historical, social, and material contexts.[58] Such infantilization can also affect other marginalized groups whose lives and experiences are made sense of through metaphors that compare them to children. For example, metaphors for women, Indigenous people, and enslaved Africans have compared each of these populations to children, with the effect of disempowering racialized, sexualized, gendered others while simultaneously reiterating children's essential vulnerability and lack of agency.[59]

Yet the agency of childhood, as it is exercised and/or refused across the chapters in this book, is never fixed; rather, it unfolds in fluid and ambivalent relation to vulnerability, with vulnerability sometimes foreclosing agency (as we saw in Rutledge's comments about trans youth in this introduction's opening anecdote), but at other times, vulnerability opening new possibilities for agency. Although children are often not granted the same rights as adults, the very qualities of children that disqualify them from the privileges and responsibilities of adulthood also make them eligible for a supplemental, conditional set of rights; as Sánchez-Eppler describes, the "dependent state" of children generates "the right of dependency, the right to care, protection, and guidance."[60] This second form of rights, a temporary remedy for childhood's perceived vulnerability, is defined differently and contextually in various cultures, locations, and historical moments, and is arbitrarily and inconsistently inscribed into institutions through legal designations of minor status and adulthood. This right of dependency is intended to dissolve when a young person reaches legal adulthood and is unique in that it does not confer a right

---

57. Gill-Peterson, *Histories of the Transgender Child*, 9–10.
58. Amar, "The Street, the Sponge," 571, 573.
59. Duane, *Suffering Childhood*, 4–5. See also McCann, "Lonely Young American."
60. Sánchez-Eppler, *Dependent States*, xxiv.

to act but rather a different kind of agency: a right to be less responsible for one's actions, a right to be consistently acted upon.

The vulnerability of childhood also enables the agency of adults insofar as controversies regarding young people's sexuality serve as a repository and site of resolution for adult desires—desires to maintain the fantasy of the idealized white, cisgender, hetero(non)sexual child, desires to deny the queerness of childhood that would threaten any clear distinction between children and adults, and desires to understand themselves as the guardians and saviors of the purity that childhood represents. As Katie Oliviero notes, adults hold affective, "sentimental" investments in childhood vulnerability: "its innocence embodies a sepia-tinged past for which we are supposed to long. The fact that we were all once children makes that past personal and tangible, sensationalizing it." Childhood vulnerability, Oliviero suggests, operates "as a placeholder, an effigy" onto which privileged adults can project their own feelings of precariousness brought on by the diversification of sexual cultures, changing norms of gender, and demands to grapple with racial inequalities of the past and present. Thus, imagining vulnerable children to save, whether earnestly or cynically, both "recuperates a sense of lost self" and recovers the fantasy of a prior national innocence.[61] Even queer adults may be invested in the pain and abjection of queer youth in order to imagine their present adulthood, in contrast, as a time of redemption and reward. A developmental narrative of queer adolescence, Susan Talburt suggests, recapitulates narratives of the progress of queer communities and politics—both of which are oversimplified as moving linearly from isolation to group identity to pride—and thus serves queer adults' desires for happy endings and political progress.[62]

I view the malleability of the category of childhood throughout this book as a generative resource that encourages us to consider the rhetorical production of vulnerability and agency. In Sánchez-Eppler's "dependent state" of childhood, for instance, we can see how the relationship between agency and vulnerability is inconsistent and manipulable: childhood vulnerability can be used to justify limitations or expansions of children's own agency, to make certain children intelligible as dependents who deserve adult protection, to empower adult or institutional actions ostensibly on children's behalf, or to restrict the freedoms of adult populations who are said to pose a threat to young people. While the malleability of childhood's meanings permit such disparate applications, the political potency of the racial figuration of childhood—in public discourse as depicted by adults—depends upon naturalizing vulnerability, not

---

61. Oliviero, *Vulnerability Politics*, 233.
62. Talburt, "Intelligibility and Narrating," 25–27.

agency, as childhood's defining characteristic. The more vulnerable the children are depicted to be, the more powerful the political claims made in their name. Children might be said to "act" most powerfully in public discourse, then, when they do not act at all: when they are at their most disempowered, when they are viewed primarily through the lens of endangerment, when they are imagined to have no agency of their own. Therefore, the political clout of the racial figuration of the child is realized through whiteness, hetero(non)sexuality, and gender normativity precisely insofar as it is opposed to a variety of racialized, sexualized, and gendered characteristics ineligible for the protections offered to the vulnerable.

Making Trouble, Solving Problems: A Rhetorical Approach to Figuration

I have been suggesting so far that when adults are confronted with the queerness of youth sexuality—which contradicts the imagined innocence of childhood—they manage that contradiction by deploying the racial figuration of childhood as a normative force. Figures of childhood do this work so powerfully by operating affectively to shape public discourse; they often are not articulated overtly, instead appearing only through their effects, functioning enthymematically to substantiate claims made on their behalf. In short, racial figurations of childhood are undoubtedly rhetorical, both arising from and creating material consequences through language practices. While the previous sections concentrated on the content of the figures of childhood—their queerness and racialization, their malleability and instrumentalization—this section turns to the rhetorical processes by which these figures are produced and reproduced in discourse.

For over two millennia, scholars of rhetoric have been concerned with classifying and defining various kinds of figural language, or "rhetorical figures," such as metaphor, alliteration, personification, hyperbole, and so on. While some have dismissed uses of figural language as mere stylistic flourishes, others treat them more seriously as inventional resources and epistemic structures that are characterized by logical patterns.[63] Although figurations of childhood certainly are shaped by figural language, my concern is more specifically focused on how "childhood," which purports to name a real state of existence defined by developmental chronology, comes to signify more flexibly and contingently, taking on cultural meanings and persuasive force that are

---

63. Poster, "Being, Time, and Definition," 116, 124.

detached from any actual children. Francisco J. Galarte illustrates this characteristic of rhetorical figures in his work with Brown trans subjects, where figuration is a means for "identifying the archetypal tropes that structure brown trans narratives and the effects that this narrative entrapment imposes upon trans subjects both living and dead." When Brown trans people are metaphorized through tropes rendering them sensational and consumable, the material and affective conditions of their lives are abstracted; figuration, for Galarte, is the critical tool through which to illuminate this process of exploitation and extraction and to foreground the agency that can emerge within the "slippages and shadows of discourse."[64]

Rhetorical figuration thus has both inventive utility and material consequences across myriad contexts. D. Robert DeChaine describes how the figure of the "border" in immigration discourse names an identifiable geopolitical site but is also an "organizing doxa" that concentrates public anxieties about the flow of migration and shapes attitudes about those who travel across it. Even when borders are mappable and undisputed, then, they are nonetheless "socially motivated constructs" that function as warrants for claims and inducements to action.[65] Philippe-Joseph Salazar emphasizes the interestedness and inducement of figuration even further, suggesting that figures are "calculations" or even "fictions" that are "aimed at producing persuasion and social action."[66] A number of rhetorical scholars have similarly considered the ways that everyday language comes to operate through culturally produced, ideologically loaded, and argumentatively impactful figures, tracing the deployment of the rhetorical figures of "unwed pregnancy," "white hipster masculinity," and "the pirate," to name just a few.[67]

I suggest that rhetorical figures of childhood are strategic and persuasive interventions in matters of public concern, to be sure, but also that they do even more specific work to assuage cultural anxieties and resolve social problems for adults. Here, I follow the lead of Bonnie Honig, who describes how the "figure of the foreigner" is a recurring "device" that appears in the classic texts used to legitimize Western democracy. Treating the figure of the foreigner as a rhetorical construction, she asks, "What problems does foreignness solve for us?"[68] This book thus similarly investigates how children serve as repositories for cultural anxieties about reproducing the social order; when

---

64. Galarte, *Brown Trans Figurations*, 13–17.
65. DeChaine, "Bordering the Civic Imaginary," 44–45.
66. Salazar, "Figures of the Republic," 244.
67. Adams, "Rhetorics of Unwed Motherhood"; Buerkle, "Adam Mansplains Everything"; and Mills, "Pirate and the Sovereign."
68. Honig, *Democracy and the Foreigner*, 12.

children cause trouble, they also solve problems, offering a means for adults to manage changing norms of sexuality, gender, and race.[69]

Rhetorical figurations are creatively fashioned and strategically manipulated, reflecting what Robert Asen calls "processes of collective imagining," in which participants collaboratively produce shared values and perceptions of groups and ideas through discursive interactions. These collective symbols can be explicit or implicit and work both descriptively and prescriptively, especially as they affect the implementation of policies and programs related to the groups being imagined.[70] Hesford notes that when certain figurations of childhood innocence become politically expedient, they "delimit public understanding of and responses to structural injustices," thus emphasizing rhetoric's material force and asserting the co-constitutive nature of the discursive and the material.[71] Or, as Castañeda argues, figurations have a "double force": simultaneously semiotic and material, they have constitutive effects and they generate circulation.[72] Figurations of childhood therefore serve a variety of interconnected functions, substituting an undeniable emotional appeal for rational deliberation, influencing or justifying policy decisions, distilling complex social transformations to simple terms, and standing in as proxies for larger anxieties about everything from expanding vocabularies for gender nonconformity to rapidly proliferating modern technologies to uncomfortable awakenings to systemic racism.

Throughout *Minor Troubles* I often use the term "figuration" rather than the more common "figure" in order to emphasize the *process* of figuration—the act of determining or reinforcing a recognizable form—over the *product* of the figure itself. Figuration refers to representing or making a likeness of something, constructing a figure, symbol, or "nonliteral form of speech"; it is the "action or process of forming into figure," or "the action of representing figuratively."[73] Rhetorical figures, I suggest, are always contingent responses to real demands, and as such are subject to modifications, novel applications, and reinvention as they are adapted across various contexts. As an act rather than an object, figuration also points to the agency of the speaker—not as the origin or inventor of the figure but in whose words the figuration proceeds, and as one who is implicated in the consequences of its circulation. Figures are never fully or finally constituted, always depending on repetition

---

69. Elman, *Chronic Youth*, 2–3; and Acland, *Youth, Murder, Spectacle*.
70. Asen, "Women, Work, Welfare," 286–87.
71. Hesford, *Violent Exceptions*, 22.
72. Castañeda, *Figurations*, 3.
73. Oxford English Dictionary, "figuration"; Merriam-Webster.com Dictionary, "figuration"; and Merriam-Webster.com Dictionary, "figure."

and reiteration to (re)produce effects, and therefore more precisely named by the continual and strategic act of figuration.

I am particularly invested in illuminating how rhetorical figurations of childhood are used strategically to assign vulnerability and enable agency specifically through racialized and sexualized logics; to emphasize the centrality of race to the (re)production of the category of childhood, I refer to rhetorical figurations of childhood as *racial figurations of childhood*. I use this phrase not to suggest a one-dimensional understanding of childhood viewed only through the lens of racialization (of course, gender, sexuality, class, ability, and so on are also crucial), but rather to insist on race and childhood as foundational designations through which *both* categories come to have cultural impact. As an advocate for what Lisa Flores has summed up in the frequently cited phrase "the imperative of racial rhetorical criticism," I offer *racial figurations of childhood* as a marker and reminder throughout this book that rhetorical figurations of childhood are animated by anti-Black exclusions and confer privileges associated with whiteness, while producing detrimental material effects for marginalized youth.[74]

My notion of the racial figuration of childhood clearly nods to Edelman's argument about how the figure of the Child shapes the political landscape and limits the positions available therein; however, while Edelman attends to the production of a (supposedly universal but already constituted through the privileges of whiteness) figure of a Capital-C Child, my concern is for the racialized production of multiple, contingent, flexible, and contextual figurations of lowercase-c children. It is this malleability of the figuration of childhood—not its universality—that makes it such a devastating tool of power: its meanings can shift to suit the most relevant categories of privilege, while the fundamental unquestionability of its emotional appeal remains intact.

Therefore, by centering the (re)production of rhetorical figurations of childhood as solutions to rhetorical problems that generate material effects, I suggest that the figurations of childhood in this book are transfer points between the symbolic functions of language and the material conditions of real children. In this way *Minor Troubles* makes a unique intervention into scholarly work on the child and its cultural significance. While queer scholarship on the child based in the humanities offers crucial insights into how the idea of childhood functions in public discourse as a means for upholding cis- and heteronormative sexual values, it tends to turn to literary and media texts as the source for figural representations of children rather than actual public discourse and policy, therefore reproducing the privileging of whiteness and

---

74. Flores, "Between Abundance and Marginalization," 5; see also Wanzer-Serrano, "Rhetoric's Rac(e/ist) Problems."

disregarding the lived experiences of queer and trans youth of color. On the other hand, education scholarship and other social scientific work on LGBTQ+ children focuses intently on the practical considerations of school policy, pedagogy and praxis, and institutional, community, and family arrangements; it centers real children, but as Meiners suggests, it may be less able to interrogate the "structures and systems that are written into these bodies and shape our wider landscapes."[75] My work in this project maintains its methodological footing firmly within rhetorical studies, but it also engages scholarship from education, childhood studies, sociology, legal studies, and other fields that examine real young people's experiences and the outcomes of relevant policies. I focus my attention at the point where these fields might be said to overlap: where figurations of childhood come into contact with the embodied and lived experiences of actual children. In other words, the racial figuration of childhood illuminates the child as a point of contact between the symbolic and the material—the malleable site of rhetorical articulation at which cultural ideas about race, sexuality, and youth are embodied and enacted.

Queer Troublemakers:
Reading Controversies in Youth Sexuality

Although *Minor Troubles* concentrates on adults' instrumentalization of racial figurations of childhood in controversies about youth sexuality, it also centers the experiences, lives, and/or deaths of the particular youths at the epicenters of those controversies. The young people who appear in the following chapters thus are not imagined, they are not fictional characters in literature, film, or television, and they are not interpretations of historical persons by analysts or theorists. They are actual young people whose stories have—in most cases, without their intention or consent—become public platforms for the negotiation of adult values about youth sexuality. They are also young people who, by virtue of being Black or mixed race, and/or being queer or trans or gender-nonconforming, bear the brunt of material betrayals of care.

These stories appear here because they are already in public circulation and seldom treated with the sensitivity they deserve, but I hope my own engagement can model an ethics of humanization and dignity.[76] As a white,

---

75. Meiners, "Problem Child," 138.
76. The Institutional Review Board at Syracuse University determined that my interviews with KIMBRITIVE and Antjuanece Brown do not meet the definition of human subjects research as defined by the Office of Human Research Protections (OHRP). In both cases, the interviewees gave explicit consent for their stories, their names, and their words to be included in this book.

queer, and these days mostly cis-passing author who was already well into adulthood by the turn of the twenty-first century, I do not pretend that I have access to the truths of the lives or experiences of these young people. But I do strive, at least in some small way, to give prominence to the ethical dilemma involved in recirculating (and in some cases, attempting to dismantle) public narratives that are not my own. Responding to Lisa B. Y. Calvente, Bernadette Marie Calafell, and Karma R. Chávez's call to action, I also recognize that my own positionality informs how I navigate these stories and that my perspective will always be partial, but it is nonetheless important that I add my voice to those leading the way "toward a process of decolonization."[77] I follow the guidance of Black queer scholars like E. Patrick Johnson and Bryant Keith Alexander, who urge researchers to engage in "critical reflexivity," which Alexander defines as recognizing "how we are always already complicit in the scholarly productions of our labor, and the effects of our positions and positionalities with the diverse communities in which we circulate." Critical reflexivity is especially crucial when crossing community boundaries, requiring humility and vulnerability in viewing research and writing as political and moral acts that "demand a clear sense of where we stand in relation to others, as well as the complications and implications of our actions."[78] As I move forward with care, I appreciate the wisdom of Marco Dehnert, Daniel C. Brouwer, and Lore/tta LeMaster, who help me to acknowledge that while these may not exactly be *my* arguments to make, because resisting racism and cis- and heteronormativity is the undeniable obligation of us all, they *must be my arguments*.[79]

To further emphasize the ethics involved in recirculating these narratives, I want to address two important points regarding naming practices and terminology. First, I have chosen to refer to all of the young people in this book, regardless of age, initially by their full names and thereafter by their first names. I make this choice in spite of my impulse—especially in cases where young people are cast as unqualified to know their own genders and desires—to underscore their rights and agency, to resist their infantilization, by granting them the formality conferred by surnames. But using first names is a humanizing gesture, reminding us that although these youths may be the subjects of media attention, legal decisions, and policy debates, they are also still youthful private citizens. Furthermore, first names are often a site of identity construction (especially in cases where trans and gender-nonconforming youth use

---

77. Calvente, Calafell, and Chávez, "Here Is Something," 204.
78. Alexander, *Performing Black Masculinity*, xviii–xix; and Johnson, "Put a Little Honey," 57–59.
79. Dehnert, Brouwer, and LeMaster, "Anti-Normativity under Duress," 319.

names other than the ones given to them), a form of personal expression that would be erased by representing them by their last names alone.

Second, the young people I feature range in age from tweens to early twenties, and the language used to describe them in the media, in policy documents, and in public discourse varies: they are called children, kids, adolescents, youths, teens, young adults, minors, and so on. Some of these terms obviously signify important distinctions in age categories and levels of maturity (e.g., children versus adolescents or teens), some offer legal designations (e.g., minors), and others (e.g., kids, youths, or even young adults) are more capacious and available for interpretation. But the particularities of any of these labels are less significant than, as Erica Meiners points out, their collective contrast with the category of adulthood.[80]

Thus, rather than attempting to pin down particular definitions for these words or adopting a rigid rubric for their use, I instead submit that the fuzziness of their borders, the slippages between them, and at times their interchangeability is an important aspect of how the racial figuration of childhood does its political work. That is, the nonspecificity and malleability of the categories allow adult fears about the corruption of childhood purity to move more promiscuously within and across discourses. Fears about the racialized sexualization of childhood can seep into arguments in unpredictable ways, revoking the quality of innocence from certain young people while ascribing it to others. To take two illustrative examples from chapter 3, Larry/Latisha King, a biracial, queer and gender-nonconforming fifteen-year-old, is accused of being sexually precocious just for performing their gender identity at school, while white, cisgender, presumably heterosexual teenage boys of the same age are cast as too innocent and fragile to share a public bathroom with a transgender classmate. Here, regardless of chronological or developmental ages, Larry/Latisha's biracial queerness is associated with an adultlike sexual awareness, while the cisgender boys are imagined with all the sexual naivete of much younger children. This slippage across terminology and chronology produces unequal access to the quality of innocence, and adult panic about youth sexuality is facilitated when the language of childhood, adolescence, and youth can slide freely across racialized referents.

In the chapters that follow, these young people's stories are woven through various cultural texts. I trace the appearance of racial figurations of childhood across multiple kinds of "official" discourses issued by powerful institutions (legal decisions, state and school policies, government guidance documents, court proceedings, scholarly research), as well as popular and vernacular

---

80. Meiners, "Problem Child," 125.

discourses (mainstream media coverage, popular culture, local community deliberations, education curricula, social media). The language of these different kinds of discourses intertwines, such that, for instance, legal documents reflect components of a shared "rhetorical culture" gleaned from popular and critical communication but also produce specific legal categories of persons who are positioned as a threat or who are to be protected from harm, which are then recirculated in subsequent media coverage and everyday talk and disseminated through local policies.[81] Reading across this variety of forms of public talk about youth sexuality demonstrates the multiple and interrelated sites at which racial figurations of childhood are constituted and deployed: they capture cultural anxieties about the supremacy of whiteness, heterosexuality, and traditional gender norms, and they also produce material effects in the world by, for instance, justifying policies about bullying and sex education, or being encoded into laws about sex-segregated bathrooms or sexting by minors.

The first two chapters of this book explore the production of vulnerability as a defining characteristic of childhood, highlighting how certain young people are excluded from or assigned to vulnerability. In chapter 1 I investigate the mass-mediated sexting panic of the late 2010s, using as a guide the story of Antjuanece Brown, a young Black woman who was prosecuted for sending consensual sexually explicit texts to Jolene Jenkins, her younger Black girlfriend. I suggest that adult concerns about teen sexting illuminate the gendered, racialized, and heteronormative assumptions upholding the innocence of youth. I examine the historical and contemporary adultification and hypersexualization of Black girls, especially as they produce racialized queerness as a scapegoat for adult anxieties about the sexualization of culture, and as they result in the disproportionate disciplining and criminalization of Black girls in general, and queer and gender-nonconforming Black girls in particular. I argue in this chapter that Antjuanece and Jolene demonstrate the founding exclusions of Blackness, female sexual agency, and queer desires that instantiate the vulnerability of the racial figuration of childhood. The category of vulnerability, that is, emerges as an effect of the dehumanization and criminalization of Blackness.

Building on chapter 1's assertion that vulnerability becomes available through its contrast with Blackness and queerness, chapter 2 describes how vulnerability comes to be occupied by whiteness. I turn to the deaths by suicide of nine cisgender adolescent boys in September 2010, which crystallized

---

81. Hasian, Condit, and Lucaites, "Rhetorical Boundaries of 'the Law,'" 326; and Canaday, *Straight State*, 216, 205.

a new mainstream awareness of the problems of anti-gay bullying and queer youth suicide. My analysis focuses on some of the ensuing federal recommendations and policy discourse that attempt to address the higher rates of bullying and suicide among queer youth, and it also takes up the scholarly work that offers critical perspectives on framing queer youth in terms of "risk" and "resilience." I suggest that the figure of the white cisgender gay boy, characterized by the privileges of white weakness and the performativity of contingent masculinity, appears as the epitome of queer susceptibility to harm and thus is imbued with vulnerability. Such a figuration of vulnerability not only obscures other material precarities of youth of color and queer, trans, and gender-nonconforming youth, but it also enables the agency of adults who imagine themselves as tolerant saviors.

The third and fourth chapters tease out vulnerability's relationship to agency, as it inheres in whiteness, as it is co-opted by adults, and as it is reimagined as a possibility for Black girls and other queer youth of color. Chapter 3 takes up the question of trans young people's rights to gender-segregated spaces at school. It focuses on two meetings of the Gloucester County School Board in 2014, where the community debated the rights of Gavin Grimm, a white transgender boy, to use the school bathroom that aligned with his gender identity. I identify two themes that emerged from this public deliberation: a skewing of the white normative temporality of childhood development that makes transness into a sexual threat, and an invocation and disavowal of Blackness as means for making white trans rights intelligible within a framework of racial discrimination. I argue that the racial figuration of childhood that emerges here enables adult agency to refuse the temporal distortions that trans identities are perceived to introduce, and to displace the racialized surpluses of transness onto a Blackness that is perpetually deferred. I end this chapter with the brief life of Larry/Latisha King, a biracial, Black-identified queer and gender-nonconforming teen who was murdered at school by a classmate. In contrast to Gavin's legal legibility, Larry/Latisha's Black and trans excesses are stifled, but they are also a condition of possibility for trans identity and for the figuration of childhood innocence.

Having painted a rather dismal portrait in the first three chapters of the racial figuration of childhood that dominates public discourse, chapter 4 offers an alternative example in KIMBRITIVE, a sexual-wellness program that reconfigures vulnerability and facilitates youthful sexual agency. I begin by tracing the ideological commitments of American sex education programs from the early twentieth century to today, demonstrating their tendency to advocate for abstinence, to promote a eugenicist model of the white, heteropatriarchal, nuclear family, and to deny female sexual desire. I suggest that

KIMBRITIVE "talks back" to the racist, sexist, and heteronormative assumptions of this history, offering instead a Black feminist version of sexuality education dedicated to the sexual wellness of Black women, girls, and femmes. KIMBRITIVE's "black feminist love-politics," I contend, centers the embodied and erotic experiences of women of color, promotes self-care as a radical community practice for marginalized people, and facilitates intergenerational relationships among Black women and girls. As such, KIMBRITIVE challenges both the substance and the style of speech presumed in sex education, emphasizing the processes of rhetorical invention through which childhood can be figured queerly as a site of embodied knowledge and agency.

The conclusion revisits the question of the figuration of childhood in the reproduction of the future, suggesting queerness as a resource for alternate innovations rather than a source of stigma and weakness, and Blackness as a site of possibility for imagining survival otherwise. Here, hoping that vulnerability and agency need not always be antagonists, I suggest the possibility for vulnerability as an agency of its own, where a kind of critical vulnerability—an openness to relationality with others—can be a source of empowerment and action. Calling back to the second chapter's attention to the construction of queer youth vulnerability through concerns for bullying and suicide, I offer a brief analysis of the Beyond Bullying Project, an unconventional strategy for supporting queer youth by centering their own agency, forms of identification, and relational possibilities. Recognizing that figurations of childhood are not static and universal, and that vulnerability may be a means for intimate connection as well as injury, we can imagine survival into Black and queer futures otherwise: where the queerness of childhood desires, delights, and astonishments are embraced rather than squelched, where Blackness is inseparable from queer relations, and where "allow[ing] a child to be a child" means fighting for racial, gender, reproductive, and sexual justice so that children can dream futures of their own.

CHAPTER 1

Illegal Desires

*The Sexting Panic and the
Criminalization of Queer Black Girls*

Jolene Jenkins was "moonstruck" when she met Antjuanece Brown on October 10, 2009, a date that she would mark in her calendar with "dozens of loopy hearts." Jolene, a sixteen-year-old high school student in Portland, Oregon, and Antjuanece, a nineteen-year-old call-center worker in a nearby town, met through mutual friends; the two young Black women were quickly smitten, began spending more and more time together, and eventually started dating. Their sweet relationship, in which both girls participated happily, responsibly, and consensually, might have been a model for queer teenage romance. However, their love story took a darker turn when Jolene's mother confiscated her cell phone and discovered that the girls had been sending each other flirtatious and suggestive texts and photos. She turned the phone over to the police and on October 12, 2010, Antjuanece was arrested. Because she was legally an adult and Jolene was a minor, the law was harsh: Antjuanece was indicted by an Oregon grand jury for the felony crimes of producing child pornography, luring a minor, and sex abuse.[1]

At the time of Antjuanece's indictment, the two young women had been in a relationship for a full year, all of the images and texts were exchanged consensually, and they were never publicly shared or disputed until Jolene's mother handed them over to the police. As it turns out, the district attorney of

---

1. Slovic, "Sext Crimes."

Antjuanece's county was known to be the most aggressive in Oregon in pursuing child pornography charges against young people; he defended his prosecution of Antjuanece even though other counties took a more lenient approach.[2] Although this application of the law was supposedly meant to protect Jolene as a minor, she vehemently opposed the charges brought against her girlfriend. An aspiring lawyer, Jolene dressed the part for Antjuanece's day in court, presenting herself with her characteristic maturity and self-assurance, and stating eloquently through her tears, "I feel victimized by the state, not [Antjuanece]." Jolene even set up a crowd-funded campaign to help pay off Antjuanece's fines and legal fees.[3] Jolene's mother, who put the whole case in motion, did not appear that day. Antjuanece's conviction thus did nothing to protect or vindicate the victim of a crime, or even to prove that such a victim existed. Instead, Jolene consistently presented herself as an agentive and consenting partner, and when she finally turned eighteen and achieved legal adult status, the two women had a joyful and much anticipated reunion and later began living together.

The troubling inequalities for racialized and queer youth that Antjuanece and Jolene's story reveals were highlighted by local journalists. For instance, Beth Slovic's cover story about Antjuanece for *Willamette Week* specifies that while Jolene's mother had not minded when she dated older boys (her previous boyfriend was four years her senior), she never accepted Jolene's relationship with Antjuanece.[4] Slovic stops short of explicitly naming homophobia as a motivating factor in the case, but in an article for qPDX.com, a queer news resource in the Pacific Northwest, Alley Hector argues more pointedly that anti–child pornography laws tend to arbitrarily target youth of color and queer youth, and urges, "Now it's our job to make sure that parental homophobia or a prosecutor's racism, bias, morality or zeal doesn't ruin the lives of other young people already struggling to cope, make connections and come out in such a dangerous world."[5] Blogger Brendan Adkins situates Antjuanece and Jolene's narrative in relation to his criticism of a recently passed Oregon state ballot measure that imposed mandatory minimum sentencing for those convicted of displaying a sexually explicit image of a minor. Adkins calls Antjuanece and Jolene "kids" who met, fell in love, and "had the misfortune to do so while on the bottom rung of every social ladder: female, gay, black, working-class and, crucially, young." He concludes acerbically, "Naturally it was in the best

---

2. Slovic, "Sext Crimes."
3. Adkins, "Being Aggressive"; and "Support Antjuanece Brown."
4. Slovic, "Sext Crimes"; and Brown, interview with author.
5. Hector, "Oregon Sex Crime Laws."

interests of the citizens of Oregon to throw one of them in jail."[6] Kate Kendall, an attorney and the executive director at the National Center for Lesbian Rights, called the outcome of Antjuanece's experience "appalling," and says, "I've never seen a case that was such a nauseating miscarriage of justice as what happened to Antjuanece Brown."[7]

Rather than an exercise in safety or justice for youth, then, Antjuanece and Jolene's case might be better understood in terms of its uneasy positioning within what Amy Adele Hasinoff refers to as a mass-mediated "sexting panic," fueled by the convergence of adult anxieties about digital technologies and youth sexuality and undergirded by pernicious cultural discourses of racism and cis- and heteronormativity.[8] It results in minors being ensnared by child pornography laws which were intended to protect youth, not prosecute them, and makes the private sexual interactions of teenagers the subject of adult public discourse. But the sexting panic also showcases white, hetero(non)sexual youth and shores up normative expectations about gender, race, and heterosexuality.

Even a cursory survey of the most circulated national stories about teen sexting reveals that the cases are remarkably similar to each other: generally, white, middle-class, heterosexual girls produce suggestive images of themselves, which are then distributed more widely (with varying degrees of malicious intent) by their white, middle-class, heterosexual boyfriends and/or platonic female friends.[9] In the context of this flurry of worry about teen sexting, it is striking that Antjuanece and Jolene's case was not picked up by a single national news source, in spite of it occurring at the height of the sexting panic and resulting in dramatic consequences for Antjuanece. Even after Michelle Maher, at the time a professor at Lewis and Clark College, produced a documentary about the couple and featured them in a mini-conference on the surveillance of racialized sexualities, their story was not visible outside of brief mentions in academic treatments of sexting—and then usually only as a counterexample to confirm the white, heterosexual, middle-class nature of the rest of the sexting panic.[10]

Antjuanece and Jolene, in other words, are significant to the sexting panic not because they are central to its expansion but rather because they are mostly erased from its history. Their disappearance is by design: the exclusion of their Blackness, female sexual agency, and queer desires instantiates the sexting

---

6. Adkins, "Being Aggressive."
7. Maher, "Unlawful Justice."
8. Hasinoff, *Sexting Panic*.
9. Hasinoff, *Sexting Panic*, 8.
10. See, for example, Karaian, "Policing 'Sexting'"; and McClelland and Fine, "Over-Sexed."

panic's racial figuration of childhood vulnerability and hetero(non)sexuality. Because they willingly engaged in sexting as an uncoerced expression of sexual agency as Black, queer, young women, they neatly reveal the sexting panic's conceit: at stake is not so much the actual harms that may befall teens who sext, but rather maintaining the racial figuration of childhood sexual innocence by emphasizing the vulnerabilities of privileged youth. Thus, vulnerability is a special dispensation for which not all youth qualify; young women like Antjuanece and Jolene are much more likely to be perceived as deviant troublemakers and risk-takers who are not entitled to sexual agency, whose consensual erotic pleasure is vilified, and who do not deserve to have their privacy protected. They are made intelligible in the context of the sexting panic only through the pathologization and criminalization of their consensual sexual expression.

This chapter is guided by Antjuanece and Jolene's absence from the sexting panic narrative. I weave bits of their story throughout my analysis, but I focus primarily on the structures that render them incomprehensible as sexual agents and as vulnerable youth: the racialized and gendered contours of the sexting panic and the discourse of sexualization, the adultification of Black girls, and the criminalization of queer youth of color. I argue that Antjuanece and Jolene demonstrate the founding exclusions that inaugurate the racial figuration of childhood vulnerability: Black female queer sexual agency is not just subjugated but pathologized and criminalized in order to render white hetero(non)sexual vulnerability legible. That is, vulnerability is instantiated as a characteristic of racial figurations of childhood, available to be occupied by whiteness, insofar as it is understood *against* Blackness.

I begin by describing the ways that sexting behaviors among young people have been taken up by researchers and popular discourse, and how the ensuing cultural panic has illuminated the gendered, racialized, and heteronormative assumptions about the supposedly natural innocence of youth. I pay particular attention in this section to how the "sexualization" of culture is blamed for girls' sexting, arguing that the scapegoating of racialized queerness produces the white, feminine, hetero(non)sexual vulnerability in need of protection. Next, widening my analytic lens beyond the specific context of the sexting panic, I explore the historical and contemporary figurations of Black girlhood that naturalize the hypersexualization and adultification of Black girls. I demonstrate that such dehumanizing figurations of Black girlhood have produced devastating effects by legitimizing the disproportionate punishment and incarceration of LGBTQ+ youth of color, especially Black queer girls and gender-nonconforming youth like Antjuanece. Finally, in an effort to reintroduce Antjuanece's dignity and personhood to this account, I end with a brief description of her life in the aftermath of her conviction.

Girls, Technology, and Sex:
The Racialized Contours of the Sexting Panic

Antjuanece and Jolene's relationship was technically in violation of both federal child pornography statutes and state age of consent laws. Antjuanece was indicted for producing child pornography, luring a minor, and sex abuse not because of her actual relationship with Jolene, but because of the suggestive photographic representations of that relationship in the texts the two young women exchanged. In Oregon, where the age of consent is eighteen, Antjuanece was also disallowed from having a sexual relationship with sixteen-year-old Jolene. The state law provides a defense from charges for relationships between adults and minors as long as their age difference is less than three years, but Antjuanece and Jolene exceeded this age difference by a scant three and a half months. The young women both vehemently maintain that they did not have sex; if they had, Antjuanece also could have been charged with statutory rape.[11]

Child pornography laws, unlike age of consent laws, do not make exceptions for consensual sexting between adults and minors or even for consensual sexting between two minors. It is illegal for anyone, regardless of age, to produce, possess, or distribute a sexually explicit image of a minor.[12] Federal child pornography laws apply to sexual depictions of minors under the age of eighteen irrespective of the age of consent set by individual states, and have been interpreted to apply not just to adults' creation or possession of child pornography, but also to youth-generated images such as nude selfies shared with other minors in the context of consensual sexting.[13] To be clear, this means that even if Antjuanece were also a minor, both she and Jolene could have faced child pornography charges. The confusion of overlapping state age of consent laws and federal child pornography laws is clearly illustrated by turning to Antjuanece and Jolene's neighboring state of Washington: the legal age of consent in Washington is sixteen, so a minor like Jolene could legally engage in sexual activity with a similarly aged partner. However, she could not legally consent to be the subject of a sexual photo; in fact, the same sixteen-year-old could face felony charges and fifteen to thirty years in prison for merely possessing an explicit photo of the minor partner with whom they were having legal and consensual sex.[14]

---

11. Oregonlaws.org; and Pirius, "Oregon Statutory Rape Laws."
12. US Dept of Justice, "Citizen's Guide." In some cases, it can be illegal to claim to possess child pornography even if no such images exist, or to suggest that an image represents a minor even if it does not. Rand, "PROTECTing the Figure of Innocence."
13. Primack, "Youth Sexting," 2918.
14. Albury and Byron, "Queering Sexting," 141.

These discrepancies between age of consent laws and child pornography laws demonstrate the ineffectiveness of child pornography laws to deal with teen sexting. Child pornography laws were written to protect minors from exploitation by adults; they were never intended to apply to (because legislators could not foresee the possibility of) minors sharing explicit images of themselves.[15] That is, child pornography laws cannot account for young people's sexual agency, and they penalize rather than protect consensual sexual expression. As some youth advocates have pointed out, bringing young people into contact with the criminal justice system, forcing them to register as sex offenders, and labeling them child pornographers may conform to the letter of the law (which prohibits sexually explicit images of minors) but clearly contravenes its spirit (to safeguard minor subjects from harm and trauma).[16] As John Humbach puts it, "something is profoundly amiss when a system of laws makes serious felony offenders of such a large proportion of its young people." The injustice is only multiplied by the fact that only a select few are prosecuted for a "crime" that so many youth commit.[17]

Antjuanece's case underscores the devastating material consequences of the clumsy and discriminatory application of child pornography laws to youth sexting, as well as the discrepancies in punishment of racialized and queer youth. She faced six years in prison and mandatory registration as a sex offender if she were to be convicted of the charges against her. Rather than going to trial, Antjuanece chose to plead guilty to the lesser crime of luring a minor because although it is still a felony, this crime does not require sex offender registration. In the end, Antjuanece was relatively lucky that the terms of her sentence were not as severe as they could have been: three years of bench probation, $3,000 in court fees, and no contact with Jolene until she turned eighteen. However, because she could not afford her $50,000 bail, she had already spent over a month in the Washington County jail, which she described as "horrible." She says, "I got called a child molester," and "I was told I should kill myself. We were only allowed out of our cells six to eight hours a day. It was lonely and scary." Additionally, her conviction resulted in losing her job at the call center, which would not employ felons, and jeopardized her dreams of one day becoming a children's social worker.[18]

While Antjuanece and Jolene are certainly not the only young people to find their lives upended by ordinary adolescent expressions of sexual desire, their story brings into stark relief the rhetorical effects of the sexting panic.

---

15. Davis, "'Sext' Education."
16. Davis, "'Sext' Education"; and Humbach, "'Sexting' and the First Amendment."
17. Humbach, "'Sexting' and the First Amendment," 438.
18. Slovic, "Sext Crimes."

That is, the sexting panic is a site at which vulnerability is constructed against Blackness, queerness, and female sexual agency, and where the rhetorical figuration of childhood puts legal and public discourse in contact with the racialized, gendered, and sexual bodies and lives of young people. This rhetorical work is accelerated by the sensationalistic and alarmist tone adopted in mainstream media attention to teen sexting. Thus, informed more by social anxieties than by reason, the public conversation about teen sexting might be best understood as what researchers call a "media panic." Building on the notion of moral panics, a media panic specifically refers to apprehension about new media forms and suggests that mass media incites and proliferates public reactions. In other words, media coverage does not necessarily *reflect* the objective importance of an issue but instead can *cultivate* the public's perception of importance, and in the case of the sexting panic, media coverage also forwarded what would prove to be its indelible association with child pornography.[19]

Technological advancements ranging from the emergence of cinemas to the introduction of home telephones to the advent of the internet have often been a site of concern about the perceived loss of parental control over children, and the ability of young people to independently seek entertainment and pleasure. As Lippman and Campbell note, media panics "tend to focus on the effect new technologies have on youth, who are portrayed as vulnerable and in need of protection."[20] Media panics thus cast youth as barometers of social unrest; they symbolize larger ideological struggles piqued by new technologies and position young people as the site of endangerment.[21] In the case of sexting, the digital technologies that enable teens to easily take and send explicit photographs with cell phones seems to pose an outsized threat not only to young people's safety and privacy but also to sexual morals and the social order. As an expert quoted in a 2009 article arguing that the panic is "overblown" puts it, "Sexting is the latest way adults are getting panicky about teen sexuality and for mainstream culture to get panicky about technology. . . . And when you mix the two together, there's always a lot of anxiety and misunderstanding."[22]

The concern about sexting in the United States began in 2008 when the results of a "Sex and Tech" survey by the National Campaign to Prevent Teen and Unplanned Pregnancy were widely reported in newspapers nationwide. That survey found that 20 percent of teenagers had sent or posted a nude or

---

19. Podlas, "'Legal Epidemiology,'" 22–23.
20. Lippman and Campbell, "Damned If You Do," 371.
21. Draper, "Is Your Teen at Risk?," 222.
22. Berton, "Are Lots of Teens 'Sexting'?"

seminude photo of themselves.[23] Subsequent studies have produced a wide variety of statistics on the prevalence of teen sexting, with results ranging from only 2.5 percent to as much as 40 percent of adolescents reporting that they had ever sent a sext, and as many as 31 percent of teens reporting that they had received a sext from a peer. The discrepancies are related to, among other factors, the definitions of "sexting" used (e.g., whether it includes only cell phone transmission or any digital communication, and whether sexual language without images is counted as sexting), the age and other demographic features of the young people surveyed, and how likely respondents were to admit to a behavior that meets with such intense social disapproval.[24] Black and LGBTQ+ youth, as well as youth who are sexually active, are more likely to admit to sexting, although this may better reflect a difference in their willingness to report sexting activity than a difference in actual frequency.[25]

Some of the scholarly research on sexting follows the lead of the media panic about sexting, utilizing a "risk" framework, in which the primary concern is the potential for harmful outcomes of sexting (such as unprotected sex or negative impacts on mental health). But other scholars employ a "rights" or "social justice" framework, focusing on sexting as sexual expression and taking a more critical approach to not just the findings of the various surveys but also the surrounding public discourse and assumptions about teen sexuality and technology.[26] For example, Hasinoff understands teen sexting as an exercise of adolescent sexual agency and an instance of intimate communication that must be negotiated in relation to the new questions of consent and privacy introduced by technological innovations. She points out, for example, that since sexting is often discussed in relation to other social problems such as cyberbullying among adolescents and online political scandals and leaked celebrity photos among adults, it is presented as a public problem with wide-ranging dangers rather than as a potentially harmless form of sexual exploration. Furthermore, the application of child pornography laws to teen sexters not only "makes sexting *seem* more dangerous and deviant" but also, as Antjuanece can attest, quite literally defines it as a criminal act.[27] Even when experts oppose bringing child pornography or other serious charges against

---

23. "Sex and Tech."
24. See, for example: Lippman and Campbell, "Damned If You Do," 372; Humbach, "'Sexting' and the First Amendment," 436–37; Hasinoff, *Sexting Panic*, 173n1; and Lorang, McNiel, and Binder, "Minors and Sexting," 73.
25. Lorang, McNiel, and Binder, "Minors and Sexting," 74; and Karaian, "Policing 'Sexting,'" 286.
26. Setty, "Rights-Based Approach"; Dir et al., "Understanding Differences"; Dobson, "Sexting in Context"; and Van Ouytsel et al., "Sexting."
27. Hasinoff, *Sexting Panic*, 1, 14; emphasis added.

teens who sext, it is still usually taken for granted in mainstream media that sexting is foolish, "stupid," and "wrong" and that the frequency of teen sexting can and should be reduced; in other words, sexting rarely appears as a normal means of sexual exploration or a legitimate form of adolescent sexual expression.[28]

Although surveys of sexting behavior show that boys and girls engage in sexting with roughly equal frequency, the sexting panic highlights adolescent girls' creation and distribution of images of themselves. As Hasinoff explains, adult concerns about youths' production of sexual images focuses nearly exclusively on girls, whose behaviors are cast as "irresponsible and out of control." Meanwhile, adolescent boys are not perceived to be at similar risk: if adults worry over the sexual perils of digital technology for boys, it is to be concerned with their access to pornography, rather than their creation of it. These perspectives on teen sexting obviously reinforce the double standards of a binary gender system and compulsory hetero(non)sexuality, where teenage boys' sexual activity is expected, considered a normal part of growing up, and even praised, while girls' sexual activity is criticized, treated as a danger to be avoided, and shamed.[29]

Unable to imagine sexting as a valid or healthy form of sexual expression for girls, the very possibility of female sexual agency and desire is treated as a problem in the sexting panic. As Hasinoff puts it, "the reason boys or adults sext often goes without saying: sexual desire and communication. But for girls, the reason somehow does not seem so simple." Instead, digital technologies are imagined as "dangerous catalysts" that "threaten to destroy even the most strong-willed girl's valiant attempts to resist and delay sexuality."[30] Adults believe their "hapless teens are merely falling victim to the national disease of sexting rather than engaging in it voluntarily," and that if it were not for external pressures to sext, girls would avoid—or at least delay—becoming involved in sexual relationships of any kind.[31] Thus, sexting is understood in terms of girls' deficiencies or weaknesses, which might include, for example: girls' vulnerabilities to the damaging influence of new technologies and their inability to withstand the draw of the latest digital trends; girls' biological immaturity and lack of self-discipline, which leave them unable to control their impulses or anticipate the repercussions of their actions; or girls' psychological shortcomings, such as low self-esteem or susceptibility to peer pressure. By this logic, girls' sexting behaviors cannot be understood as articulations of desire,

---

28. Hamill, "Students Sue Prosecutor"; and Berton, "Are Lots of Teens 'Sexting'?"
29. Hasinoff, *Sexting Panic*, 57.
30. Hasinoff, *Sexting Panic*, 57.
31. Hasinoff, *Sexting Panic*, 64.

as meaningful forms of personal expression, or as means of pleasure, but only as a "problem" arising from personal inadequacies or as evidence of their failure of sexual restraint. Crucially, as Hasinoff argues, whether this "problem" is treated sympathetically or pathologically has everything to do with adult assumptions about sexuality, race, and class.[32]

Girls are not only expected to control their own sexual urges; they are also held liable for others' violations of trust and digital etiquette. When a girl's private images are received by and nonconsensually distributed by another party (often a girl's friends, current or former boyfriend, or in Jolene's case, her mother), it is frequently the girl who is blamed for creating and sending the images in the first place, even if she did so with the understanding that those images would be kept private. As Lara Karaian puts it, this is a form of victim-blaming in which "teenage girls are responsibilized for managing not only their own potential experiences of humiliation, sexual violation and criminalization, but also the criminalization of their peers."[33] The self-control expected of a consensually sexting girl, in other words, is not similarly expected of those who do not restrain themselves from nonconsensually forwarding her nude photos.[34]

Since sexting is presumed to be the result of coercion and insufficient self-confidence, anti-sexting campaigns often frame abstaining from sexting as the only truly "free" choice available to girls. For instance, Karaian describes a Canadian "internet safety initiative" called "Respect Yourself," which purports to teach adolescents—all adolescents, regardless of gender—about the risks of digital sexual expression and the dangers of sending or posting sexual images or videos. But the initiative's target audience, she points out, is the girls who consensually create and send sexual images, not the boys who are statistically more likely to nonconsensually forward or redistribute them.[35] Thus, Karaian reads the campaign's call to "respect yourself" as a demand for girls to abstain from sexting by asserting personal boundaries and learning to say no, based on the assumption that girls would never willingly, enthusiastically, or autonomously say yes to such sexual expression on their own.[36] This duplicity, in which female sexual expression is framed only in terms of the strength to say no, is common to anti-sexting programs; as Hasinoff explains,

---

32. Hasinoff, *Sexting Panic*, 13.
33. Karaian, "Policing 'Sexting,'" 284.
34. Hasinoff, *Sexting Panic*, 150. Hasinoff suggests rethinking the "problem" of sexting by centering questions of consent in the distribution of private information.
35. Karaian, "Policing 'Sexting,'" 286; and Peskin et al., "Prevalence and Patterns of Sexting."
36. Karaian, "Policing 'Sexting,'" 287–88.

While appearing to promote empowerment and free choice, the kind of sexual agency this offers to girls is quite narrow: It gives girls the power to say "no" to sexuality but also the obligation to do so. Refusing sexual advances requires and asserts a kind of power, but without genuine choice about whether or not to refuse, the campaign barely offers girls any agency at all.[37]

Therefore, the responsibility for the sexting panic falls squarely on the shoulders of adolescent hetero(non)sexual girls, who are the site of an impossible contradiction: they are accused of being duped by the influences of media and their peers, they are blamed for foolishly distributing sexual images of themselves without anticipating future violations of their privacy by the recipients, but they are also denied the agency and sexual desire that might motivate their choices to sext or not to sext, or for that matter, to make any other sexual choice.

The Sexualization of Culture and the Racialization of Vulnerability

When girls' own desires cannot be imagined as the source of their sexting activities, the blame must fall elsewhere on some external influence; one of the most frequently invoked culprits is the so-called sexualization or pornification of culture. The discourse of sexualization points to the onslaught of hypersexualized media messages that suggest that women's value is defined primarily in terms of sexual appeal, physical attractiveness, and objectification by others, and that promote an excessive, public, and commercialized female sexuality. The sexualization of culture impacts everyone, but it is the influence of sexual media content on children—girls in particular—that most troubles adults. The worries over sexualization are evidenced by an abundance of both popular and scholarly texts published between 2005 and 2010, such as Pamela Paul's *Pornified: How Pornography Is Transforming Our Lives, Our Relationships, and Our Families,* Feona Attwood's *Mainstreaming Sex: The Sexualization of Western Culture,* Diane E. Levin and Jean Kilbourne's *So Sexy So Soon: The New Sexualized Childhood and What Parents Can Do to Protect Their Kids,* and M. Gigi Durham's *The Lolita Effect: The Media Sexualization of Young Girls and What We Can Do About It.* These authors worry that the "toxic mix" of sexual media and commodities, which introduces girls to mature content they are too young to consume, will goad them into practices of self-objectification

---

37. Hasinoff, *Sexting Panic,* 93.

and lead to unhealthy relationships and issues with physical and emotional well-being.[38]

The discourse of sexualization, like the sexting panic, does not acknowledge any healthy role for sexuality or even any ability to make choices about sexuality for girls. The "problem" of sexualization is actually a construction by adults which does less to protect girls from real harms than it does to manage adult anxieties about the eroticism of children.[39] Indeed, imagining girls as victims of media's inescapable sexualization denies them any agency or critical media literacy of their own—their media consumption is assumed to be passive rather than willful, such that they are perceived to be unable to consent to, reject, or otherwise interact with or manipulate media messages. As R. Danielle Egan contends, the sexualization panic "unwittingly creates a vision of girlhood that can only ever be damaged, sexualized, and self-subjugating."[40] The widespread worries over the victimization of girls, in other words, ends up producing that victimization as an essential component of the meaning of girlhood. In the remainder of this section I explore the discourse of sexualization through one of its most recognizable and infamous objects—Bratz dolls—in order to emphasize the racialized logics through which this panic gets its grip. The sexualization discourse, as both context and impetus for the sexting panic, is a key site at which racialized female sexual agency is framed as an unspoken threat and the vulnerability of white, hetero(non)sexual girls is naturalized.

The popular concern regarding the sexualization of culture in the early 2000s was taken seriously enough that the American Psychological Association (APA) created a Task Force on the Sexualization of Girls. According to the task force's 2007 report,

> in the current environment, teen girls are encouraged to look sexy, yet they know little about what it means to be sexual, to have sexual desires, and to make rational and responsible decisions about pleasure and risk within intimate relationships that acknowledge their own desires. Younger girls imbued with adult sexuality may seem sexually appealing, and this may suggest their sexual availability and status as appropriate sexual objects.[41]

The APA report argues that sexualization leads to a range of negative consequences for girls, including body dissatisfaction, low self-esteem, depression,

---

38. Egan, *Becoming Sexual*, 2.
39. Egan, *Becoming Sexual*, 17, 48.
40. Egan, *Becoming Sexual*, 47.
41. APA, "Report on the Sexualization of Girls," 2.

and diminished cognitive ability, and that being exposed to objectifying messages hinders their ability to develop a sense of themselves as sexual beings during adolescence.[42]

Without a doubt, it is easy and tempting to single out media messages as a primary influence that corrupts girls' innocence, leading them to become promiscuous and emotionally stunted. There is no shortage of affectively compelling and seductively self-evident examples of early 2000s television and film, music videos and lyrics, video games, advertising, consumer products, and other forms of media that seem to contribute to the sexualization of girls. These include a variety of distasteful objects, including teen magazines offering advice about how to solicit male sexual attention; advertising that blurs the lines between girls and adult women (where girls are made to look sexily mature and women to look sexily childlike); the influence of "hot young stars" like the Spice Girls, Britney Spears, and Christina Aguilera who offer provocative lyrics, choreography, and styles for girls to emulate; and sexualized slogans on girls' clothing ("eye candy" and "wink-wink" on bras and panties, or "so many boys, so little time" on T-shirts).[43]

But no other piece of popular culture or single consumer product in the early 2000s provoked such concerted adult panic as Bratz dolls. Adult unease coalesced so fervently around these plastic toys that they have become metonymically linked to the idea that young people were degraded and impaired by sexual media and products. The APA report, for example, names Bratz dolls "dressed in sexualized clothing such as miniskirts, fishnet stockings, and feather boas" as one of the worrying components of sexualization, while Levin and Kilbourne lament girls playing with Bratz dolls, "dressed in sexually revealing (or practically non-existent) clothing," to put on fashion shows or pretend to go on dates.[44] Although it may seem unrelated to sexting, I want to pause for a moment with this fixation on Bratz dolls as a pivotal instrument in the sexualization of girls because it reveals something crucial about the role of sexualization in the sexting panic: namely, adults' distress about Bratz is as much about the race and class implications of the dolls as it is about their sexual appearance. Bratz dolls offer a material representation of the threatening racialized sexuality that must be condemned, that is, in order to shore up the vulnerability of white femininity in the sexting panic.

---

42. APA, "Report on the Sexualization of Girls," 34.
43. APA, "Report on the Sexualization of Girls," 4–14; and Levin and Kilbourne, *So Sexy So Soon*, 45, 42.
44. APA, "Report on the Sexualization of Girls," 7, 13; and Levin and Kilbourne, *So Sexy So Soon*, 31–32.

When Bratz dolls debuted in 2001, they were distinctive not only for their hip and sexy streetwear fashion but also because of their racial diversity: the original line of four dolls included a white doll, a Black doll, an Asian doll, and a more ambiguously racialized doll who could be read as Latina, Filipina, South Asian, or mixed race. The representation of racial difference and the emphasis on urban-inspired fashion are what made Bratz appealing to girls: in contrast to Barbie's traditional white aspirational femininity, Bratz offered a more relatable version of contemporary youthful femininity and sexual empowerment. Lisa Guerrero contends that Barbie's feminine subjectivity is "tied to the traditional middle-class values of home, family, and career," but the focus of Bratz is on "pleasure and indulgence" among a group of friends who highlight the "performative possibilities" of femininity (as tomboys, punks, sports stars, and so on) and who are free of domestic, familial, or employment responsibilities.[45] As Guerrero argues, the racial diversity of Bratz dolls simultaneously makes them available for wider identification, while also reifying racial stereotypes (by using eye shape and lip size as recognizable markers of racialization, for example). The dolls' racial difference is what signifies their "hipness," so that race becomes a form of fashion that can be commodified but disconnected from real-world consequences of racial identification.[46] Indeed, as Angharad N. Valdivia argues, the dolls are strategically racially muddled, all of them looking "possibly and ambiguously" Latina, precisely in order to signal a marketable racial otherness without the specificity of actual racialization.[47]

Even though the racial characteristics of Bratz were commodified, their value for the young people who play with the dolls should not be ignored; indeed, for girls of color, Bratz's racial characteristics may be more salient and compelling than their sexualized clothing and may produce unanticipated forms of agency. For example, in an observational study, Rebecca C. Hains notes that Black girls drew on the affordances of Bratz's racial diversity to act out histories of racism and slavery and to narrate their own experiences of everyday race relations at school. Hains describes the girls designating two Black dolls as "slaves" using the Underground Railroad to escape to freedom, and agreeing to pretend their clothes were "raggedy" rather than cute and fashionable. In short, even if the marketing of Bratz commodifies their sexual provocativeness and racial ambiguity, Hains suggests that children may find in these characteristics the ability to "create new scripts not intended by

---

45. Guerrero, "Can the Subaltern Shop?," 191.
46. Guerrero, "Can the Subaltern Shop?," 189–90.
47. Valdivia, "This Tween Bridge," 99.

the manufacturer" and not predicted by adults.[48] The single-minded focus on girls' vulnerability to Bratz's sexual pollution, then, obscures their possibilities for enacting racialized and gendered forms of agency and discovery.

It is precisely this intersection of racial difference and sexual expression in Bratz dolls that raised concerns for media critics, educators, psychologists, parents, and scholars of popular culture. Some critics have observed, for example, that Bratz look "at home on any street corner where prostitutes ply their trade" or like "pole dancers on their way to work at a gentlemen's club." Media scholar M. Gigi Durham recalls seeing a girl dressed as a Bratz doll for Halloween in an outfit that "projected a rather tawdry adult sexuality" and evoked a memory of "a child prostitute [she] had seen in Cambodia."[49] The frequent invocations of sex work to describe the Bratz aesthetic speaks to the impossibility of female sexual agency outside the framework of a cis- and heteronormative market economy: to dress provocatively cannot be read as an independent assertion of self-confident eroticism but is understood only within a transactional context and denigrated as such. Most importantly in relation to the larger discourse of sexualization and its impact on sexting, however, the racial difference of Bratz dolls plays a significant role in adults' perception of their sexiness. As Lisa Orr notes, the stereotyping of women of color as hypersexual and exotic is deeply engrained in Western culture, so the race of Bratz dolls "stands as one more signifier for sexy."[50]

While there is a great deal more complexity to the broader cultural phenomenon of Bratz dolls than I can address here, I see it as both a touchstone of the discourse of sexualization and an illuminating model for how sexualization serves as an alibi for race, class, and queerness in the sexting panic. Bratz dolls cause trouble for adults because their markers of raced and class otherness (their phenotypical differences and their edgy streetwear styles) are read as sexual excess—an excess that is imagined to be not merely expressive but persuasive, impelling girls to mimicry. Unlike baby dolls that train girls in the practices of mothering or Barbies that model a glamorous and refined version of white femininity, Bratz dolls offer a grittier kind of gendered and sexual agency that celebrates racialized and alternative gender performances. They defy Barbie's narrow view of femininity through the ambivalent commodification of the aesthetics of Black and Brown communities. To claim that Bratz dolls sexualize girls, then, is to fear girls' exposure to the hypersexualization,

---

48. Hains, "Afternoon of Productive Play," 132, 136.
49. LaFerla, "Underdressed and Hot"; Talbott, "Department of Marketing"; and Durham, *Lolita Effect*. See also Lamb and Brown, *Packaging Girlhood*; and Womack, "Generation of 'Damaged' Girls."
50. Orr, "'Difference That Is Actually Sameness,'" 24.

the queerness of gender performativity, and the economies of sexual trade associated with racialized women's bodies. Likewise, these fears define the vulnerability of the girl who would be corrupted by such exposure through her innocence of such characteristics; in other words, vulnerability takes shape in white hetero(non)sexuality precisely insofar as it is defined against these racialized threats.

Of course, no one directly blames Bratz dolls for girls' sexting activities, but the discourse of sexualization is central to the sexting panic, and both formations of adult angst depend upon an imagined sexual excess that takes a specifically racialized figuration. Egan suggests that sexualization discourse operates according to a scapegoating logic, whereby the innocence of certain white, presumably heterosexual girls is perceived to be in danger, while racialized, working-class, and queer girls are perceived as sexualized and damaged, the site of the sexual danger, and thus further marginalized.[51] Whether expressed in concerns about Bratz dolls or about teen sexting, race need not be explicitly named in order to (re)produce the figuration of youthful vulnerability through the antagonism of racialized hypersexuality. The desirable and supposedly natural state of naivete and innocence in girls—and the panic about protecting their delicate sensibilities from the dangers of sexting—is thus only available for white, hetero(non)sexual, middle-class girls, and this vulnerability is constructed through its opposition to racialized queerness and hypersexuality and articulated through the veiled language of sexualization.

Strategies of Exclusion: Figurations of Black Girlhood

The popular worry over the sexualization of girls demonstrates that the association with innocence conferred by the racial figuration of childhood warrants both leniency and protection for hetero(non)sexual white girls.[52] Meanwhile, the treatment of queer Black youth like Antjuanece and Jolene reveals some of the flexible and strategic ways in which childhood and its privileges are figured and deployed according to racial logics. Since the sexting panic is built on the presumption of the vulnerability of the white hetero(non)sexual girl, in this section I elaborate on some of the specific rhetorical figurations of Black girls—and queer and gender-nonconforming Black girls in particular—that disqualify them from adult protection but bolster their apparent need for heightened discipline. Namely, the adultification and hypersexualization of

---

51. Egan, "Sexualizing Girl Troubles."
52. Meiners, *For the Children?*, 3.

Black girls, stereotyped and sedimented throughout history, are mechanisms through which Blackness is not just devalued but dehumanized, and therefore strategically positioned as vulnerability's antithesis.

The caricatures of Black womanhood—the asexual and self-sacrificing Mammy, the promiscuous Jezebel, the domineering Sapphire, the emasculating Matriarch, the deviously progenerating Welfare Queen—are easily recognizable archetypes of US American racism. Each of these stereotypes defines Black womanhood in terms of sexuality, reproduction, and motherhood, denying Black humanity and, as Dorothy Roberts argues, highlighting the "incurable immorality" of Black women. Roberts contends that Black motherhood's "corrupting tendency" is also blamed for damaging Black children, who are interchangeably marked by race, poverty, and drugs, and are presumed to be predisposed to criminality, "inevitably consign[ed] . . . to a worthless future."[53] Within this white supremacist logic, Black girls are burdened with the indictment that they are the result of their mothers' reckless reproduction and with the destiny to embody the next generation of Black female degeneracy. These myths of Black female sexuality shape not only representations in popular music and cinema but also public policies about issues like welfare, health and reproductive justice, controlled substances, and child-rearing.[54]

Black girls thus have very limited options for agency and self-actualization, especially when it comes to sexual expression. As Nikki Jones describes, "good" Black girls who want to avoid being perceived as "ghetto" "must manage their interactions and gender displays in ways that mirror mainstream notions of appropriate femininity and challenge stereotypical notions of Black femininity."[55] Specifically, "good" Black girls "do not look or act like men or boys," "do not run wild in the streets," "are appropriately deferential to the men in their lives," and "are not sexually promiscuous, nor are they anything other than heterosexual."[56] To be a "good" Black girl, then, requires performances of white femininity coupled with constant vigilance to avoid any resemblance to the stereotypes of Black femininity. Indeed, teachers' criticisms of Black girls, whom they tend to perceive as "loud," "defiant," "precocious," and "unladylike," clearly call out girls' failures to properly conform to the expectations of white femininity by invoking the characteristics of the Jezebel and the Sapphire.[57] The agency of Black girls is thus severely constrained: any assertion of

---

53. Roberts, *Killing the Black Body,* 8, 20. See also Hill Collins, *Black Feminist Thought,* 70–78; and Harris, "'Whores' and 'Hottentots,'" 253–57.
54. Morris, *Pushout,* 115–16.
55. Jones, *Between Good and Ghetto,* 48.
56. Jones, *Between Good and Ghetto,* 48–49.
57. Morris, *Pushout,* 11.

will or perceived youthful misbehavior is read in terms of racist stereotypes of adult Black women and disciplined without the leniency usually accorded to childhood.

The blurring of Black womanhood and Black girlhood is also complicated by the tendencies to view Black girls as being older than they actually are and to hypersexualize their bodies and their actions. The age compression of Black girls means that they are treated more like adults than children and perceived to be willingly engaging in adult behaviors such as parenting or sexual activity. Monique Morris characterizes this compression as "both a reflection of deeply entrenched biases that have stripped Black girls of their childhood freedoms and a function of an opportunity-starved social landscape that makes Black girlhood interchangeable with Black womanhood."[58] The propensity to view Black girls as always already mature is, as we saw in the previous section, one of the linchpins in defining the threat of sexualization: while white hetero(non)sexual girls are vulnerable to the impending dangers of being prematurely sexualized, Black girls (and Black queer and gender-nonconforming girls, especially) physically and metaphorically embody that danger, no matter their actual age, stage of sexual maturation, or sexual activity.

Researchers first identified these patterns of age compression, which they refer to as "adultification," in Black boys, noting that because Black boys are seen as less "childlike" than white boys of the same age, they are often misperceived to be older than their peers of other races and more culpable for their actions. Behaviors that might be understood as childish carelessness or youthful indiscretions in white boys are read through fantasies of Black masculinity as willful, destructive, irrational, and violent. Thus, Black boyhood is always framed through racist fears of the menacing Black man.[59] As a result, as Phillip Atiba Goff et al. describe, Black boys are "prematurely perceived as responsible for their actions during a developmental period where their peers receive the beneficial assumption of childlike innocence." The adultification of Black boys has been found to be linked to the implicit dehumanization of Blackness and, more specifically in criminal justice contexts, to racially disparate police violence toward Black boys.[60] Indeed, Aneeta Rattan et al. note that the law usually offers some protection to minors by viewing them as less culpable for their actions and therefore less deserving of severe punishment than adults. However, they contend that Black youths have a much more "fragile" claim to juvenile status in legal settings because the cognitive association between

---

58. Morris, *Pushout*, 34.

59. Breslow, "Adolescent Citizenship," 483; Dancy, "Adultification of Black Boys"; and Vargas and James, "Refusing Blackness-as-Victimization," 196.

60. Goff et al., "Essence of Innocence," 540.

Blackness and criminality in American culture can override the assumption of youthful innocence.[61] The devastating consequences of denying the innocence of childhood to Black boys can be witnessed most explicitly, of course, in the murders of young people such as Trayvon Martin and Tamir Rice, and most recently Ryan Gainer, all of whom were described by their killers as embodying the physicality and the threat of adult Black men.[62]

Studies of adultification began with Black boys because of their overrepresentation in the criminal justice system, but Black girls also experience similar forms of adultification. A study entitled "Girlhood Interrupted: The Erasure of Black Girls' Childhood," by Georgetown Law Center, found that compared with white girls of the same age, Black girls are viewed as needing less nurturing, protection, support, and comforting, being more independent, and knowing more about sex and other adult topics. The adultification of Black girls begins as early as five years old and continues through age nineteen; the most significant differences in the perception of Black and white girls occurs in mid-childhood (ages five through nine) and early adolescence (ages ten through fourteen), which are critical periods of identity development.[63] Just as it does for Black boys, the adultification of Black girls "contributes to a false narrative that [their] transgressions are intentional and malicious, instead of the result of immature decision-making—a key characteristic of childhood."[64] This misunderstanding of Black girls as more intentional in their misbehaviors and more knowledgeable about the consequences of those behaviors is one of the factors contributing to their teachers viewing them as "defiant" and "precocious" and to their disproportionate disciplining in schools and contact with the juvenile justice system. The authors conclude that Black girls thus do not have the same opportunity to learn and grow from their mistakes that white children are afforded.[65]

While the adultification of Black boys tends to view them through the lens of violent Black masculinity, the adultification of girls occurs at the intersections of racism and sexism, through the hypersexualization of their bodies and actions. The hypersexualization of Black womanhood is rooted in a historical myth that helped to justify the enslavement of Black women: understood as inherently licentious, sexually insatiable, and immoral, Black women were thought to require the control of their white enslavers but to deserve none of the respect or protection that white women were offered. Mitchell

---

61. Rattan et al., "Race and the Fragility."
62. Levin, "'Talented, Goofy Kid.'"
63. Epstein, Blake, and González, "Girlhood Interrupted," 1, 8.
64. Epstein, Blake, and González, "Girlhood Interrupted," 6.
65. Epstein, Blake, and González, "Girlhood Interrupted," 6.

asserts that the slave economy also demanded that the sexuality of Black girls be overt: since the value of enslaved Black women depended in part on their fertility, even prepubescent Black girls were evaluated at sale in terms of their imminent sexuality.[66] Thus, the sexualized bodies of Black girls, in which the future sexuality of the mature woman is collapsed into the current body of the girl, have long been seen as objects for judgment, use, and possession.

Today, as the age of the onset of puberty in Black girls has dropped dramatically since the mid-twentieth century (25 percent of Black girls now begin developing breasts by age seven), the sexualization and stereotyping of their bodies has only intensified. Trends in early maturation have been tied to chemicals in everyday consumer items such as dairy and meat, plastics, pesticides, and beauty products, and the exposure to the negative effects of these chemicals is known to be distributed along lines of race and class.[67] In other words, the adultification and hypersexualization of Black girls does not occur only through stereotyping and cultural myth but takes material form when their future reproductive capacities are exchanged as chattel or when the development of their bodies is disproportionately modified by capitalism's toxic residues.

As a consequence of adultification and hypersexualization, Black girls are not imagined to be vulnerable to the sexualization of culture or its objectifying media messages, because they already embody the racialized sexual threat from which white hetero(non)sexual girls must be protected. Black girls are presumed, like Black women, to be "unrapeable," to possess adultlike knowledge and experience with sex, and to find their bodies being objectified and policed by adults. For example, Morris cites multiple examples of Black girls who were reprimanded for being in violation of school dress codes while wearing garments identical to those of their white peers. Clearly, the lesson being taught to these girls is that regardless of what they wear, their Black female bodies are "too sexual" or "distracting"; the adult vigilance of their bodies both performs and perpetuates the objectification of the sexualized Black female body.[68] The girls Morris talked to also reported that sexual advances from adult men, even when those men were fully aware of the girls' ages, were commonplace. As Tressie McMillan Cottom chillingly describes, simply existing in a Black young woman's body is understood as offering consent to attention or overtures from adult men, such that "puberty becomes permission."[69] Regardless of their age, size, body type, clothing choices, or

---

66. Mitchell, *Raising Freedom's Child*, 80.
67. Henning, *Rage of Innocence*, 103.
68. Morris, *Pushout*, 124–28.
69. Cottom, *Thick and Other Essays*, 184.

behavior, then, Black girls are vulnerable to being objectified and sexualized unwillingly, and their assertions of youthful agency, read through the limiting stereotypes of Black womanhood and the adultification of Black girlhood, are perceived as defiant and immoral.[70]

Black youth like Antjuanece and Jolene are therefore granted neither the innocence of childhood nor the rights of adulthood. Adolescence—not quite childhood, not quite adulthood, defined by temporal suspension—illustrates the underlying queerness of the expected developmental chronology of maturation: it highlights the ambivalence of protection and punishment. As Kristin Henning argues, adolescence is a particularly "efficient" stage at which to inculcate white supremacy's lessons: "Black youth are dehumanized, exploited, and even killed to establish the boundaries of Whiteness before they reach adulthood and assert their rights and independence."[71] For queer Black girls like Antjuanece and Jolene, the act of sexting, perceived as precociously sexual and inappropriate for children, is coupled with the hypersexualization and adultification of Black girls, and further layered with the apparently inappropriately advanced sexual awareness of queerness, rendering both young women ineligible for the innocence and indulgence granted to childhood. But at the same time, the fact that they participate in such temporally disjointed behaviors also demonstrates their apparent lack of the good judgment and self-discipline of adulthood, and that they therefore require the paternalistic hand of the law to rein in their childish impulses. Within this ambivalent status of adolescence, not worthy of the patience and care extended to childhood or the responsibility and rights granted to adulthood, their Blackness, their queerness, and their female sexuality render their subjectivity unintelligible and their desires illegal.

Disciplining Difference: The Criminalization of Queer Youth of Color

The rhetorical figurations of Blackness and childhood that render Black youth as particularly in need of discipline and correction, while also ineligible for the indulgences and protections that are usually offered to young people, have dire material consequences. As this section will show, youth of color, queer and gender-nonconforming youth, and low-income youth are systematically targeted by the criminal justice system for disproportionate policing and

---

70. Morris, *Pushout*, 129–32.
71. Henning, *Rage of Innocence*, xv.

discipline; meanwhile, young people with financial resources and cisgender, white, male, heterosexual privilege are more likely to avoid prosecution and be treated leniently.[72] These discriminatory patterns of prosecution and conviction are even more pronounced in sex offenses, where adult biases become more consequential.[73] For example, the application of statutory rape laws depends upon the extent to which the parents of the younger party disapprove of the relationship—if the relationship is consensual, parents' and prosecutors' opinions about appropriate youth sexuality determine whether a charge is brought against the older party or not. This means that young people in queer, interracial, cross-class, or otherwise "improper" pairings are more likely to find their consensual sexual activity criminalized, as Antjuanece and Jolene understand all too well.[74] Likewise, a study of public opinion on appropriate sanctions for sexting found that adults are more likely to support sex-offender registration for teens who sext within a same-sex relationship than for those whose sexting is heterosexual.[75]

In spite of queer youth of color being disavowed in the public panic over protecting children from the dangers of sexting, then, their participation is more likely to be closely scrutinized and punished as a sexual offense. Thus, it is not surprising that a Black, queer young woman such as Antjuanece found her life being turned upside down for relatively tame sexting—a behavior engaged in by many adolescents and adults, usually with absolutely no legal repercussions. Andrea J. Ritchie cites Antjuanece's punishment as an example of the racially discriminatory policing of sexual offenses, as well as how sex-offender registries are used to punish sexual and gender nonconformity. She elaborates that the stories of women like Antjuanece and Jolene "reflect a pattern of systemic criminalization and punishment of sexual and gender nonconformity," especially as gendered and sexual norms are used to facilitate white supremacy and colonization. Their experiences

> are central, yet often invisible points in a systemic arc of police brutality and state-sanctioned violence against Indigenous, Black and Brown women and gender nonconforming people, beginning with the first colonizing armies and the advent of slave patrols, and continuing through the systematic rape, denial of reproductive autonomy, and theft of children of Indigenous and African descended women, to the enforcement of the nation's borders on the bodies of immigrant women.[76]

---

72. "Unjust," 10; Hasinoff, *Sexting Panic*, 36–39; and Meiners, *For the Children?*, 31–37.
73. Godsoe, "#MeToo and the Myth," 338.
74. Hasinoff, *Sexting Panic*, 37–38.
75. Comartin, Kernsmith, and Kernsmith, "'Sexting' and Sex Offender Registration," 45.
76. Ritchie, "#SayHerName," 195, 191.

Histories of sexuality typically focus on the overt policing of sexual and gender nonconformity among men (sodomy laws, for example), obscuring the ways that female bodies and sexual practices are regulated through different means. In addition to the specific violations of Indigenous and Black and Brown women that Ritchie describes above, women's transgressions of sexual and gender norms have been (and continue to be) punished through what Mogul, Ritchie, and Whitlock describe as the "multipurpose, criminal legal archipelagos of fornication, prostitution, vagrancy, disorderly conduct, and 'lewd, lascivious, and unseemly' behavior." While poor women, immigrant women, and women of color tend to face public penalties, wealthy white women are more likely to be corrected privately within their families or religious communities and to be protected from public shaming.[77] Thus, the criminalization of queer and gender-nonconforming bodies and practices emerges not only as a mechanism of heteronormativity but also quite clearly as a tool of white supremacy and colonialism.

Antjuanece's unduly harsh punishment, in other words, might reveal something about the whiteness and heterosexuality of the sexting panic, but it is also just one example of a much larger pattern of Black, queer, trans, and gender-nonconforming youth being disproportionately targeted for in-school discipline, police intervention, criminalization, and incarceration. Morris's book, *Pushout,* tackles the criminalization of Black girls specifically in school environments—often the first site of institutional correction, and often an instigating factor for future contact with the law. Her central argument is that Black girls' experiences at school are too often degrading and marginalizing, leaving both their education and their humanity in jeopardy, and frequently leading to conditions that ultimately push them out of school altogether.[78] Morris's titular key term, "pushout," offers an alternative to the more common "dropout," redirecting attention from the student's supposed lack of motivation to finish school to the structural problems that make schools unsafe sites of surveillance, discipline, and hostility, and that disproportionately discourage Black girls—regardless of their personal desire for education and achievement—from graduating high school. Morris notes that the problem of school pushouts and the school-to-prison pipeline, facilitated by the presence of law enforcement in schools, zero-tolerance policies, and suspensions and expulsions, has largely been understood in terms of its effects on Black boys.[79] Morris extends this analysis by centering the experiences of Black girls: she expands the "school-to-prison pipeline" to "school-to-confinement pathways" to recognize the multiple ways that Black girls and women experience

---

77. Mogul, Ritchie, and Whitlock, *Queer (In)Justice,* 16–17.
78. Morris, *Pushout,* 8.
79. Morris, *Pushout,* 9. See also Morris, "Race, Gender, and the School-to-Prison Pipeline."

confinement beyond actual prisons (such as detention centers, house arrests, electronic monitoring, and other forms of social exclusion); she also interrogates the uniquely gendered and sexualized ways in which perceptions of Black femininity and sexuality are used to justify the lowered expectations for and heightened discipline of Black girls in schools.[80]

Morris identifies the Gun Free Schools Act (GFSA) of 1994 as one of the factors contributing to the disproportionate surveilling and disciplining of Black youth. Created in response to a series of school shootings, the GFSA requires schools to expel for at least one year a student who brings a weapon on to school grounds. Although protecting students from gun violence is certainly a reasonable and important goal, the GFSA's emphasis on school safety has been used to justify zero-tolerance policies for an expanding list of infractions, including bringing drugs to campus, fighting on or near school property, and threatening students or teachers with physical violence. Not only do these offenses allow a wide degree of variable interpretation (for instance, determining what counts as a threat of physical violence), but they also dramatically escalate the punishments students face. Even for nonviolent misbehaviors, automatic suspensions and contact with law enforcement replace more moderate forms of in-school correction.[81]

Schools thus become sites of increasingly disproportionate policing and punishment of Black youth in general, but the disparities are greatest for Black girls, whose race and gender produce punitive inequalities. One study found that while Black boys are twice as likely as white boys to be disciplined for a range of minor or moderate offenses in school, Black girls are three times as likely as white girls to be disciplined for the same violations.[82] According to the *New York Times*' analysis of data from the Department of Education, "Black girls are over five times more likely than white girls to be suspended at least once from school, seven times more likely to receive multiple out-of-school suspensions than white girls and three times more likely to receive referrals to law enforcement." On each of these measures, the discrepancies between Black and white boys' punishments were smaller than those for girls.[83] Morris notes that there is a sharp upward trend in Black girls' suspensions: while in the year 2000 Black girls represented 34 percent of girls given an out-of-school suspension, that number rose to 43 percent by 2006, and by 2009, 52 percent of girls with multiple out-of-school suspensions were Black.[84]

---

80. Morris, *Pushout*, 12.
81. Morris, *Pushout*, 67.
82. Morris and Perry, "Girls Behaving Badly?," 143.
83. Green, Walker, and Shapiro, "'Battle for the Souls of Black Girls.'"
84. Morris, *Pushout*, 68.

Even more chilling, the "Black Girls Matter" report, which offered a gendered perspective on data released by the Office of Civil Rights Data Collection, indicates that during the 2011–12 school year, of all girls expelled from school, 90 percent of those in New York City and 63 percent of those in Boston were Black girls, while *none* of the expelled girls in either city were white.[85]

Importantly, the increasingly severe discipline of Black girls is not actually linked to heightened rates of misconduct or seriousness of misbehavior. Rather, this trend speaks more to the tendency to discipline Black girls harshly for minor infractions such as dress code violations or inappropriate language. As Subini Annamma et al. note, "In general, racial disparities in exclusionary school discipline outcomes appear to be driven by minor infractions and subjective categories of student misconduct, rather than more objective and serious behaviors such as bringing a weapon to school."[86] Indeed, the minor and subjective misbehaviors for which Black girls are targeted allow teachers and school staff to exercise more discretionary judgment (compared with more serious misbehaviors like possession of drugs or weapons, which are less ambiguous and more likely to result in standard sanctions), opening more opportunity for implicit racial and gender biases.

Queer and Gender-Nonconforming Black Girls

The disparities in discipline faced by Black girls are further amplified when those girls are queer and/or gender-nonconforming. According to "Unjust: How the Broken Juvenile and Criminal Justice Systems Fail LGBTQ Youth," a 2016 report by the Center for American Progress and the Movement Advancement Project, LGBTQ+ youth are up to 300 percent more likely than heterosexual youth to experience some sort of official sanction—ranging from expulsion from school to being arrested or convicted.[87] Often LGBTQ+ youth are targeted specifically because of their same-sex sexual attractions and behaviors, even when their straight peers engage in identical behaviors without reproach. As a result, LGBTQ+ youth are vastly overrepresented in juvenile justice centers, making up 20 percent of the population of incarcerated youth, but only 7 to 9 percent of all American youth. A whopping 40 percent of girls in juvenile justice centers identify as LGBTQ+ or gender-nonconforming. Black, Latinx, and multiracial LGBTQ+ students are even more likely to be disciplined in school than their LGBTQ+ peers who are

---

85. Crenshaw with Ocen and Nanda, "Black Girls Matter," 23.
86. Annamma et al., "Black Girls and School Discipline," 4.
87. "Unjust," 4.

white: of all the LGBTQ+ and gender-nonconforming youth in juvenile justice centers, 85 percent are youth of color.[88]

LGBTQ+ youth of color are also more likely to be targeted outside of school contexts by "quality of life" or "broken windows" policing, in which police departments crack down on minor offenses and legal but "unwanted" activities in the belief that they will prevent more serious crimes. Because LGBTQ+ youth of color are more likely than white and non-LGBTQ+ youth to use drugs and alcohol, to be homeless, to be involved in sex work for survival, and to be poor, they are more visible in public spaces and especially vulnerable to being stopped by police for minor infractions.[89] Being arrested or incarcerated as a young person is associated with future arrests and incarcerations as an adult: Black and Pink surveyed incarcerated LGBTQ+ adults and found that 66 percent of Black, Latinx, and mixed-race respondents were arrested for the first time when they were minors.[90] Therefore, the overrepresentation of LGBTQ+ youth of color in the juvenile justice system produces lifelong consequences not just for individuals but also for entire queer communities and communities of color.

A crucial component of the intersectional disciplining of LGBTQ+ youth of color is the way that gender presentation is deployed as a modality of both racism and heteronormativity, such that violations of gender norms index other kinds of violations. As Ritchie explains, "police interactions are informed by perceptions of women and queer people of color as literally embodying a racially gendered and sexualized disorder—which often translates directly into a charge of disorderly conduct, unreasonable noise, or loitering for the purposes of prostitution simply for being present in a public space." Gender-nonconforming young women of color are profiled as gang members, while gay and gender-nonconforming men of color are profiled for lewd conduct in public parks and restrooms based solely on racialized, gendered, heteronormative, and transphobic assumptions and regardless of their actual behavior.[91]

Therefore, gender nonconformity in Black girls, especially in combination with the pressures of adultification and hypersexualization described earlier, emerges as a significant site at which not only their behaviors, but also their embodied existence, is identified as a problem and criminalized.

---

88. "Unjust," 12, 1, 4.
89. "Unjust," 13.
90. Lydon et al., "Coming Out of Concrete Closets." Of incarcerated LGBTQ adults, two-thirds of respondents had been incarcerated in the past, and 58 percent had been arrested for the first time when they were under eighteen years old. Black, Latinx, and mixed-race LGBTQ respondents were significantly more likely than white respondents to have had their first arrest occur when they were under eighteen (66% compared with 51%).
91. Ritchie, "#SayHerName," 198.

As Joel Mittleman contends, "more masculine, 'unladylike' gender expression may be interpreted by adults as threatening," leading queer and gender-nonconforming girls to be treated with suspicion and presumed to be the aggressors in conflicts.[92] For Black girls, simply being outspoken in class, wearing "masculine" attire, or playing sports might be identified as gender-nonconforming attributes—whether the girls identify as LGBTQ+ or not—that prompt heightened discipline. In other words, Black girls' behavior is more likely to be scrutinized and thought to violate gendered norms of decorum in school because the "appropriate" femininity of "good" Black girls, as I described earlier, is coded as white. As Morris and Perry speculate, "the perceived misbehavior of African American girls is often behavior that breaches gender assumptions of standard femininity."[93] In short, particularly for Black girls who already contravene white standards of femininity, perceived gender nonconformity can lead adults to view normal acts of youthful agency as defiant or disruptive, and to impute criminality to typical nonviolent teen misbehaviors.

Given this tendency to punish the gender nonconformity of Black girls in general, and Black queer girls especially, it is important to pay particular attention to the ways that Antjuanece's and Jolene's gender presentations are portrayed. In the *Willamette Week* article, Slovic describes Jolene as sporty, wholesome, all-American, a "typical teenager" and a "nice, sweet girl." Slovic tells us that Jolene's "heart-shaped face" is framed by straight black hair, that she keeps her clothing casual but "often wears a trace of makeup and two sets of glittering gemstone earrings." Antjuanece, in contrast, is presented as "stocky, with a round face and a slouchy carriage," an introvert, "the funny one" who keeps her family together. In photos, Antjuanece has very close-cropped hair, a pierced eyebrow and lower lip, and is usually wearing hoodies or T-shirts, baggy pants, a chunky watch, and sometimes a hat.

Although it is never stated directly in the descriptions of Antjuanece, the images of her clearly depict a gender-nonconforming masculine style and comportment; of the two young women, it is only in Antjuanece's body that queerness is rendered public and visible, while Jolene's queer desires are invisible in a heteronormative framework where femininity signals heterosexuality. The representations of Jolene seem to fit the expected gendered patterns of the sexting panic, in which sexual agency and femininity are mutually exclusive. But they also traffic in long-standing stereotypes of lesbian desire which assume "authentic" lesbians are masculine or butch women (whose deviant

---

92. Mittleman, "Sexual Orientation and School Discipline," 185–87.
93. Morris and Perry, "Girls Behaving Badly?," 144.

desires are manifested in deviant gender presentation), while the objects of their seductions are otherwise heterosexual women (whose queerness is understood in terms of mental illness or a weakness of will, but not in terms of genuine desire).[94] Jolene and Antjuanece's own narrative of their relationship complicates this facile categorization of their roles: the two say that it was Jolene who set the pace of their relationship, who instigated their first kiss and set the boundaries on their physical intimacy, and who, after six months of dating, chose to get a small tattoo of Antjuanece's initials inside a heart on her hip. Antjuanece says, "Jolene took the lead in almost everything we did."[95]

Nevertheless, Antjuanece is conscious of the ways her gender presentation and race frame her as a predator, explaining that people sometimes think she seems "intimidating" and "aggressive" not just because she "looks a certain way" but also because she is "chunky" and Black. This is part of the reason she opted for the plea bargain rather than taking her chances with a jury who might be influenced by these intersections of her physical appearance. She says, "I mean, I look intimidating and stuff, and that's fine. . . . But I'm not this, like, hardcore person. . . . I'm sweet, and I'm kind, and I know that I'm a good human being . . . and I love who I am. . . . But when you look at me you don't see that." She also points out that had she and Jolene both been feminine girls, their sexting would likely have been perceived as just girls "messing around or exploring," or "being silly."[96] In other words, Antjuanece's gender nonconformity, her Blackness, and her queerness lend a serious and adultlike, or even sinister quality to what might otherwise be dismissed as adolescent play, no more harmful than a game of spin-the-bottle.

The disproportionate discipline and incarceration of Black girls and other queer youth of color like Antjuanece clearly points to systemic discrimination in our educational, policing, and legal systems. However, this is not merely a matter of those systems needing to be reformed; rather, as Egan argues, it points to the ways that these systems are functioning as they were intended to do, to scapegoat those who are already marginalized in order to protect white, middle-class, heterosexual girls. By viewing queer youth of color as too sexual for their age, out of control, immoral, and troublesome, they become a site of transference for cultural anxieties. Adults decide, as Egan puts it, "who is acceptable, who should be sanctioned, and who is in need of psychological, medical or spiritual intervention," identifying queer youth of color as damaged and pathological, and therefore constructing white hetero(non)sexual girlhood as normal, natural, and innocent.[97]

---

94. Walker, "How to Recognize a Lesbian," 881–82; and McCann, "Beyond the Visible."
95. Slovic, "Sext Crimes."
96. Brown, interview with author.
97. Egan, "Sexualizing Girl Troubles," 57.

When these forms of scapegoating result in the excessive policing and incarceration of youth of color, they participate in (re)producing the Black criminality that defines the limits of white vulnerability. These practices work alongside other violent traditions like lynching that, as Ersula Ore argues convincingly, performatively constitute the whiteness of American national identity and exclude Black people from full citizenship. The disproportionate surveillance and discipline of Black girls' gendered and sexual expression and the criminalization of queer Black youth collude with the incarceration and police killings of Black men as modern-day lynchings. As material practices and rhetorical performances, they demonstrate "an ideological belief regarding black inferiority, white superiority, and the need to keep blacks in their racially prescribed place."[98] In other words, the disciplining of Antjuanece's sexual expression and behavior might be productively viewed not as an idiosyncratic instance of overzealous prosecution but rather, alongside other historical and contemporary practices that disenfranchise, confine, and kill Black bodies, as a more systematic denial of full citizenship to Black and queer youth. As a result of this dehumanization of Blackness and queerness, vulnerability emerges as a quality defined by Blackness's exclusion and available only as a privilege of whiteness, thus (re)producing the racial figuration of youth.

Queering the Sexting Panic

I began this chapter with Antjuanece and Jolene's story in order to demonstrate the ways that their Blackness, queerness, and female sexual agency have been disavowed in order to shore up the figuration of vulnerability available to white, hetero(non)sexual girls in the context of the sexting panic. In contrast to other scholarly treatments of sexting, which tend to focus on the most visible examples of straight white kids and include Antjuanece's prosecution only to corroborate the overwhelming homogeneity of the mainstream treatment of the sexting panic, I have sought to bring her disavowal to the center, to situate Blackness and queerness as the key features whose absence and erasure are necessary to the production of white vulnerability. Although my primary focus in this book is on the public narratives about young people that are used to justify adult decisions about law and policy, I can make at least a small effort to counter the dehumanizing criminalization of Black queer youth by recentering Antjuanece as the subject of her own story. As I conclude, then, I offer a brief analysis of Michelle Maher's documentary, "Unlawful Justice: The Story of Antjuanece Brown and Jolene Jenkins," in which Antjuanece

---

98. Ore, *Lynching*, 13–16.

describes her experience in her own words, and then provide an update on Antjuanece's life beyond her entanglements with the sexting panic.

"Unlawful Justice," a "mini-documentary" published to YouTube at the beginning of 2012, features Antjuanece, labeled in a chyron as a "cool chica," and Jolene, described as "lawyer-to-be," sitting outside on what appears to be the concrete curb of a parking lot, and later side by side at a restaurant table. It opens with Jolene, wearing a pink scoop-neck tank top and a necklace, her hair pulled back, recounting the day that Antjuanece was arrested and she could not get ahold of her. Antjuanece, in an unzipped striped hoody and baggy gray pants, remembers her confusion at finding herself suddenly in jail and thinking, "I didn't do anything wrong. All I did was love somebody. . . . I flipped out and then I started crying for, like, ever." The two young women reflect on how Antjuanece's indictment has impacted both of their lives: Antjuanece, of course, lost her job and found her employment prospects, her ability to sign a lease, her options for going to college, and so on, severely constrained by her felony and her bench probation. Jolene struggles with feeling responsible for Antjuanece's fate and laments the deterioration of her relationship with her mother, concluding sadly, "It did cost me my family." The video then cuts to Kate Kendall of the National Center for Lesbian Rights, who contends that Antjuanece's lawyer knew that the district attorney's vigorous prosecution of child pornography cases was "off the rails." The lawyer, Kendall argues, should have recognized that the charges against her client were motivated by race and sexuality and reached out to an LGBTQ+ legal organization for help, which may have led to challenging the statute and dropping Antjuanece's charges. The documentary ends with Antjuanece and Jolene in a restaurant, recounting their happy reunion on Jolene's eighteenth birthday after ten months of court-mandated separation, while "Everlasting Love" plays in the background. Jolene leans her face on Antjuanece's shoulder as Antjuanece describes how she brought Jolene a cake and gifts and sang happy birthday to her. Antjuanece says, "It felt very unreal. . . . I felt like it was a dream, like at any moment I'd wake up and she'd be gone." In the final scene Jolene playfully grabs a corn chip away from Antjuanece, they giggle with each other, and then embrace.[99]

After reuniting, Antjuanece and Jolene moved in together and continued dating for another three years before eventually breaking up. I had the opportunity to speak with Antjuanece Brown as part of my research for this chapter; here, as I document her perspective as an adult looking back on the experiences of her youth, I use her last name to refer to her. Brown recalls

---

99. Maher, "Unlawful Justice."

that thirteen years ago when she was arrested, she herself was barely an adult, yet the consequences of her teenage romance continue to affect her life. She describes, for example, how she worked as a sign-spinner and then at a series of "dead end" food service jobs because, as a felon, her options for employment were limited. When Brown started getting serious with her now wife, who ran a daycare business out of her home, she could not move in because her criminal record would jeopardize the business. Eventually, Brown was able to pay to have her record expunged (she recounts a sweet story about her wife surreptitiously saving money for this purpose), and now she is a licensed preschool director. Brown and her wife have been married for four years; she has a son and is a foster parent to six more children.

However, Brown continues to worry about how her past lives forever on the internet. One of the first results when you google her name is the 2010 cover photo from *Willamette Week*; it shows young Antjuanece in the courtroom, eyebrows raised and chin lowered, her shoulders hunched in a loose-fitting, jail-issued orange shirt, her wrists shackled to her waist, the headline "SEXT CRIMES" spelled out in bold letters next to her face. Brown emphasizes that she is not ashamed of her past and will not change the name she uses personally or professionally (in part because her son's name is a variation on hers); but she is well aware that any perceived association with pedophilia or other sex offenses against a minor would put her business and her family at risk. In 2010 she was relieved simply to avoid prison, but now she recognizes that she will feel the repercussions of her arrest forever, anticipating a seemingly endless number of difficult conversations if people she loves happen to look up her name: "It sucks that . . . my son is probably going to find it one day, and then . . . my grandkids, and you know, on and on." Even Maher's documentary and now this chapter as well, even though they argue that Antjuanece's case was an appalling miscarriage of justice, are lingering pieces of evidence that follow her into adulthood, marriage, motherhood, and her career, perpetually connecting her to an adolescent relationship and to the sexting panic.

Although today adult anxieties about the sexting behaviors of teenagers are not driven by a media panic like they were at the time of Antjuanece's case (contemporary media panics seem to have moved on to worrying over "gender ideology" and queer and trans youth), sexting certainly has not disappeared as an adolescent pastime or as a source of adult concern. As the initial alarm has died down, experts have begun to recognize that many of the harms that arise from teen sexting are due not to the actual act of sexting itself but to the various ways in which sexting can be nonconsensual. For instance, young people experience negative mental health outcomes such as depression and anxiety when they feel coerced to send nude images, when they receive unwanted nude images or sexual language, or when their consensual sexts are distributed nonconsensually to other parties. But several studies have found that youth who sext consensually can feel happy, surprised, and amused by the practice, and report experiencing attraction, pleasure, and respect in their relationships.[100] Both the risks and the benefits of sexting, in other words, seem consistent with the effects of any kind of sexual activity, both for adolescents and adults. Thus, Justin W. Patchin and Sameer Hinduja argue for a harm-reduction approach to sexting, in which adults acknowledge that it is normal for young people to engage in potentially risky behaviors and offer strategies for reducing the likelihood of negative outcomes. Just as kids can be taught to plan for a designated driver if they expect to drink alcohol or to use a condom to have sex, they can also be taught practices for safer sexting.[101]

In addition, because more states have passed laws specific to sexting, young people are less likely to be subjected to the blunt instrument of federal child pornography charges as Antjuanece was. As of 2022, twenty-seven states have sexting laws with specific provisions for minors who send and/or receive explicit material.[102] These laws produce fewer spectacular instances of teenagers facing prosecution for felonies and can offer more reasonable and age-appropriate sanctions, such as educational or counseling programs.[103] Although state laws have thus calmed some of the public panic about sexting, they still subject normal teenage sexual behavior to legal penalties, and most importantly, are still enforced according to the racist, classist, heterosexist, and gender-normative biases I have described throughout this chapter. While teen sexting may no longer be provoking the public media panic it did fifteen years ago, then, concern for and policies about sexting certainly continue to shape adult perspectives on youth sexuality, especially for queer youth, gender-nonconforming youth, and youth of color.

The sexting panic of the aughts was clearly born from a specific confluence of technological advancement and cultural anxiety about the sexualization of young people, but the pathologization and criminalization of Black female sexuality, queerness, and gender nonconformity are certainly not new. Indeed, Antjuanece and Jolene's case is a digitally mediated contemporary instance, situated within a long and diverse history, of Black women carving out viable erotic options—of Black women literally writing their desire—within and

---

100. Bronfenbrenner Center, "Complex Consequences"; and Del Rey et al., "Sexting among Adolescents."
101. Patchin and Hinduja, "It Is Time."
102. Patchin, "Status of Sexting Laws."
103. Patchin, "Status of Sexting Laws."

against the narrow and terrorizing archetypes of Black female sexuality. They assert themselves as sexual subjects in spite of being framed as inherently deviant and in need of external control, leaning into the ways that, as Ritchie puts it, Black women's sexuality "is queered in deeply racialized ways."[104] The queer intervention of Antjuanece and Jolene, although emerging from the peculiarities of the sexting panic, is therefore also a response to centuries-long legacies of violence inscribed into the bodies and desires of Black women and girls.

The sexting panic, arising from racist ideas about (white) childhood innocence, sexist assumptions about girls' sexual agency, and heteronormative expectations of adolescent sexuality, excludes Antjuanece and Jolene from the media narrative, but even more importantly, it depends upon Antjuanece's criminalization to justify the threat of sexualization to white hetero(non)sexual girls. In their unabashed embodiment of queer desire in young Black female bodies, Antjuanece and Jolene disrupt the framework of the sexting panic narrative at every turn. Antjuanece's masculine style and history of queer relationships present precisely the kinds of Black gender-nonconforming challenges to white, heterosexual norms of femininity that are targeted for discipline and control. Meanwhile, Jolene cannot easily be positioned as Antjuanece's "victim" because her Blackness, her femininity, and her queer desire suggest a sexual maturity and excessiveness that trouble her innocent and childlike victimhood. And because there is no heterosexual male desire in their story—the sexual agency that supposedly coerces diffident hetero(non)sexual white girls to send naked photos of themselves—Antjuanece and Jolene lay bare the realities of girls' sexual agency. Antjuanece's behavior is criminalized not just because Jolene is underage, then, but also because both women embody a Black, queer, female sexuality that is overdetermined by the trope of Black women's sexual excessiveness. In the adolescent liminality between Black girlhood and Black womanhood, Antjuanece and Jolene find themselves caught up in a performative scene of anti-Black punishment that repeatedly and relentlessly inaugurates the possibility of white childhood innocence.

Ostensibly about safeguarding the virtue of minors in the context of rapidly proliferating digital technologies, the sexting panic therefore does the rhetorical work of (re)producing the vulnerability so central to the racial figuration of childhood. This is a vulnerability that privileges white innocence and hetero(non)sexuality, offering up female sexual agency and racialized queerness as scapegoats for the troubles of today's youth, and wrapping its violence in the warm embrace of parental concern for the figural child. As we have seen

---

104. Ritchie, "#SayHerName," 194.

in this chapter, the privileges of perceived vulnerability are crucial to young people's experiences with law enforcement, with the juvenile justice system, and in the courtroom—Antjuanece's felony conviction makes painfully evident the extent to which her access to innocence was compromised by the racist, classist, and homophobic biases that shaped her case. I want to emphasize, however, that I am not proposing vulnerability as a white characteristic from which Blackness is barred; instead, the very possibility of vulnerability is premised on a distinction between Blackness and humanness, where the creation of (white) vulnerability is an effect of the dehumanization of Blackness. In other words, the critical point is that we cannot simply learn to think about vulnerability more capaciously in order to include racialized children, but that we must recognize how the category of vulnerability, generated through anti-Blackness, becomes available for white occupation. I pursue this question in the next chapter's analyses of how the perceived weaknesses of whiteness and the performativity of masculinity are highlighted in popular, policy, and scholarly discourses about the bullying and suicides of cisgender gay boys.

CHAPTER 2

Wounded White Boys

Figuring Queer Vulnerability to Bullying and Suicide

In the spring of 2020, as the COVID-19 pandemic was ramping up in the United States and schools across the country were pausing in-person instruction and activities, youth service organizations issued a number of warnings about what young people might be missing at school—not just education but also crucial resources like free or reduced-cost meals for those without enough food at home, a warm and safe place to spend the day for those who were unhoused, important socialization and assistance for those with special needs, and so on. One group often mentioned were queer youth, who were losing access to school resources such as counselors or gender sexuality alliances (also called gay-straight alliances or GSAs), who were cut off from supportive peers and adults at school, and who may be facing quarantine with trans- and homophobic families. For instance, UNICEF USA noted that "actions taken to fight coronavirus' spread, such as school closures and quarantines, are disrupting children's routines and support systems in ways that may have disproportionate negative consequences for LGBTQ youth." The Trevor Project, a suicide-prevention and crisis-intervention organization for LGBTQ+ youth, warned that queer youth may be "particularly vulnerable to negative mental health impacts," including suicide, related to COVID-19 precautions and added that transgender and nonbinary individuals, as well as Black and other youth of color, were at even more elevated risk.[1]

1. Sasse, "Case for Intersectionality"; Trevor Project, "Implications of COVID-19"; and Trevor Project, "Black LGBTQ Youth."

These warnings were important and apt, calling attention to the unique mental health challenges of queer youth, especially queer youth of color and those who are trans or gender-nonconforming, and suggesting that they may require additional support from schools, youth programs, and families. But while it is crucial to recognize how queer young people face greater degrees of precarity and to strive to remediate their risk factors, I am often troubled by such warnings because I wonder whether their earnest emphasis on the vulnerability of queer youth may also naturalize the very dangers they seek to mitigate. In the absence of other compelling messages, have queer kids come to matter in the popular imagination primarily insofar as they are susceptible to mental health struggles, self-harm, and suicidality? That is, have queer youth—whose existence was so recently invisible to mainstream attention—become publicly legible only in terms of a racialized fragility rooted in vulnerability's association with whiteness? I certainly do not mean to downplay the material precarities of youth at the intersections of transphobia, homophobia, and racism—my point is not that these vulnerabilities are overstated. Rather, I want to inquire into the ways that these vulnerabilities are ascribed to certain queer subjects, and how they become intelligible in public discourse, official guidance and policy documents, and in scholarly explorations and recommendations. In short, in this chapter I turn a critical eye to the racial figuration of queer vulnerability through which adults come to understand the lives of queer young people, and I seek to understand the work that the category of vulnerability does for the adults who deploy it.

This chapter takes up these questions by investigating the rhetorical production of the racial figuration of queer youth at risk for bullying and suicide. I begin by looking back at the suicides of nine cisgender adolescent boys in September 2010, which garnered an unprecedented amount of media attention, as well as official and popular responses to the problem of anti-gay bullying. In this moment of dawning public awareness and intense public feeling—perhaps captured most unmistakably in the launch of the It Gets Better Project—the figuration of the sympathetic vulnerability of queer youth crystallizes. I sketch this figuration's influence across two institutionally supported areas of discourse about queer youth, bullying, and suicide: federal guidance information and scholarly conversation. First, in the popularization of the federal government's recommendations on bullying policy, I suggest bullying is naturalized as a causal factor for suicide, and the risk for both is located in the desexualized and racially undifferentiated identities of queer youth. Second, in scholars' and researchers' attention to queer young people, I trace how queer youth are positioned as uniquely and innately vulnerable to suicide, and how this positioning impacts the interventions made on their behalf as well as their own possibilities for self-understanding. I suggest that the racial figuration of queer youth at risk is premised on the vulnerabilities of whiteness and masculinity, such that the narratives of white gay boys and their homophobic bullies become the model through which the challenges of all queer youth are imagined.

Throughout this book I treat vulnerability as one of the foundational characteristics of the racial figuration of childhood, and in this chapter I grapple with the notion of vulnerability as a specifically rhetorical phenomenon—that is, not as an undeniable quality of life but as an ascription composed strategically and inequitably. In the previous chapter I demonstrated how the protections of childhood are produced through the exclusions of young people like Antjuanece and Jolene, whose Blackness, queerness, and agentic assertions of female sexuality threaten the racial figuration of childhood rooted in hetero(non)sexuality. Having established the anti-Blackness that founds childhood's imagined vulnerability, in this chapter I now turn to how certain qualities—namely, whiteness and masculinity—are *imbued with* vulnerability. I engage here more specifically with vulnerability itself in order to understand how it can name both a state of structural precarity as well as a political designation that depends on and confers privilege.

This chapter thus makes two interrelated claims about vulnerability in relation to public, governmental, and scholarly discourse on queer youth, bullying, and suicide. First, I argue that the heightened risks for bullying and suicide of queer, trans, and gender-nonconforming youth are strategically situated in the identities of young people—in other words, as an inherent weakness related to sexuality—rather than in structures of trans- and homophobia, racism, sexism, ableism, and so on. By framing vulnerability in this way, concerned adults are relieved of responsibility: they can feel sympathy and even imagine themselves as benevolent saviors of fragile queer youth, but they need not address their complicity with the relentless racism and cis- and heteronormativity that put those young people at risk. Second, I suggest that the vulnerability of queer youth is figured compellingly through the white masculinity of the cis white gay boy; the wounded white boy, that is, occupies—fills up and seizes—the category of vulnerability. Taken together, these two claims compose this chapter's purpose in this book: to establish the vulnerability that is so crucial to the racial figuration of childhood as a characteristic most easily ascribed to categories of privilege and assumed to arise from the queer child's intrinsic deficits. Ultimately, I contend that this figuration of queer youth—with its conflation of bullying and suicide, its presumption of the riskiness of queerness, and its white and masculinist underpinnings—persists in part because it does important work for adult understandings of youth sexuality, even as it has constraining effects for how we can imagine the agency, resilience, sexual expression, and queer resourcefulness of queer youth.

My thinking on vulnerability is indebted to Katie Oliviero's work, which investigates how the politics of vulnerability are deployed toward both progressive and conservative ends. Corporeal vulnerability is a shared and inescapable human condition, but it is also produced in and distributed across demographic groups unequally. That is, vulnerabilities are structurally and socioculturally produced; the designation of vulnerability is "politically malleable" and can be translated into political affect and political action.[2] Oliviero is specifically interested in how conservative arguments have co-opted the language and experience of vulnerability, claiming that, for example, American citizens are threatened by migrants, that the heterosexual nuclear family is threatened by legal same-sex marriage, and that the future of human life itself is threatened by safe and affordable abortion.[3] Thus, she offers a helpful framework for noticing that vulnerability might be conferred as a "sympathetic status" that provides protection when racialized, gendered, sexualized, classed, and citizenship narratives are constructed in particular ways, but that vulnerability's ambivalent effects also include the possibility for increased surveillance and regulation.[4]

I draw on Oliviero's understanding of vulnerability to examine the ways in which queer youth are figured in popular, scientific, scholarly, and policy discourse about bullying and suicide as uniquely vulnerable on the basis of their LGBTQ+ identities. Although this figuration is not constructed as strategically (or as disingenuously) as the conservative arguments Oliviero traces, it does nonetheless comport with Oliviero's assertion that "vulnerability politics' seemingly universal appeal tends to primarily protect more privileged groups," such that the vulnerability of "queer youth at risk" emerges as a kind of "privileged status" that is available only to certain queer youth.[5] That is, the vulnerability in the racial figuration of queer youth at risk is a characteristic that is premised on the privileges of whiteness and the precarious performance of masculinity, and thus renders unintelligible the specific kinds of vulnerabilities experienced by queer youth of color, queer girls, and trans and gender-nonconforming youth.

---

2. Oliviero, *Vulnerability Politics*, 12–13.
3. Oliviero, *Vulnerability Politics*, 7.
4. Oliviero, *Vulnerability Politics*, 6.
5. Oliviero, *Vulnerability Politics*, 150, 22.

Assembling a Queer Epidemic: The September 2010 Suicides

In September 2010, a decade prior to the warnings about queer youths' mental health prompted by the COVID-19 pandemic, nine young men died by suicide and made headlines across the country. None of these boys knew each other, and their suicides occurred sporadically throughout the month, but they have been indelibly linked together in the media through an emerging discourse of anti-gay bullying and its tragic consequences. For example, *WitnessLA*, an independent, nonpartisan source of criminal justice news, reported the list of nine names with clickable links to more information about most of them, framing the group in a manner that emphasized their association with gayness but flattened some of their differences: "The nine young men listed below are members of a tragic fraternity. They were all tormented, teased and/or bullied for being gay. They all killed themselves—most of them just after a particularly bad bout of teasing or social humiliation."[6] Likewise, in a story titled "Suicides Put Light on Pressures of Gay Teenagers," which featured the deaths of four of the boys, the *New York Times* describes "several suicides in recent weeks by young gay teenagers who had been harassed by classmates, both in person and online."[7] These boys are linked, the narrative goes, by being presumed to be gay and being bullied; cultivating this apparent sameness offers adults a means for understanding the tragedies and, most importantly, for identifying the specific source of their vulnerability.

Three of the boys fit this public narrative well: Seth Walsh, a thirteen-year-old from California, Tyler Clementi, an eighteen-year-old from New Jersey, and Asher Brown, a thirteen-year-old from Texas, were all engaging in same-sex relationships and/or open about their queer identities and were also known to be targeted by anti-gay bullying. But the rest of the boys' stories were a bit more complicated. For instance, two of them—Cody J. Barker, a seventeen-year-old from Wisconsin, and Raymond Chase, a nineteen-year-old college student in Rhode Island—were also both out as gay. However, Raymond's friends emphatically deny that he was bullied and assert that his death should not be connected to the other September suicides; his best friend referred to him as "the life of the party" and insisted that no one was ever mean to him. Cody was an anti-bullying activist at school, and although his parents and his GSA peer mentor suggested that he may have faced harassment and name-calling, the superintendent of his school flatly denied that

---

6. Fremon, "Why Did So Many."
7. McKinley, "Suicides Put Light on Pressures."

he had been bullied. Indeed, the superintendent specifically rebuffed efforts to make Cody a "poster child" for anti-gay bullying and suicide, saying that people were "connecting dots that weren't there."[8] Two others, fourteen-year-old Caleb Nolt and fifteen-year-old Billy Lucas, both from Indiana, experienced anti-gay bullying but did not self-identify as gay. Caleb's obituary and the coverage of his death mention his girlfriend prominently, suggesting that establishing his heterosexuality was important to his family and community. Billy is often referred to as a "gay teenager" in news stories, even as they also admit that he never identified himself as such.[9] And for two of these young men—Harrison Chase Brown, a fifteen-year-old from Colorado, and Felix Sacco, a seventeen-year-old from Massachusetts—there is no suggestion that they were perceived to be gay, and there is conflicting evidence about whether they were bullied or whether bullying may have been a factor in their suicides. To further complicate the narrative, not all of these boys have received equal media coverage or name recognition; some sources refer to only five or six of them, either because the less publicized stories are easy to overlook or because reporters made different decisions about which were the most relevant.

Nonetheless, all nine deaths have been connected and remembered as evidence of the problem of bullying (which almost always implies at least a whiff of anti-gay sentiment in these stories) and suicide, and they are often used to mark a moment of dawning public awareness and action. The media coverage during this time referred to the shocking frequency and apparent surge in suicides, calling them, for instance, a "recent eruption of gay teen suicides," a "recent rash of suicides among gay youth," an "alarming suicide spike," or even an "epidemic," emphasizing a sense of growing alarm that these deaths were unprecedented.[10] Of course, as many researchers and experts in LGBTQ+ youth and suicide prevention were quick to point out, there was nothing new or surprising about the elevated rates of suicide among queer youth. Leigh Powers, head of Information Services at the Suicide Prevention Resource Center, stated flatly, "This isn't news. This is an issue that has been going on for a long time."[11] What was unprecedented, however, was the extent to which the issues of bullying and suicide among queer youth were suddenly being highlighted in mainstream media and stirring public response. Many of the news stories noted that the September 2010 suicides "captured the attention of the nation," were prompting a "national call to action," or were "provok[ing]

---

8. Howorth, "Raymond Chase"; "Cody Barker"; and "Two More."
9. "Caleb R. Nolt Obituary"; and Savage, "Bullied Gay Teenager."
10. Hubbard, "Fifth Gay Teen Suicide"; Graves, "Gay Teen Suicides Pervasive"; Howorth, "Raymond Chase"; "Raymond Chase Commits Suicide"; and "Recent Youth Suicides."
11. Graves, "Gay Teen Suicides Pervasive."

nationwide introspection about bullying, and how gay teens are treated, from the heartland to Hollywood."[12]

Indeed, an official national response came almost immediately: US Secretary of Education Arne Duncan issued a statement on October 1, 2010, in which he referenced five of the previous month's suicides, saying that the young men "took their own lives for one unacceptable reason: they were being bullied and harassed because they were openly gay or believed to be gay." These "unnecessary tragedies," he continued, occurred "because the trauma of being bullied and harassed for their actual or perceived sexual orientation was too much to bear."[13] Later that month, Duncan sent a "Dear Colleague" letter to schools, colleges, and universities nationwide describing educators' obligation to shield students from certain kinds of harassment protected by federal education anti-discrimination laws. It also announced the anti-bullying initiatives planned for the next year by the White House, the Department of Education, and other federal agencies.[14] Then, on December 16, 2010, Duncan distributed a "technical assistance" memo to state leaders to offer guidance on best practices in bullying legislation. This memo began with a direct reference to the "recent incidents of bullying [that] have demonstrated its potentially devastating effects on students, schools, and communities and have spurred a sense of urgency among State and local educators and policymakers to take action to combat bullying."[15] Within the next few years, in fact, every US state had some version of anti-bullying legislation on the books.

Meanwhile, more popular responses also abounded. Dan Savage and his partner Terry Miller founded the It Gets Better Project with a hopeful video in which they recounted favorite happy memories as evidence that their lives as queer adults had become better than they could have imagined when they were being bullied as young people. They invited others to contribute their messages of hope, and the project took off immediately: over a thousand videos were submitted by the end of the first week, and two months later, ten thousand more people had uploaded videos. As the numbers and diversity of the videos continued to expand, millions of people viewed them through YouTube or the It Gets Better website.[16] Videos came from public figures like President Barack Obama, Vice President Joseph Biden, Secretary of State

---

12. Hubbard, "Fifth Gay Teen Suicide"; Graves, "Gay Teen Suicides Pervasive"; Howorth, "Raymond Chase"; and "Raymond Chase Commits Suicide."
13. US Dept of Education, "Statement by U.S. Secretary of Education"; and "Education Secretary Calls for Tolerance."
14. US Dept of Education, "Guidance Targeting Harassment."
15. US Dept of Education, "Key Policy Letters."
16. It Gets Better Project, "How It All Got Started"; and Krutzsch, "A History."

Hillary Clinton, and troves of other celebrities, actors, musicians, athletes, and organizations, as well as countless regular people, including young queer people themselves. The critiques of the privilege showcased in Savage and Miller's video and of the entire project's neoliberal progress narrative are, by now, well known, but its impact in the aftermath of the September 2010 suicides is undeniable.[17] As West, Frischherz, Panther, and Brophy point out, the "vernacular video" format of It Gets Better—in which private individuals can disseminate messages and interact with one another in a public forum—created a unique opportunity for queer community-building and especially for queer intergenerational communication.[18] Because of its accessible and participatory nature and the vast recirculation of its videos, It Gets Better became not only one of the most prominent responses to the immediate exigence of the September 2010 suicides, but it also fueled continued media coverage. As Brett Krutzsch asserts, the success of It Gets Better was a key factor promoting reporting on anti-gay bullying, homophobia, and suicide among queer youth as issues that Americans should care about and that needed to be addressed.[19]

Other popular culture responses also followed the September 2010 suicides. For example, the rock band Rise Against released a single entitled "Make It Stop (September's Children)" in May 2011 that specifically addresses the bullying and suicides of gay youth, even listing the names and ages of five of the boys who died in September. Tim McIlrath, who leads the band and wrote the song, says that he felt it was important to speak up about "the wave of gay-teen suicides" because the "male-dominated, testosterone-driven" world of rock music does not tend to comment on issues like this, and perpetuates homophobia.[20] The music video for "Make It Stop," produced in collaboration with the It Gets Better Project, portrays three high school students being bullied at school and then contemplating suicide. As each of them is on the brink of pulling the trigger, affixing the noose, or jumping from the bridge, brief clips from other youths' It Gets Better videos are interspersed with imagined future successes (a career in politics, a successful art exhibition, a same-sex wedding) for each of the featured young people. All three decide against suicide as McIlrath sings, "But proud I stand, of who I am. I plan to go on living." The song was well received by critics and reached number eight on the Billboard Hot Rock Songs chart, and the music video was nominated

---

17. See, for example, Gray, "It Doesn't Get Better"; Halberstam, "It Gets Worse . . ."; and Puar, "In the Wake."
18. West et al., "Queer Worldmaking," 51–52.
19. Krutzsch, *Dying to Be Normal*, 86.
20. Montgomery, "Rise Against's 'Make It Stop.'"

for "Best Video with a Message" at the 2011 MTV Video Music Awards (it lost to Lady Gaga's "Born This Way," another LGBTQ+ anthem).

The documentary film *Bully* (formerly titled *The Bully Project*) also premiered in 2011. Filmed during the 2009–10 school year, *Bully* follows five students ranging in age from eleven to seventeen and their families, highlighting the relentless bullying they faced from peers. Viewers learn that two of the five featured young people, including the eleven-year-old, die by suicide within the school year chronicled by the film. The arrival of *Bully* was timely, landing in the aftermath of the September 2010 suicides and their media coverage, with sympathetic audiences stimulated by It Gets Better and other poignant portrayals of queer youth, bullying, and suicide. But its release was complicated by the Motion Picture Association of America (MPAA) giving the film an R rating for language. This rating meant that the film was inaccessible to young people like the ones whose stories it tells, and that it could not be used by schools or other youth organizations as part of educational programs on bullying. Eventually *Bully* was released with no rating (which still prevented it from being shown in most American movie theater chains), and then later an edited version with less profanity was offered a PG-13 rating. The controversy over the rating, as well as its incredible irony—young people not being allowed to see footage of the violence that so many experience in their daily lives on the school bus or in the lunchroom—added to the sense of urgency and outrage about bullying and suicide itself.[21]

This moment of cultural awareness and reckoning was also symbolized by the proliferation of new language to refer to the problem of bullying and suicide: the use of the term *bullycide* spiked in the aftermath of the September 2010 suicides. This neologism was coined in 2001 by Neil Marr and Tim Field in their book, *Bullycide: Death at Playtime*, but it became a convenient way in 2010 and beyond to mark the apparent connection between bullying and suicide. Headlines referred to, for example, "The Grief of Bullycide" and "'Bullycide' A Sadly New Pandemic," and articles described "bullycide victims" and young people "literally bullied to death"; a *48 Hours* special presentation even used "bullycide" as a substitute for "suicide," as in "committed bullycide" or a "bullycide attempt." The term was taken up in the title of a play, *The Bullycide Project*, which was based on the stories included in Brenda High's 2012 book, *Bullycide in America: Moms Speak Out about the Bullying/Suicide Connection*, and even in a piano sextet called "Bullycide" by composer David Del Tredici.[22] Rhetorical scholars have noted that neologisms arise in order to "present

---

21. "New Film"; Holmes, "'Bully' Problems"; and Douglas, "Interview."
22. Moody, "Mother on Mission"; Kessler, "Grief of Bullycide"; "'Bullycide'"; Smith, "Bullying"; and Swed, "Gay Bullying."

the unpresentable," or to offer a new interpretation or framing of a subject; "bullycide" does this by quite literally fusing bullying to suicide, presenting suicide as an inevitable and overdetermined outcome of bullying.[23] This conflation suggests not just a relationship between bullying and suicide but a specifically causal relationship, implying that concerns about youth suicide might be best and most naturally addressed by focusing on bullying.

What we can see in the news coverage and mainstream responses to the September 2010 suicides, then, is a vivid snapshot of a moment of cultural anxiety and a response to what was often treated as a newly emergent crisis. It was an attempt to grapple—for many Americans, likely for the first time— with the realities of the inequalities present in school settings, the myriad forms that homophobia takes, the stressors faced by young people who do not conform to the expectations of heterosexuality or traditional gendered behaviors, and even the very existence of queer youth. Linking together the deaths of these nine boys might be understood as a means for making public sense of what would otherwise be private moments of loss and grief.

This moment of crisis did important rhetorical work to shape the contours of subsequent discussions of bullying, suicide, and the vulnerabilities of queer youth: it helped to naturalize the connection between suicide and bullying and to identify queer youth as being particularly at risk for both. Especially given the dearth of prior media coverage of queer youth, this culturally and temporally specific moment illuminates how queer youth were constructed as a social group through the dissemination and institutionalization of the news about bullying and suicide. As Tom Waidzunas explains, "new kinds of people such as 'gay youth' are not merely discovered by experts, but rather, such human kinds come into being at the same time that human classifications are invented through a process of 'making up people.'"[24] Thus, taking September 2010 not as an origin but as a moment of crystallization, I use the articulation of these nine suicides to demonstrate how a particular rhetorical figuration of queer youth—where queer youth are inherently vulnerable to bullying and suicide—helps queer youth become intelligible in mainstream discourses that previously disregarded and erased them. Later in this chapter, I trace how this figuration continues to develop and is institutionalized across subsequent discourse: federal recommendations and policies about bullying and scholarly attention to queer youth at risk for suicide. But first, in the next section I investigate the production of vulnerability itself, noting that the privileges of vulnerability in this context arise from whiteness and masculinity's precarious performance.

---

23. Nuyen, "Role of Rhetorical Devices," 190.
24. Waidzunas, "Young, Gay, and Suicidal," 203.

Privilege and Precarity: Racial Figurations of Masculine Vulnerability

Recognizing the tension between material precarities and the rhetorical ascription of vulnerability means understanding vulnerability not as a quality of a particular group but as a contextual and political marker. As Oliviero suggests, "vulnerability is more a subjectivity and political context rather than an identity: it may be a universal ontological condition, but it is also experienced unequally and shifts in a way that both clings to and exceeds identity-based categories."[25] Vulnerability can become tightly associated with particular groups of people, while also remaining malleable enough to be attributed strategically to others, producing affective appeals, reworking categories of belonging, and refiguring which lives deserve protection.[26] Thus, it can be deployed tactically and flexibly to imagine dominant populations and institutions as imperiled and in need of protection, even if their vulnerability is not based in—and possibly even co-opts others'—actual material precarities.

The most familiar and insidious manifestation of the manipulation of vulnerability to instantiate and reinforce cultural hierarchies is the construction of the apotheosis of studied defenselessness: white femininity. Feminist and critical race scholars have long noted the usefulness of white womanhood's vulnerability in upholding white supremacy and patriarchy, in part through its contrasting production of predatory Black and Brown masculinity (often with violent and deadly consequences for men of color). Rooted in the contexts of settler colonialism and slavery, the supposedly inherent innocence and purity of white womanhood remains on display in countless contemporary contexts, ranging from white celebrity women garnering public attention to sexual harassment and assault in the #MeToo movement, to missing and murdered Aboriginal women in Canada who do not receive the same kind of compassionate and thorough news coverage that white victims are granted.[27] White femininity is often perceived to be—or strategically and convincingly positioned to be—vulnerable even when no real threat exists. As Carol Mason points out, anti-trans "bathroom bills" seek to deny trans people equal access to public restrooms by manufacturing fears about white women and girls being preyed upon by sexual predators, and in anti-abortion bills, "white women and girls are portrayed as being victimized by all sorts of predators—moral, financial, sexual, racial, Semitic, and satanic—or a conglomeration of all of these."[28] Dreama Moon and Michelle Holling describe these discursive

---

25. Oliviero, *Vulnerability Politics*, 47.
26. Oliviero, *Vulnerability Politics*, 9.
27. Gilchrist, "'Newsworthy' Victims?"
28. Mason, "Opposing Abortion," 666–67.

strategies of "white victimhood" at some length in the context of white feminism, where they result in whiteness being recentered, women of color and their experiences being ignored or made invisible, and white supremacy being reproduced.[29]

Even when it does not specifically invoke femininity, whiteness can depend on the quality of vulnerability in "white innocence myths" to uphold systems of white supremacy.[30] As Anastasia Kanjere explains, "white vulnerability is one component of the logic by which a notion of innocence is recruited as a means of protection and justification of whiteness." Robin DiAngelo has famously named a certain version of this vulnerability "white fragility," and describes how it protects white people from anti-racist criticisms by privileging their potential hurt feelings over the actual harms done to people of color.[31] This emphasis on whiteness's vulnerability, as Mary Bucholtz argues, "strategically and affectively positions whiteness as beleaguered in order to maintain the white-supremacist racial order for all white people"; whiteness thus justifies its own defense.[32]

Whiteness's association with vulnerability not only provides a framework for understanding how certain populations are protected while others remain precarious, but also has material consequences for who can be perceived as a victim. Put bluntly, white victims are more easily recognized and white people, regardless of gender, are more easily imagined as being the targets of persecution, abuse, and oppression. For example, in a study of Los Angeles news reporting, Travis L. Dixon found that white people were significantly overrepresented as homicide victims on local television news in comparison to their actual rates of victimization according to crime reports. By contrast, the news coverage of Black victims was proportionate to their actual victimization, while the news coverage of Latinos vastly underrepresented their victimization (whites made up only 13% of actual victims but composed 35% of the television coverage, whereas Latinos were 50% of actual homicide victims but only 10% of the news coverage).[33] These findings comport with numerous studies on racial bias in bystander responses and the unequal application of hate-crimes laws depending on the race of the victims and the perpetrators.[34]

---

29. Moon and Holling, "'White Supremacy in Heels,'" 256.
30. Lacy, "White Innocence Myths."
31. The phenomenon of "white women's tears" functions similarly, emphasizing whiteness's inability to withstand confrontation or critique. Kanjere, "Defending Race Privilege," 2161.
32. Bucholtz, "Public Life of White Affects," 488.
33. Dixon, "Good Guys," 784. Similarly, as Tommy J. Curry reports, Black men are sexually assaulted at higher rates than white women, but due to raced and gendered assumptions about vulnerability they are often overlooked as victims. Curry, "Expendables for Whom."
34. Kunstman and Plant, "Racing to Help"; Katz et al., "White Female Bystanders' Responses"; and Spieldenner and Glenn, "Scripting Hate Crimes."

The contemporary racialized and gendered form of what Rey Chow calls the "cultural capital of victimhood" depends upon previous iterations through a variety of historical social problems.[35] For instance, Julian Carter identifies "the construction of whiteness as weakness" in the late nineteenth-century medical formulation of neurasthenia, or "nervous exhaustion." The predilection toward nervousness among bourgeois white people was an indication of their physical, intellectual, and moral sensitivity and their refinement; in short, it signified their evolutionary superiority over the racialized laboring classes whose stout, brawny, vigorous bodies were not susceptible to nervous disorders.[36] The weakness of whiteness, in other words, worked paradoxically as an asset in demonstrating white superiority; it was "a way for whites to talk about whiteness as both precious and vulnerable" and "helped to disguise the power relationships embedded in its constructions of racial and national modernity."[37] Emphasizing the vulnerability of whiteness both bolstered white claims to natural dominance and obscured the actual maldistribution of material vulnerabilities among nonwhite and working-class populations.

Of course, the discourse of neurasthenia was particular to its time; by the 1920s, the construction of whiteness as weakness was recalibrated around different vulnerable figures, which Carter identifies as the "contemptible (if sometimes fascinating) cultural figures of the degenerate 'fairy,' the mannish or man-hating woman, and the primitive pervert."[38] These figures might be thought of as the antecedents to the contemporary framing of queer boys at risk for bullying and suicide, offering a historical context for vulnerability's queerness and implicit whiteness. The cultural capital of victimhood, especially in its association with whiteness, thus provides a particular figure (the neurasthenic, the fairy, the bullied queer boy) in which the anxieties of maintaining whiteness's supremacy can be located, while also offering ever-evolving examples of whiteness's vulnerability and need for protection. Therefore, even though not all of the nine boys who died by suicide in September 2010 were white—Raymond Chase was Black, and Billy Lucas's (unspecified) ethnicity was named as one of the reasons he was bullied in the wrongful-death lawsuit his family filed against his school district—the whiteness of the figuration of vulnerability arises from the rhetorical ascription of vulnerability as a category of relative privilege.[39]

But how does white masculinity—in general, the category enjoying the greatest degree of protection from embodied forms of gendered and raced

---

35. Chow, *Protestant Ethnic*, 180.
36. Carter, *Heart of Whiteness*, 43, 47–48.
37. Carter, *Heart of Whiteness*, 44.
38. Carter, *Heart of Whiteness*, 73.
39. "On Anniversary."

precarity—come to make convincing claims on vulnerability? And how does the vulnerability of the figure of queer youth at risk depend on this particular vulnerability of white masculinity? As norms of gender shift and some aspects of male privilege are exposed, we can see not just whiteness in general but white masculinity in particular cast as vulnerable and imperiled because, as Bucholtz puts it, privilege "is inherently unstable and thus requires regular fortification."[40] Thus, the most vulnerable aspect of white masculinity is located precisely in its constant exertions to perform and maintain privilege in contexts of changing racial formations and gender norms. Sara Ahmed describes this "defense system" of white male fragility as constantly anticipating a future potential loss or injury that justifies preventative or avoidance measures in the present.[41]

The vulnerability of white masculinity is often rehearsed in popular and political contexts. For instance, Casey Ryan Kelly describes the filmic representation of the "wounded man" who is imagined to be harmed by the marginal gains made by women, people of color, immigrants, and queers. Kelly explains that the figure of the "wounded man" can build political communities on the basis of a (perceived) shared victimhood, "encourag[ing] white men to speak about common human vulnerability as if it were structural oppression." Crucially, the "wounded man" does not relinquish power through vulnerability; as Kelly writes, this figure "appropriates victimhood even as it celebrates white male primacy."[42] In fact, the claims to white masculinity's victimhood function to consolidate power, as Paul Johnson demonstrates in regard to Donald Trump's use of victimized white masculinity to facilitate demagoguery, manufacture precarity, and ultimately destabilize liberal democracy.[43]

I highlight these examples of how white masculinity can be seen as vulnerable not to suggest that any such intentional process is at work in the framing of white queer boys as vulnerable to bullying and suicide—indeed, the visibility of queer youth in the last decade is part of the supposed threat to white (hetero)masculinity's dominance, as well as the precarity that it appropriates as its own. Rather, Kelly's and Johnson's work demonstrates the performative and contingent nature of white masculinity, which must continually work to establish dominance.[44] Joseph A. Vandello and Jennifer K. Bosson characterize this demand for the repeated performance of masculinity as "precarious manhood." They explain that, in contrast to womanhood, which is typically

40. Bucholtz, "Public Life of White Affects," 488.
41. Ahmed, *Living a Feminist Life*, 179, 276n1.
42. Kelly, "Wounded Man," 163–64.
43. Johnson, "Art of Masculine Victimhood."
44. Johnson, "Walter White(ness) Lashes Out."

understood as more closely linked to embodiment and ascribed because of biological changes, manhood is a social status that is hard won, easily lost, and requires continual public performances. Thus, masculinity is an elusive status that must be earned, it is always "tenuous and impermanent," and it must be publicly enacted because it can only be confirmed by others.[45] The vulnerability particular to white masculinity, then, is not so much about material precarity as it is about the looming danger of not properly performing and therefore losing access to the privileged status of the category.

In the next two sections, I bring this understanding of the conferral of vulnerability to bear on federal recommendations and policies about bullying and researchers' attempts to account for queer youths' risk for suicide. I inquire into the conflation of bullying, homophobia, and suicide, delving into the tensions between, on one hand, the very real precarities experienced by queer, trans, and gender-nonconforming youth (especially youth of color) in a cis- and heteronormative culture and, on the other hand, the ascription of a vulnerability that is justified by the privileges of whiteness and the performativity of masculinity. Attending to the racial figuration of vulnerability calls into question the assumption of this characteristic as an inherent quality of queer youth and forces us to reckon with the ways in which the rhetorical consolidation of the vulnerability of certain young people (white cis gay boys) appropriates but ultimately obscures the specific precarities of others—especially youth of color, girls, and trans and gender-nonconforming youth.

Natural Targets: Defining the Problem of Bullying and Queer Youth

Contemporary statistics on bullying and suicide among queer youth vary from one study to another, but the general patterns that emerge are fairly consistent: while about 20 percent of all young people report being bullied at school, among LGBTQ+ students the rates are higher, with 70 percent being bullied verbally, 29 percent being bullied physically, and 49 percent experiencing cyberbullying.[46] According to the Trevor Project's National Survey on LGBTQ+ Youth Mental Health in 2021, over half of all LGBTQ+ youth have experienced bullying in the past year. Trans and nonbinary students reported more bullying (61%) than their cisgender LGBQ peers (45%). This bullying disproportionately targets LGBTQ+ youth who are Native/Indigenous

---

45. Vandello and Bosson, "Hard Won and Easily Lost," 101.
46. US Dept. of Education, "Student Reports of Bullying"; and PACER, "Bullying Statistics."

(70%), multiracial (54%), white (54%), and Latinx (47%), while Asian American / Pacific Islander (41%), and Black (41%) LGBTQ+ youth face slightly lower but still alarming rates of bullying. Queer and trans youth are also at significantly higher risk than their heterosexual peers for considering suicide, making a plan for suicide, attempting suicide, and being injured in a suicide attempt.[47] For example, the Trevor Project's survey found that in the past year, 42 percent of LGBTQ+ youth and 52 percent of trans and nonbinary youth seriously considered suicide, and 20 percent of trans and nonbinary youth attempted suicide.[48] LGBTQ+ youth of color were particularly at risk, with Native/Indigenous (31%), Black (21%), multiracial (21%), and Latinx (18%) youth all reporting higher rates of suicide attempts than white (12%) and Asian/Pacific Islander (12%) youth.[49] There seems to be no question, then, that queer and trans youth experience more bullying than heterosexual and cisgender youth and that queer and trans youth of color, in particular, report heightened rates of suicidal ideation.

However, simply identifying these trends does not address how this data functions rhetorically. For example, the representations of LGBTQ+ young people in these statistics often obscure their intersectional racial and gender identities, therefore depicting bullying and suicide as one-dimensional problems affecting queer kids. The correlation between bullying and suicide is clear in statistics amalgamating all LGBTQ+ youth, but that correlation becomes more complex when race and gender identity are specified (for instance, Native/Indigenous LGBQ youth and trans and nonbinary youth do experience heightened rates of both bullying and suicide, but while white youth are bullied more than Black youth, the rate of suicide attempts among Black youth is nearly double that of white youth). In spite of these nuances, which suggest that neither bullying nor suicide behaviors can be explained only in terms of sexuality, policy and popular discourses tend to make sense of LGBTQ+ youths' relationship to these risks primarily through their queerness, treating it as an inherent characteristic that makes them uniquely vulnerable. Thus, in the remainder of this section, I first examine the relatively sophisticated guidance on bullying offered by the federal government in the "Bullying Surveillance" report, and then turn to the popular interpretation of this report on the bullying.gov website, which (re)produces the hetero(non)sexuality of youth and contributes to the figuration of queer youth as predisposed to vulnerability to bullying and suicide.

---

47. CDC, "Youth Risk Behavior Survey . . . 2011–2021."
48. Trevor Project, "National Survey."
49. Trevor Project, "National Survey."

State Policies and Federal Guidance on Bullying

There are no federal laws to regulate bullying behavior; rather, it is handled at the state and local level through a variety of different laws and policies. The first anti-bullying state law was passed in Georgia in 1999, partially in response to the Columbine school shooting of the same year. The perpetrators, Eric Harris and Dylan Klebold, were often described as having endured constant and severe bullying, notably including being frequently called "queer" and "faggots."[50] The link between being bullied and acting violently was the subject of much investigation and discussion in the aftermath of Columbine, and although the veracity of Eric's and Dylan's bullying is contentious (some sources report that they were, themselves, bullies), many states followed Georgia's lead in passing new laws about bullying. In fact, from 1999 to 2010, more than 120 separate bills that either introduced or amended bullying statutes in states' education or criminal codes were enacted.[51] The number of new or amended state laws spiked again in 2010 and the following years, in response to the September 2010 suicides highlighted here. Tyler Clementi's suicide, in particular, was a catalyst for his home state of New Jersey to pass nearly unanimously the "Anti-bullying Bill of Rights"—often recognized as the most stringent of all state laws against bullying—within two months of his death.

By 2015 every American state had passed laws about bullying that offered at least a statement that bullying behaviors were unacceptable, although states define what counts as bullying slightly differently. Many, but not all, of these state laws require schools to implement bullying-prevention programs, but most do not offer any oversight or assistance with creating these programs, nor any means for ensuring that schools are in compliance. In general, state laws also do not dictate consequences for bullying behavior or classify it as a criminal offense. Only in cases where bullying overlaps with discriminatory harassment based on race, national origin, color, sex, age, disability, or religion is it subject to federal civil rights laws enforced by the US Department of Education and the US Department of Justice.[52] Notably, harassment based on sexual orientation has only recently been determined to be prohibited by civil rights laws and educational laws such as Title IX; according to a January 2021

---

50. I recognize the potential for the word "faggots" to cause injury and perpetuate violence. I include it in full here because that violence is central to my claims about the (re)production of the racial figuration and hetero(non)sexuality of youth. Later in the chapter, I return to this particular epithet and the "fag discourse" as a means for reinforcing the white supremacist and misogynist underpinnings of hegemonic masculinity.
51. US Dept. of Education, "Analysis of State Bullying Laws," 16.
52. "Federal Laws."

executive order, sexual orientation, gender identity, and intersex traits are all included under these laws' protections based on "sex."[53]

But state-level anti-bullying laws and federal discrimination laws mainly have a symbolic aim and are not intended to be the primary point of intervention for preventing bullying. As Deborah Temkin, a director of education research at Child Trends, a nonpartisan, nonprofit research organization, and formerly a member of the US Department of Education's federal initiative on bullying, explains, "the purpose of anti-bullying laws is to demonstrate that the legislature recognizes bullying as something that must be addressed, but the laws do not and cannot serve as the mechanism by which to actually address the behavior."[54] Furthermore, bullying behaviors are unlikely to decrease through the punishment of individual bullies or the criminalization of acts of bullying. Indeed, as Temkin argues, criminalizing bullying is more likely to have detrimental effects in terms of the school-to-prison pipeline (which, as we saw clearly in the previous chapter, already disproportionately impacts youth of color and queer youth) and offers nothing in the way of support for mental health or to change bullying behaviors.[55]

In light of the lack of uniformity across state bullying legislation and the inability (and inadvisability) of these laws to directly address bullying behavior, as well as the nonexistence of federal bullying legislation, the US federal government offers research-based guidance on how best to study and prevent bullying. The effort to address bullying at the federal level began in 2008, when the Federal Partners in Bullying Prevention Steering Committee was established; the committee convened the first Federal Partners in Bullying Prevention Summit in August 2010, just prior to the September suicides that would soon make their work much more publicly visible. Discussions at the summit among nonprofit and corporate leaders, researchers, practitioners, parents, and youth, as well as a subsequent review of the CDC's bullying assessment tools, revealed that inconsistent definitions of and measurement tools for bullying were hampering efforts at prevention. As a result, the CDC, in collaboration with the Department of Education and the Health Resources and Services Administration (HRSA), produced a report entitled "Bullying Surveillance Among Youth: Uniform Definitions for Public Health

---

53. "Federal Laws"; White House, "Executive Order." This executive order is based on the Supreme Court's 2020 ruling in *Bostock v. Clayton County* that laws prohibiting "sex" discrimination also protect individuals from discrimination on the basis of sexual orientation, gender identity, and sex stereotyping. The interpretation of "sex" in federal civil rights and education laws is taken up in more specificity in chapter 3.
54. Temkin, "All 50 States."
55. Temkin, "Why Criminalizing Bullying."

and Recommended Data Elements, Version 1.0." Released in 2014, the "Bullying Surveillance" report offered the first federal definition of bullying in the United States. It also included an extensive list of data elements that can be translated into survey questions or data collection items, and provided a framework for monitoring bullying as a public health issue.[56]

As the "Bullying Surveillance" report asserts, a uniform definition of bullying is necessary to "understand the true magnitude, scope, and impact of bullying and track trends over time" and to "improve public health surveillance of bullying and inform efforts to address bullying."[57] As such, the uniform definition indicates that bullying has three key characteristics: it is (1) unwanted aggressive behavior from another youth or youths that (2) involves an observed or perceived power imbalance and (3) is repeated multiple times or is highly likely to be repeated. Bullying can be carried out directly (face-to-face aggression or aggressive communication delivered to the targeted youth) or indirectly (spreading rumors about the targeted youth), and might include physical force, verbal aggression (taunts, threats, offensive or inappropriate comments), relational bullying (isolating or ignoring, spreading false or harmful rumors, publicly displaying embarrassing images), and damage to property. Bullying can occur in multiple contexts, both in school and outside of school, and of course, can also happen on social media and in other digital forms.[58] Specifically excluded from this definition is aggressive behavior or violence directed toward youths by adults, by siblings or other family members, or by romantic or dating partners. However, noting that youths who are involved in or targeted by bullying are often also the victims of other forms of violence, including sexual violence, the report strongly recommends that those concerned for youth safety attend to a broad range of threats.[59]

The report also points out that simply understanding the magnitude of bullying is not sufficient to address it as a public health problem. Unlike much of the mainstream media discourse of the 2010s, which sutures together queer identity (or perceived queer identity), bullying, and suicide risk, the report calls for the importance of understanding why bullying occurs and which factors make young people more or less vulnerable to being bullied. In other words, the connections between identity and bullying need to be proven, rather than assumed. Another report released by the CDC in 2014 emphasizes that framing bullying as a single, direct cause of suicide can have multiple harmful effects, including normalizing suicide as the natural response to

---

56. Gladden et al., "Bullying Surveillance," 2.
57. Gladden et al., "Bullying Surveillance," 1.
58. Gladden et al., "Bullying Surveillance," 7–8.
59. Gladden et al., "Bullying Surveillance," 1.

bullying, encouraging copycat behavior among youth, promoting sensationalized reporting, and ignoring other important risk factors like mental illness, substance abuse, family violence, and so on.[60]

Furthermore, the "Bullying Surveillance" report contends that bullied youths cannot be understood in isolation from their social, cultural, and community contexts:

> it is critical to recognize that bullying behavior emerges not only from the characteristics of youths themselves, but is affected by the responses of youths and adults who witness bullying, community and school norms, and larger social factors.... The most effective prevention programs will respond to the range of contributing factors instead of solely focusing on the individuals engaging in or experiencing bullying behaviors.[61]

Even the power imbalances that are a defining feature of bullying behavior should not be assumed to be static characteristics of the youths involved, the report cautions; instead of viewing certain individuals as "powerless" or "powerful," based on aspects of their identities or by virtue of their social standing, power is conceptualized as fluctuating and relational, not belonging to particular people, but changing across situations and over time.[62]

In short, the recommendations and warnings of the "Bullying Surveillance" report paint a complex picture of the terrain of bullying. This guidance suggests there are no easy ways to identify young people who are likely to be bullied or to be bullies themselves, that sanctions for individual behaviors cannot be imagined as solutions to the problems of systems of aggression, and that bullying and suicide do not have a predictable relationship.

The Popularization of Federal Guidance on Bullying

The cultural nuances of bullying behavior and risk factors that the "Bullying Surveillance" report describes are not typically captured in more popular treatments of bullying in the media, and they are not reflected in advice offered to the public or in policy decisions in schools. Indeed, the federal government's own website on bullying, stopbullying.gov, managed by the US Department of Health and Human Services in cooperation with the Federal Partners in Bullying Prevention Steering Committee—the same committee

---

60. CDC, "Relationship."
61. Gladden et al., "Bullying Surveillance," 4–5.
62. Gladden et al., "Bullying Surveillance," 8.

that produced the "Bullying Surveillance" report—simplifies and distorts the report's recommendations, rendering bullying as a problem of identity risk factors rather than contexts and communities, and drawing explicit connections among queerness, bullying, and suicide. In this translation from the "Bullying Surveillance" report to the stopbullying.gov website, we can begin to see how adults' insistence on the hetero(non)sexuality of youth and assumptions about whiteness and queerness have material effects for queer and trans youth of color.

The stopbullying.gov website offers information on bullying, cyberbullying, and prevention, resources for both young people and adults, and a set of videos on bullying for kids. Although some of the website's materials are targeted toward young people (for instance, there are tips for teens who want to intervene in bullying behavior or join anti-bullying efforts in their schools), its primary audience is educators, parents, and other adults who work with youth. There is much to be explored in this website, but I am most interested here in the ways it frames the question of "risk" and how risk attaches to particular youths' identities. Under its information on bullying there is a "Who Is at Risk" tab that categorizes "children at risk of being bullied" and "children more likely to bully others." This page begins by cautioning that "No single factor puts a child at risk of being bullied or bullying others," and that it "can happen anywhere." But then in the very next sentence it offers a short list of specific groups—LGBTQ youth, youth with disabilities, and socially isolated youth—who may have an increased risk of being targeted by bullying. This statement is then followed by a longer list of the more general risk factors that bullied children tend to share: being "perceived as different," being "overweight or underweight," being "perceived as weak," being depressed, anxious, or having low self-esteem, and being "less popular than others and hav[ing] few friends."

These statements paint an ambivalent picture of which youths are most likely to be bullied, simultaneously particularizing the problem to specific identity groups and universalizing it to a set of supposedly non-identity-based characteristics. The claims about the general characteristics of bullied youth and the multiplicity of factors involved contradict the singling out of specific groups (LGBTQ youth and youth with disabilities; "socially isolated youth," unlike the other two categories, is not a quantifiable demographic or a meaningful identity) who seem to be at increased risk simply by virtue of membership in these groups. Furthermore, some of the characteristics of youth who are bullied—depression, anxiety, low self-esteem, having few friends— also map perfectly onto what the website identifies as *effects* of bullying, and might also be reasonably assumed to be consequences of a heteronormative and ableist environment. Thus, is a queer kid bullied because they are queer? Because they have low self-esteem? Or do they have low self-esteem because they have been bullied? Or because they feel marginalized in the heteronormative spaces at school? In other words, there is a conflation of the risk factors for bullying (which are located in the identities, personalities, or social interactions of the bullied youth, not in the environments that permit or promote bullying) with the effects of bullying. And although queerness and disability are invoked, neither heteronormativity nor ableism are acknowledged as the real factors that make certain kids more vulnerable.

The confusion about risk is further exacerbated by an additional series of tabs on the stopbullying.gov website that name particular groups of young people; separate pages for "Race, National Origin, & Religion," "LGBTQI+ Youth," "Military Connected Youth," and "Disabilities & Special Needs" are intermingled with more general pages on, for instance, "Warning Signs for Bullying," "Bullying and Trauma," and "The Roles Kids Play." Singling out these four groups of young people certainly seems to suggest, contrary to the assertion that bullying is not predicted by identities, that they are uniquely overrepresented as victims. Each of these pages explains the specific characteristics of the named group that might lead to bullying and the supports needed to create a safer school environment. By treating each identity as a separate category of risk, however, they do not acknowledge the interaction of characteristics; kids are bullied, it seems, on the basis of one-dimensional identities, not because they are, for example, nonbinary, biracial, and autistic. In spite of trans, gender-nonconforming, queer, and intersex kids being invoked by the "LGBTQI+ Youth" label, the statistics offered only address lesbian, gay, and bisexual youth. Trans, nonbinary, gender-nonconforming, intersex, and queer youth are specifically mentioned only in a box describing "gaps in the data"—an especially egregious oversight given trans and gender-nonconforming students' reports of disproportionate rates of bullying.

Furthermore, the "LGBTQI+ Youth" page also figures LGBTQI+ youth differently than the other groups of presumably at-risk youth described on the stopbullying.gov website. The other pages carefully explain why or how the group in question might be targeted by bullying behavior: for instance, for military-connected youth, the stressors of frequent moves and school changes, worrying about parents who are deployed and potentially in danger, and increased family responsibilities are all listed as reasons that these youth may feel vulnerable, anxious, and less engaged with their peers, their classes, and their community, and therefore at risk for bullying. For youth with disabilities, their difficulties moving around their school, their differences in physical appearance, their cognitive abilities, their modes of communicating or ways of interacting socially, and their potential signs of vulnerability or distress may all contribute to their being perceived as different and at risk for aggression from peers (but again, "ableism" is not named as the source of these problems). Finally, bullying based on religious differences is described in terms of the way certain kinds of religious garb (e.g., hijabs, turbans, and yarmulkes) identify those young people as different from their (presumably Christian) peers, and may be the site of physical aggression, such as when these religious markers are forcibly removed. Significantly, this page also points out that anti-Muslim and anti-Sikh bullying has been on the rise in recent years due to the perceived association of these groups with terrorism.

By contrast, there is no similar effort to explain why or how queer, trans, and gender-nonconforming youth might be targeted by bullies. Unlike the other groups described, there is no discussion of, for instance, the specific stressors that LGBTQI+ kids might face and that may make them appear more vulnerable and anxious to their peers, or the kinds of behaviors or social interactions that might make LGBTQI+ kids seem "different" from their heterosexual and cisgender classmates. There is certainly no suggestion that the bullying of LGBTQI+ youth might be part of larger cultural patterns of stereotyping, transphobia, and homophobia, let alone recognition of how LGBTQI+ youth of color may experience bullying inflected by racism. Indeed, the qualities of LGBTQI+ youth that are most commonly associated with these identity categories and most frequently targeted by bullies—that is, failure to perform gender in accordance with a binary and traditional model, modes of dress and bodily comportment, romantic or sexual interests and activities, and so on—are completely absent from the page. The sexual behaviors and markers of sexual identities of queer kids, and the very existence of trans kids and LGBTQI+ youth of color, are veiled rather than acknowledged, as if even in discussions of bullying prevention the realities of youth sexuality and gender nonconformity must acquiesce to the pretense of white hetero(non)sexuality.

What is mentioned, however, is the particular vulnerability of queer kids to suicide: beginning with a statement that being bullied—regardless of a young person's identity—puts them at "increased risk for depression, suicidal ideation, misuse of drugs and alcohol, risky sexual behavior, and can affect academics as well," the page then asserts, "For LGBTQI+ youth, that risk is even higher." This brief concluding sentence seems to suggest that LGBTQI+ youth are somehow more naturally vulnerable to the negative outcomes of bullying, including suicide, than other youth who are bullied, but offers no further explanation for that risk.

This figuration of queer youth at risk for bullying on the stopbullying.gov website, in which the corporealities and experiences of queerness are obscured more than they are illuminated, has at least two potential effects. First, even though queer, trans, and gender-nonconforming identities are clearly defined in terms of self-recognition, presentation, attraction, and/or behavior that is gendered and/or sexual in ways that deviate from heterosexual and cisgender norms, the failure of the LGBTQI+ youth page to even so much as allude to these characteristics dehumanizes and desexualizes the young people it is meant to protect. This silence—kids identified specifically by their sexual orientations are stripped of sexuality—is the awkward outcome of the demands of hetero(non)sexuality, in which queerness cannot (yet) be known by young people. As a result, LGBTQI+ youth are defined solely in terms of the label applied to them, rather than in terms of the agency they exercise to embody and declare their queer sexualities and/or gender-nonconforming identities. Furthermore, although these categories are obviously sexual and/or gendered in nature, the page does not acknowledge the ways in which the bullying of LGBTQI+ youth may take on sexual and/or gendered characteristics as well (for instance, through the use of specifically gendered or sexualized name-calling, nonconsensual "outing" to peers or adults, using sexually explicit language or images, and unwanted advances, touching, or sexual assault). This refusal to recognize bullying's frequent homophobic and misogynist incarnations is especially ironic given the conflation of bullying and anti-gay sentiment I described in the media coverage of the September 2010 suicides. Here, the figuration of the bullied and potentially suicidal queer or gender-nonconforming youth is a degendered and desexualized figure who has somehow acquired the label of "LGBTQI+" without actually exercising any gendered or sexual agency of their own.

Second, the increased risk of bullying for LGBTQ+ youth is attributed to *who they are,* rather than, as for the other groups of youth identified, to perceptions of differences in their behavior or appearance. As I described earlier, the bullying of military-connected kids, youth with disabilities, and racial-, ethnic-, and religious-minority youth is depicted as targeting specific actions or characteristics, and even acknowledges the potential role played by misinformation about religious expression or shared ethnic or racial traits. In short, the bullying of these kids, and the distress that they might feel in reaction to bullying's threat, is not portrayed as inherent in the young people themselves. But for LGBTQ+ kids, the heightened risk of bullying appears to be self-evident and tautological: queer kids are bullied for being queer. As a result, the risk of being bullied—and the risk of bullying's corollary, suicide—is embedded into the figuration of queer youth that circulates in policy discourse.

These depictions of LGBTQ+ kids in federal guidance documents matter not only in terms of the way they encourage readers to understand and interact with queer youth but also in terms of the policy decisions that they justify. The racial figuration of queer youth vulnerability that is (re)produced, in other words, is the transfer point between the representational, persuasive work of language and the material conditions of real children. Adults' interpretation and application of these guidelines shape actual queer young people's experiences in school and with peers, and perhaps most importantly, they lead adults to recognize (or not) queer youths' sexual agency, and to respect (or not) queer youths' articulation of their gendered and sexual identities. These effects are certainly not limited to the narrow selection of federal guidance I have surveyed here; in the next section I explore how scholarly research on queer youth also tends to participate in comforting narratives about queer youth vulnerability and resilience.

Risky or Resilient: Scholarly Narratives of Queer Youth

Eve Kosofsky Sedgwick begins the first essay of her 1993 book *Tendencies* with the assertion, "I think everyone who does gay and lesbian studies is haunted by the suicides of adolescents." Citing a 1989 US Department of Health and Human Services report that found queer teens—and especially queer teens of color—to be significantly more likely to consider, attempt, and die by suicide, she continues, "The knowledge is indelible, but not astonishing, to anyone with a reason to be attuned to the profligate way this culture has of denying and despoiling queer energies and lives."[63] Sedgwick's statement, written long before the awareness of queer youth suicide had reached the mainstream American public, echoes eerily in later academic accounts that similarly note how the suicidal fate of queer kids is stubbornly inscribed in the popular and scholarly imagination. For example, in Rob Cover's 2012 book, *Queer Youth Suicide, Culture and Identity: Unliveable Lives?*, he describes reading about the September 2010 suicides as "both distressing and strangely familiar." He names this sense of familiarity "resigned expectation," and describes it as the feeling that "we could not really imagine queer lives untouched by suicide," and that suicide "continue[s] to seem like a logical outcome for queer youth."[64] Cover asks, "What is it that makes it culturally 'comfortable' for people to see a young queer life as an unliveable life?"[65] Cover's feeling of "resigned expectation" resonates with Sedgwick's sense of the haunting "but not astonishing"

---

63. Sedgwick, *Tendencies*, 1.
64. Cover, *Queer Youth Suicide*, ix, x.
65. Cover, *Queer Youth Suicide*, xi.

knowledge of queer kids' suicidality, suggesting that vulnerability is prominent in figurations of queer youth not only in media coverage and official federal recommendations but in academic discourse as well.

In this section I turn to scholarly treatments of queer youth and their risks for suicide, treating academic discourse itself as my object of analysis, in order to draw out how scholars who study queer youth have both participated in and sought to expose the racial figuration of queer youth vulnerability. I argue that the ways researchers perpetuate and/or contest this figuration, like the preceding guidance and policy documents, has important material effects for queer youth: it determines the kinds of research that are valorized, it justifies funding and programs that target queer youth in terms of their risk, and it influences the ways queer youth learn to narrate their own identities, struggles, and agency. I end this section by attending to the scholarly turn from vulnerability to resilience, an impulse that I suggest may shift scholarly focus from queer youths' fragility to their strengths, but that nonetheless reasserts a white neoliberal narrative of success.

The figuration of queer youth as victims builds upon a history of representations of queer youth in both popular culture and research that treats them primarily through the lens of what Cover calls "vulnerabilization."[66] For instance, Richard Dyer identifies the figure of the "sad young man," a young, white, beautiful, sensitive, melancholic stereotype of homosexuality that appeared repeatedly in many forms of high and low culture from the 1940s to the 1960s.[67] Although the "sad young man" could also be an object of secretive desire, more contemporary figurations of queer youth tend to obscure their eroticization or sexual objectification (and thus their sexual agency) beneath their victimization. Daniel Marshall explains, "Queer youth have been variously caricatured as victims of adult homosexual predators, of over-bearing mothers, of too much exposure to popular culture and of the evil metropolis itself." As Marshall describes them, these popular figurations of victimhood have been central components of homophobic campaigns against the "proliferation" of homosexuality, in which the only role available to a queer kid is as the victim of a predatory queer adult. Marshall cites Anita Bryant's notorious Save Our Children campaign as one of the more recognizable examples of "the homophobic conflation of the queer youth with the figure of the always-already victim"; this reference is particularly apt given the contemporary conservative panic over adults "grooming" children by merely acknowledging LGBTQ+ lives.[68] As the figurations of queer youth have shifted over the years,

---

66. Cover, *Queer Youth Suicide*, 3; and Rand, "'Gay Boys.'"
67. Dyer, *Matter of Images*, 40–42.
68. Marshall, "Popular Culture"; and Riedel, "Why Are Republicans."

in other words, the association with the fragility of whiteness has remained consistent, but the recognition of erotic potential—the ability to view queer young people as sexual agents in their own right rather than merely as victimized by adult queer influence—has actually been squelched even further.

Empirical studies of queer youth have similarly subscribed to what Ritch Savin-Williams calls the "suffering suicidal script." Savin-Williams describes how some of the earliest studies of queer youth from the 1970s and 1980s found high rates of emotional distress, suicidality, truancy and poor grades, substance abuse, and sexually transmitted infections among this population. However, he points out that these studies typically had small sample sizes and recruited their participants from organizations offering crisis intervention, counseling, and other social services. In other words, researchers began with a population of young people who had sought out or been referred to services for crises and mental health support, but drew conclusions about queer youth more broadly, concluding that all must have the same struggles and that those struggles were due to their sexual identities.[69] Even as the scholarship on queer youth expanded throughout the 1980s and especially the 1990s, and as innovations in research methods led to more inclusive definitions of sexual behaviors and identities and more representative pools of research participants, the topics of research on queer adolescents repeated earlier patterns of "clinicalization." By focusing on suicide, HIV/AIDS and other sexually transmitted infections, victimization and violence, and sexual abuse, Savin-Williams argues, researchers continue to depict queer youth as "exceptionally vulnerable individuals leading high-risk lives."[70]

Even for researchers and teachers who are queer themselves and who understand themselves as advocates for queer youth (including myself and perhaps many readers of this book), the "Martyr-Target-Victim" model, as Eric Rofes has identified it, can be difficult to resist as a means for impressing on students and other audiences the perils faced by young queer people.[71] Rofes describes teaching a course where students, after hearing the statistics about queer youth suicide repeated one too many times, challenged his own reliance on the Martyr-Target-Victim model. In trying to communicate to students the structural challenges faced by queer youth in the context of a social justice–oriented course, Rofes realized that he had compiled a syllabus based on pathologization and tragedy rather than "the potential talents of queer youth, their strategies for survival, and their lives outside of the persecution

---

69. Savin-Williams, *New Gay Teenager*, 53–55.
70. Savin-Williams, *New Gay Teenager*, 58–60, 63, 181, 183.
71. Rofes, "Martyr-Target-Victim," 47.

framework."[72] He notes the difficulty of preparing a syllabus and assignments that do not rely on the "hegemonic narratives of depression, substance abuse, homelessness, and suicide" but that also do not merely replace the trope of vulnerability and victimhood with an equally constraining trope of survival.[73]

This representation of queer youth at risk in research and scholarship is not simply a matter of how young people are framed and understood by investigators; it also has important effects on queer youth themselves and on the policies that affect them. Namely, it locates the source of risk internally in the young queer subject while locating the source of rescue externally in the well-meaning adult. As Cover asserts about the heightened risk of suicide, "the circulation of those commonly cited statistics present an impression that *all* queer youth are vulnerable, and that of this vulnerable population a percentage are *likely* to attempt suicide." This vulnerabilization of queer youth suggests that the risk of suicide is inherent in queer identity and universally applied to all queer subjects.[74] By framing queer youth in this way, the multiplicity of contexts and experiences are all flattened, such that the singularity of sexual identity is put forward as the only significant facet of identity and the only predictor of suicidality. The intersecting pressures of racism, ableism, transphobia, sexism, and so on that many queer youth face are obscured or—in the case of the CDC's Youth Risk Behavior Survey, which I discuss in the next section—not measured or reported at all. Naturalizing the suicidality of queer youth in this way forecloses their ability to do or be otherwise, but it also suggests that the resistance to this tendency, or the possibilities for strength, resilience, and coping, must be external to the subject, fostered socially by concerned others. As the agency of queer youth is limited, in other words, the agency of adults is expanded—not to dismantle the structures of oppression that do harm to queer young people but to save queer youth from their own suicidal predispositions.

Indeed, it is not surprising that when the homogeneity, the vulnerability, and the lack of agency among queer youth is taken for granted, these assumptions shape the way educators and advocates imagine possible action on their behalf and produce material effects for youth in terms of the kinds of funding sought and the kinds of programs developed for them. For example, Audrey Bryan's work turns a critical eye toward "what happens when discourses of LGBTQ+ vulnerability, victimhood and suicidality become the key discursive frame through which queer lives are understood and through which LGBTQ+ visibility is achieved in schools and other educational settings."[75] Bryan refers

---

72. Rofes, "Martyr-Target-Victim," 50.
73. Rofes, "Martyr-Target-Victim," 57.
74. Cover, *Queer Youth Suicide*, 3.
75. Bryan, "Queer Youth and Mental Health," 76.

to the commonly accepted idea that queer youth are at heightened risk of mental health struggles and self-harm as the "suicide consensus." She suggests that the suicide consensus, widely disseminated through mainstream media and by LGBTQ+ advocacy groups, serves "an important legitimizing function" for LGBTQ+ organizations and services, educational interventions, further research, and policymaking insofar as it can help mobilize financial and political support by demonstrating an undeniable exigence.[76] While the suicide consensus seems to provide a sympathetic and poignant portrayal of vulnerable queer youth in need of help, then, Bryan emphasizes that deploying this discourse casts queerness as a "problem that needs to be managed" rather than as a positive, creative, and joyful expression of gender and sexuality. And again, understanding queer youth as always already victims de-emphasizes their agency and the pleasures of exploration and self-fashioning.[77]

Seduced by these risk-based or "deficit" models of queer youth, schools and policymakers tend to favor anti-bullying and suicide-prevention programs aimed at protection and risk mitigation while continuing to overlook queer young people's needs for relevant and comprehensive sexuality education and honest conversations about sexual health, consent, sexual violence, and pleasure. As Bryan explains, talking openly about sexuality with young people is considered controversial and political, while "responding to individual instances of homophobic bullying is perceived to be a more manageable, and far less controversial response."[78] Focusing on bullying and suicide risk also sustains an illusion of liberal tolerance, within which schools, parents, and teachers can believe they are being inclusive of queer youth without having to question structures of racism and cis- and heteronormativity, or look too closely at their own racial privilege and homophobic and transphobic assumptions. Gilbert, Fields, Mamo, and Lesko make this point rather bluntly, venturing that using the framework of bullying to (not) talk about queerness in schools "might provide cover for nervous educators or researchers."[79] Risk-based perspectives also fit seamlessly with the public education system's increasing reliance on measurable outcomes, certainty, predictability, and risk avoidance—all of which are antithetical, as Harris and Farrington point out, to the uncertainty, unpredictability, and nonlinearity of "real activism, real youth leadership . . . and effective political mobilization."[80]

Finally, when queer youth are depicted universally as at heightened risk for suicide, and when their sexuality is understood as the primary (or

---

76. Bryan, "Queer Youth and Mental Health," 77–78.
77. Bryan, "Queer Youth and Mental Health," 79.
78. Bryan, "Queer Youth and Mental Health," 79–81.
79. Gilbert et al., "Intimate Possibilities," 180.
80. Harris and Farrington, "'It Gets Narrower,'" 156.

only) factor by which to assess suicidality, the narrative produced is not only descriptive but also potentially didactic. Tom Waidzunas describes the "looping effects" that result from the classification of groups, whereby people learn to behave according to the characteristics of the category to which they have been assigned, reinforcing or even producing new evidence for the categorization.[81] In other words, the public figuration of queer youth at risk for suicide offers a means for young people to make sense of their lives: prior to this figuration, Waidzunas explains, "many youths in the United States simultaneously experiencing themselves as oppressed, as LGBT, and also experiencing angst may have made connections between these phenomena, but they may not have understood them in the language of the specific high risks of suicide for 'gay youth' or 'gay teens.'" The figuration of queer youth at risk thus offers young queers a certain kind of guidance, suggesting that suicidality is an expression of queer identity and an ordinary, even expected, part of queer youth experience.[82] The rhetorical figuration of queer youth at risk helps queer youth make sense of their lives, and also provides a kind of roadmap for their actions—whether to actually attempt suicide or at least to report what they perceive to be the expected suicidal ideation.

Rugged Resilience and the White Restorative Agenda

In order to resist the figuration of queer and trans youth as victims, some researchers turn their attention not to the risks that these youth face but rather to the qualities that make them resilient in the face of hardships and inequalities. The study of resilience as a psychological trait is often traced back to Norman Garmezy's work on schizophrenia in the early 1970s. Garmezy was particularly interested in what he called "vulnerability research," which attempted to determine why certain children with a high risk for schizophrenia (because of genetics, family environment, or sociocultural factors) exhibited adaptive characteristics that seemed to protect them from developing schizophrenia as teens or adults. He defined the manifestation of adaptive behaviors in the face of significant stressors as "resilience."[83] Garmezy called for greater attention to the children whom he named the "invulnerables"—those who demonstrated such resilience that their "intellectual and social skills are not destroyed by the misfortunes they encounter in home and

---

81. Waidzunas, "Young, Gay, and Suicidal," 202, 214.
82. Waidzunas, "Young, Gay, and Suicidal," 215.
83. Garmezy, "Vulnerability Research"; and Rolf and Glantz, "Resilience," 7.

street."[84] He laments that mental health researchers tend to concentrate on children's assumed vulnerabilities rather than their resilient behaviors, going so far as to say that in a "nation torn by strife between races and between social classes," the invulnerable children are the "keepers of the dream."[85] In short, at least as early as 1971, Garmezy was juxtaposing resilience with vulnerability, and urging researchers to concentrate on adaptation and survival rather than only on risk.

Contemporary scholarship on resilience in queer youth takes up this charge, moving from a deficit model to a strengths-based perspective. In general, this body of work does not minimize the importance of risk factors in LGBTQ+ youth but attempts to understand how—in spite of their risks—queer young people frequently grow up to be healthy and productive adults.[86] Much of the research on resilience emphasizes that resilience emerges not just from individual characteristics but also from external resources, such as caring adults, supportive school environments, friendships with LGBTQ+ peers, the availability of safer spaces, and participation in social media and activism.[87] However, as Kenta Asakura points out, the struggles of queer youth are often due to the lack of some of these common resources (such as affirming families, schools, and peers); when this support is unavailable, queer youth "have to seek alternative, sometimes unconventional resources to achieve or sustain their well-being." Asakura refers to this process as "paving pathways through the pain," suggesting that queer youth "turn[] their emotional pain into an opportunity" by engaging intentionally in strategies of resilience.[88] Even as scholars attempt to recognize that resilience is influenced and supported by social contexts, they often nonetheless still celebrate individual efforts to make do when those resources fail. As Robinson and Schmitz put it in their critique of scholarship on resilience, "the focus still remain[s] on the youth themselves in dealing with, bouncing back, and building resilience against prejudice and discrimination"; thus, they claim, this perspective "can inadvertently put the burden on youth to build resilience and navigate discrimination, instead of focusing on how to change, challenge, and dismantle the oppressive structures."[89]

---

84. Garmezy, "Vulnerability Research," 114.
85. Garmezy, "Vulnerability Research," 114.
86. Stephen T. Russell's essay is considered foundational to this shift in focus. See Russell, "Beyond Risk."
87. Robinson and Schmitz, "Beyond Resilience"; and Asakura, "Paving Pathways," 532.
88. Asakura, "Paving Pathways," 531–32.
89. Robinson and Schmitz, "Beyond Resilience," 4.

Therefore, although the turn from risk to resilience seems to offer a more affirming way to understand queer youth, it continues to forward the individual as the most important factor in survival. While the risk model suggests that vulnerability is inherent in queer and trans youth, the resilience model simply replaces individual fragility with individual strength. As Cover asserts in his critique of the form of resilience celebrated in the It Gets Better Project, the queer youth subject is presumed to be a unitary and coherent subject prior to sociality; as such, there is no opportunity to recognize how subjectivity is constituted through relations with others and through adversity. The queer youth's resilience is thus not depicted as responsive adaptability but rather as the ability to "wait out" experiences in toxic environments at school or at home. Not only does this view of resilience reproduce the idea that vulnerability or resilience are intrinsic to particular queer subjects, it also suggests that "a normative sociality of bullying culture is . . . timeless and unchangeable (rather than historical and institutional), thereby requiring queer younger persons to undertake the task of managing vulnerability, risk, resilience and identity as an individualized responsibility outside of communities of care."[90] Some scholars' penchant for a resilience model, therefore, may offer queer and trans youth only a restricted form of agency to adapt to existing oppressive structures, but not a more expansive means for imagining other possibilities.

The bias toward individualism in scholarship on resilience also reflects the white, Western lens used to define resilience as a characteristic. That is, the neoliberal foundations of resilience—in which autonomy and responsibility are ascribed to individuals who are assumed to be able to make independent choices—are rooted in the "rugged individualism" so prized in white, settler colonial narratives of progress. As Anneliese A. Singh points out, scholarly treatments of resilience maintain this privileging of individual factors like "hardiness" and intelligence as evidence of resilience. Singh therefore advocates for attending to "the role of community factors and contextual influences that threaten or support resilience," especially for queer and trans youth of color. She cites a study of trans people of color that identified community and contextual factors (such as developing racial/ethnic pride, managing family relationships, having access to healthcare and financial resources, connecting with activist communities, and nurturing spiritual beliefs) as significant strategies for developing resilience and coping with the challenges in their lives.[91] In Singh's own study of trans youth of color, she finds that these young people narrate their resilience strategies in relational terms that emphasize their

---

90. Cover, "Queer Youth Resilience."
91. Singh, "Transgender Youth of Color," 692.

racial identities. The majority of her participants, for example, reported that an important component of their resilience was the ways their racial/ethnic identities and their gender identities evolved together over time, and that they could not meaningfully separate their racial/ethnic identities from their gender identities.[92] This suggests not only the obvious conclusion that identities—especially for youths whose experiences are shaped by both cissexism and racism—are intersectional, but also that the traditional model for understanding resilience does not do justice to the more communal and relational ways that youth of color understand themselves as subjects and adapt to or resist interlocking systems of marginalization.

Whether scholars focus on risk or resilience, then, the racial figuration of youth foregrounds whiteness while obscuring processes of racialization and the particularities of racialized lives. That is, vulnerability is naturalized as a characteristic of whiteness (and as a marker of whiteness's supremacy), but resilience is also defined in the terms of white individualism, valuing personal endurance and resoluteness, with the capacity for resilience seeming to arise innately within certain subjects. This shift in scholarly discourse not only perpetuates the risk/resilience binary—obscuring the ways that these two factors are always intertwined, contextual, and in flux—but it also participates in queer studies' own normative and racialized expectations of progress. Susan Talburt and Mary Lou Rasmussen describe the "restorative agenda" of much research on queer youth: emerging out of earlier assumptions of vulnerability and woundedness, scholars are drawn to transformational projects that tell a more optimistic story of queer youth and count on the promise of the future. These restorative projects, although attractive in their hopefulness and pleasurable in the redemption they seem to offer, cannot escape the linear temporality, "regulatory narrative of progress," "relentless search for agency," and "ideas of a future made better by new imaginings" that, as Edelman has argued, are dead ends for queer politics.[93] And in a binary vulnerability/resilience framework, a resilience script may not be better for queer youth, either, if the expected narrative of suffering and suicide is merely replaced by an equally narrow one of heroic perseverance through harassment and discrimination.[94]

The restorative agenda implied by resilience research, in other words, overlaps with the prescriptive developmental temporality with which queer and trans youth find themselves so often at odds. As I show in the next chapter, this sort of narrative of progress is rooted in the normative temporalities of whiteness and cis- and heteronormativity; for now, though, I simply want to

---

92. Singh, "Transgender Youth of Color," 695–96.
93. Talburt and Rasmussen, "'After-Queer' Tendencies," 2–3.
94. Waidzunas, "Young, Gay, and Suicidal," 216–17.

emphasize that whether taking risk or resilience as the starting point, the end goal seems to be much the same: that queer and trans youth assimilate into the dominant social structures of whiteness and cis- and heteronormativity from which they have been alienated. As Robinson and Schmitz argue compellingly, the "well-being" of queer youth is often measured by their ability to pursue education, employment, and relationships on a normative timeline—in short, to succeed within a capitalist system.[95]

Because both the risk model and the resilience model presume the desirability of assimilation and assume the inherent qualities of individuals, they also both offer adults a gratifying but ultimately politically toothless role. In the former model, adults can feel like benevolent saviors who rescue fragile queer young people from the terrors of bullying and the grip of suicidality; in the latter model, adults can admire and be inspired by the heroic tenacity of queer young people who persist against all odds. Crucially, neither model demands that adults take responsibility for cultural structures of cis- and heteronormativity or racism or to make material changes in their communities, families, or schools. In this chapter's final section I return to the September 2010 suicides to demonstrate that adults' lack of responsibility for young queer lives, through which they (re)produce the racial figuration of queer youth vulnerability, finds a comfortable and crucial alibi in the imagined "wounded white boy."

Resolving Sympathy and Disgust: The Work of the Wounded White Boy

As the narrative of the nine deaths by suicide in September 2010 was assembled, the commonality most frequently (but as I described earlier, not necessarily most accurately) noted among the boys was that they all suffered anti-gay bullying. By contrast, the commonality never noted, but in my view, vital to their stories' coherence, is that they were all cisgender boys. Thus, the gendered logics through which the problems of bullying and suicide are formulated are obscured: the popular representatives of queer youths' despair are exclusively male and usually white, but this homogeneity is almost never recorded.[96] Instead, news coverage focused primarily on the question of

---

95. Robinson and Schmitz, "Beyond Resilience," 10.
96. Jackson Katz and Sut Jhally have made a similar point in relation to school shootings: the media tries to explain what could have led the shooters to violence without recognizing that what almost all of them have in common is that they are white and male. Katz and Jhally, "National Conversation."

sexuality: the anti-gay bullying the boys experienced and their own previous statements about their sexual identities. The preoccupation with sexuality resulted in the specific characteristics of the boys to be subsumed under more general concerns about the (ostensibly) gender- and race-neutral category of "queer" youth. Most reports about the suicides pivot quickly from individual stories about (usually white) cisgender boys to broader worries about "gay kids," "gay and lesbian students," "lesbian, gay, bisexual, and transgender" students, "LGBT youth," or "LGBTQ+ kids" (sometimes with a helpful definition of "queer" for the uninitiated reader).[97] The media's repetition of this story formula naturalizes the white masculinity of the figuration of queer youth, and by locating the source of vulnerability in the seemingly innate quality of sexual orientation, precludes critical questions about systems of oppression that produce such vulnerability unequally.

The federal policy documents described earlier similarly substitute the language of "sexual orientation," "sexual behavior and attraction," "sexual identity," and "transgender status" for any specific identification of the ways that bullying might target different sorts of behaviors or embodiments in girls, boys, and trans or gender-nonconforming youth, and they do not offer any means for thinking about race and racism in intersection with gender and/or sexuality. Likewise, the federal government's instruments for collecting data on actual youth experiences are just as imprecise. For example, in a summary of trends from 2009 to 2019, the CDC's Youth Risk Behavior Survey breaks down the data on bullying and suicide by gender and race in the main chapters pertaining to (unmarked) heterosexual youth. But in the separate "Sexual Minority Youth" section, there is no information on race provided, and even gender is blurred by grouping "lesbian, gay, and bisexual" or "same sex" sexual contact together into a single undifferentiated category. Unlike the heterosexual youth whose sexualities are understood as intersectional with other identity markers, the young queer people in this report are identified solely by the "lesbian, gay, bisexual" amalgam, completely stripped of gender and race.[98] This leaves no way to understand the interactions of risk factors for queer youth, as if their nonheterosexuality is the only identity that matters. The next iteration of the Youth Risk Behavior Survey, which tracks trends from 2011 to 2021, incorporates "sexual minority youth" into the main part of the report, but continues to define sexuality with two categories: "heterosexual" and "LGBQ+," which includes "gay or lesbian," "bisexual," "questioning," and "I describe my sexual identity in some other way" responses.

---

97. McKinley, "Suicides Put Light"; Savage, "Bullied Gay Teenager"; Fremon, "Why Did So Many"; and Graves, "Gay Teen Suicides."
98. CDC, "Youth Risk Behavior Survey . . . 2009–2019."

Unbelievably, although trans youths' heightened risk for bullying and suicide is noted elsewhere by the CDC (and clearly emphasized by other sources, such as the Trevor Project), trans and nonbinary identities are not accounted for in the Youth Risk Behavior Survey. Even as recently as 2021, the CDC notes the absence of information about transgender students in its data and promises a question assessing gender identity in future surveys.[99] Therefore, although "LGBTQ+ youth" may have a satisfyingly inclusive feel, the effect of this nomenclature in this context is that the erasure of trans and gender-nonconforming youth is disguised, the role of masculinity in bullying and suicide goes unmarked and uninterrogated, sexuality stands in as the only category of difference that signifies, and the gendering and racialization of the figuration of queer youth at risk is obscured.

Thus, I argue that this lack of intersectional analysis in both popular and official discourse—the failure to comment on race, failure to wonder about the role of masculinity, failure to think beyond a singular category of nonheterosexuality—means that the figuration of vulnerability that emerges is premised on the unmarked privileges of whiteness and performativity of masculinity. The wounded white boy, that is, appears as the epitome of queer susceptibility to harm. The privileges of whiteness and the performativity of masculinity occupy the category of vulnerability, by which I mean they fill or hold it, but also that they capture and colonize it, crowding out possibilities for recognizing others' vulnerabilities and limiting vulnerability's capacity to be imagined differently.

Framing the boys' deaths specifically in terms of anti-gay bullying, but not recognizing the gendered nature of this bullying, presents homophobic bullying of boys as a metonym for bullying in general. For example, the hypothetical examples of bullying offered in news stories tended to invoke the homophobic taunting of boys: "an effeminate boy being teased," or a child who "thinks another kid is a great big 'faggoty-fag-fag,' and . . . beat[s] that kid to a pulp."[100] Of course, bullying does not always target boys and is not always homophobic in nature (remember, for example, the disabilities, religious identifiers, and racial differences that are also singled out by bullies), but this public discourse sutures bullying to homophobia and to racially unmarked cisgender boys, with the risk of suicide as its naturalized consequence.

Furthermore, this framing of bullying highlights the precarity of manhood by illuminating what Vandello and Bosson identify as one of the greatest threats to masculinity: an insufficient dissociation from femininity. C. J. Pascoe argues that when boys taunt other boys by calling them "faggots," they

---

99. CDC, "Youth Risk Behavior Survey . . . 2011–2021."
100. Kim, "Against 'Bullying'"; and Pierce, "Dangerous Law."

are commenting not so much on their actual or perceived homosexuality but on their association with femininity; "achieving a masculine identity," Pascoe contends, "entails a repeated repudiation of the specter of failed masculinity." This performance of masculinity often takes the form of the "fag discourse": labeling other young men as "fags" while attempting to avoid having that label applied to themselves. The "fag discourse," for Pascoe, is a means of establishing manhood and represents a defense against being perceived as insufficiently masculine.[101] What is often understood as homophobic bullying (and representative of all bullying) thus actually emerges from the precarity of manhood. The taunting of "faggots" serves to denigrate homosexuality, to be sure, but even more it disavows the disgrace of femininity. The point is not to suggest that what is perceived as homophobia is actually femmephobia, nor to posit misogyny as the root of all oppression. Rather, it is to emphasize that when homophobic bullying stands in for all bullying, the racial figuration of queer youth at risk that emerges is premised on a white masculine vulnerability to feminization.

Finally, the vulnerability of the figure of the queer youth at risk is particularly masculine because suicide itself is often coded as a masculine act. Katrina Jaworski acknowledges that suicide is often understood as an empirically male phenomenon because more men than women die by suicide; she argues, however, that knowledge about suicide rests on a constellation of binary oppositions—male/female, masculine/feminine, active/passive—that all inscribe gender into researchers' interpretations of the act of suicide. For example, Jaworski points out that although the male rates of *completed* suicide are higher than female rates, data consistently show that more women than men *attempt* suicide. Since suicide is typically measured by mortality rates (the act of suicide is defined by completion, not attempt), the idea that suicide is a masculine act persists; meanwhile, the more common attempted but nonfatal suicides by women and girls do not register as suicides at all. In fact, attempted suicide, Jaworski explains, is understood as a "feminine phenomenon," "coded as a failure," and "translated into pathological, attention-seeking exercises, desiring rescue instead of death."[102] In other words, completed suicide can be understood as a masculine exercise of agency, a commanding of the body by the mind. Dying by suicide can even be seen as a masculine assertion of valor, "a form of mastery," or "an affirmation of autonomy and rationality in the face of unrelenting adverse circumstances." Attempted suicide, on the other hand, connotes a feminine failure of the will.[103]

---

101. Pascoe, *Dude, You're a Fag*, 5.
102. Jaworski, *Gender of Suicide*, 23–24.
103. Jaworski, *Gender of Suicide*, 103.

This gendered pattern holds true for queer youth suicide, which Jaworski also asserts "materializes as a male experience." Among queer youth, lesbian and bisexual girls report higher levels of suicidal thinking than gay and bisexual boys, although gay and bisexual boys die by suicide at higher rates; significantly, boys are more likely to see their suicidal acts as directly related to their sexuality.[104] Vandello and Bosson also note that when manhood is threatened, men are likely to engage in risky or aggressive behaviors to reassert masculinity. The most effective acts of manhood are "verifiable behaviors that are hard to fake and are perhaps even costly to the actor because they signal to others that one's manliness is genuine."[105] Vandello and Bosson do not specifically mention suicide, but given Jaworski's convincing claims about the masculinity of this action, it is easy to see how completed suicide (certainly "verifiable" and "costly") could be perceived to resecure—if only in death—the masculinity called into question by homophobic bullying.

These assumptions about the gendered nature of suicide and the relationship between suicidality and sexuality, as well as the precarity of white masculinity, contribute to the "seductive quality" of risk-based discourses about queer youth. As Bryan suggests, adults are compelled by the figuration of the vulnerable queer young person who is innocent, fragile, and endangered, and who depends upon the benevolent intervention of the adult; in other words, this framing of vulnerable queer youth is so powerful, in part, because it resonates emotionally with well-meaning adults who imagine themselves as protectors and saviors.[106] But the affects of vulnerability are complex. Recognizing vulnerability involves what Oliviero describes as an "affective ambivalence" that combines "incitement to compassion" with "disgust toward weakness," resulting in both "moral outrage and disgusted empathy."[107] By seeing queer youth as vulnerable victims, adults can imagine queerness as implying a kind of frailty, flaw, or even degeneracy, while simultaneously viewing themselves as sympathetic, tolerant, and magnanimous. Their proclamations of sympathy and self-righteous multiculturalism disguise their own traces of disgust at the violation of hetero(non)sexuality, while disavowing the expressions of gender and sexuality of actual queer youth (especially when those youth are Black, Brown, gender-nonconforming, disabled, and/or poor) and refusing to recognize them as sexual agents. And they can also assuage their anxieties about the vulnerabilities of white masculinity by situating that weakness in the figure of the queer youth at risk, whose death by suicide might be understood

---

104. Jaworski, *Gender of Suicide*, 30–32.
105. Vandello and Bosson, "Hard Won and Easily Lost," 104–5.
106. Bryan, "Queer Youth and Mental Health," 76.
107. Oliviero, *Vulnerability Politics*, 229.

as a restitutive act. Perhaps the September 2010 suicides are such a compelling spectacle, then, because they provide a poignant scene for expressing sympathy toward the perceived woundedness of white boys while also offering a satisfying reassurance of masculine dominance and mastery. These boys might have been gay in life, but the public narrative of their deaths delivers a comforting negation of the specter of the faggot and a triumph of masculinity.

Thus, the figuration of the weakness of queer youth that we have seen in this chapter—that queer youth are inherently at risk for (or sometimes inherently resilient to) bullying and suicide, that suicide is a natural outcome of being bullied and perhaps even of queerness itself—belies the supposedly gender-neutral and race-neutral "LGBTQ+ kids" under whose name it usually appears. Instead, this is a figure whose vulnerability emerges specifically from the privileges of whiteness and the performativity of masculinity. While the stories of certain queer youth are undeniably illuminated by this framework, as this figure crystallizes in the public imagination other stories of young queer lives and deaths—ones that are gender-nonconforming or trans or female, ones that are marked by racial or ethnic identity, ones that intersect with disability, mental illness, homelessness, sex work, and a whole host of other material precarities—become unintelligible and recede further from view. This figure also only tells us one story about vulnerability: this is a vulnerability that is rooted in the precarity of privilege and thus can only be viewed in terms of debility. But queer vulnerability can also, as I point to in chapter 4 and the conclusion to this book, be refigured as a site of connection, an impetus toward ingenuity, a resource for refuge, a capacity for world-making.

Here, however, the imagined wounded white boy offers a very particular version of white vulnerability that (re)produces the racial figuration of youth and manages public anxiety about young people, sexuality, gender, and race. It has important implications for the ways that queer youth are understood as a group, how their stories are told, and the kinds of research that is done and programs that are implemented on their behalf. The recognizable narrative of the bullied and suicidal cis gay boy also does significant work for adults, whose commitment to the hetero(non)sexuality of childhood depends on desexualizing and depoliticizing queer youth as subjects; the particular vulnerability of this figure, that is, opens up possibilities for adult rhetorical agency. As the next chapter demonstrates through an analysis of community deliberation about a trans student's right to gender-segregated bathrooms, adults' rhetorical agency is further enacted by asserting normative developmental temporalities and calling up but disavowing histories of anti-Black discrimination.

CHAPTER 3

Too Much to Tolerate

School Bathrooms, Trans Temporality, and Black Excess

Gavin Grimm posted on his public Facebook page on June 28, 2021, "Big news, everybody! This morning, the Supreme Court denied review of my case from the Fourth Circuit, meaning my win stands!" This somewhat anticlimactic news of a denied review was actually a "watershed moment" in *Grimm v. Gloucester County School Board*: it meant that transgender students like Gavin could, under the protections of Title IX, use the public-school bathrooms that correspond to their gender identities.[1] Gavin, a young white trans man and former student in a Gloucester, Virginia, high school, was already twenty-two years old by the time this decision was rendered; it brought over seven years' worth of complicated and protracted legal proceedings to a close by upholding an August 2020 ruling in Gavin's favor by the Fourth Circuit Court of Appeals and was "an important tactical victory for transgender individuals, especially in public schools."[2]

Prior to his notoriety for this case, Gavin was a quiet student in a small town who just wanted to "be a normal child and use the restroom in peace."[3] He began identifying as male and using men's public restrooms during his freshman year of high school. He and his mother discussed his transition with his school guidance counselor before the start of his sophomore year, and he

---

1. Hohmann, "Please, Go On."
2. Steve Vladeck, quoted in de Vogue and Duster, "Supreme Court Gives Victory."
3. Block, "'All I Want to Do.'"

agreed to use the nurse's unisex bathroom during school. However, this solution quickly became untenable because it was inconveniently located (often causing him to be late to class) and unavailable during after-school activities, and because he found it stigmatizing. Gavin asked his guidance counselor for permission to use the boys' bathroom, and in consultation with the school principal and the superintendent, that permission was granted. He used the boys' bathrooms for seven weeks without incident, until the outcry from disgruntled parents prompted the Gloucester County School Board (GCSB) to recommend a new policy. The GCSB's resolution proposed that separate male and female restrooms and locker rooms would be provided in Gloucester County schools and that "the use of said facilities shall be limited to the corresponding biological genders, and students with gender identity issues shall be provided an alternative appropriate private facility."[4] This resolution was discussed at the November and December 2014 school board meetings, with heated open-discussion periods where parents, teachers, students, and community members expressed their adamant objections to allowing Gavin to continue to use the boys' bathroom. Reflecting the sentiment of the majority, the GCSB passed its resolution by a 6–1 margin on December 9, 2014.

In light of the new policy, Gavin's restroom options included the bathroom in the nurse's office that he had used previously, newly converted single-stall unisex bathrooms unused by any other students, or, of course, the girls' bathroom; displeased with these choices and the stigma they invited, he suffered urinary tract infections from abstaining from using the bathroom and was hospitalized with suicidal thoughts. At the end of his sophomore year in 2015, the American Civil Liberties Union (ACLU) sued the GCSB on Gavin's behalf, claiming that excluding him from the boys' bathroom violated the Equal Protection Clause of the Fourteenth Amendment (which prohibits states from applying laws to different classes of persons unequally) and the provisions of Title IX (which prohibits discrimination on the basis of sex in educational programs receiving federal financial assistance).[5] During this time Gavin also began hormone therapy, and by 2016 he had undergone chest reconstruction surgery and had his birth certificate amended to reflect his gender, but the school remained unwavering in its commitment to Gavin's gender assigned at birth. Even when presented with the new birth certificate, the school refused to acknowledge Gavin's gender or update his school records and transcripts; after graduating in 2017, Gavin added this complaint about his records (which he needed in order to start college) to his lawsuit.

---

4. GCSB meeting minutes, November 11, 2014.
5. *Gavin Grimm v. Gloucester County*, 5–6.

It did not take long for Gavin's case to attract national attention and for Gavin to become, as writer and activist Janet Mock puts it, the "cherubic face" of the "debate about trans people's right to exist in public spaces without hostility, harassment and violence."[6] *Time* magazine named Gavin one of its "30 Most Influential Teens" in 2016 and "100 Most Influential People" in 2017.[7] Actress Laverne Cox plugged Gavin's case while onstage at the 2017 Grammy Awards, telling the audience to "please google Gavin Grimm, #StandWithGavin." She later authored an article about Gavin for *InStyle* magazine, in which she asserted, "It's not about bathrooms. It's about the humanity of trans people, about us having the right to exist in a public space."[8] The trans artist Cassils played audio recordings from Gavin's case to accompany their sculpture PISSED, which featured 200 days' worth of Cassils's urine stored in a glass cube. This piece was a durational performance in response to the increased media visibility of trans people and the hypersurveillance of trans bodies.[9] Among many other public appearances, Gavin rode as a "celebrity special guest" in the San Francisco Pride Parade and spoke about his experiences from the main stage in 2018. Aaron Jackson, known for LGBTQ+ activist stunts such as painting the rainbow-striped "Equality House" across the street from the homophobic Westboro Baptist Church, offered Gavin a college scholarship, calling him "the Rosa Parks of the trans bathroom debate."[10]

Gavin's case has far-reaching national implications for trans youth and adults, but it also offers a glimpse into the ways that the racial figuration of childhood is deployed by adults to make sense of trans young people as a sexual threat to vulnerable cis white children, and therefore to justify policies that restrict their rights. Thus, while much of the scholarship on Gavin's case and other trans bathroom lawsuits tends to concentrate on their complex legal precedents and ramifications, my analysis here focuses more locally on the two GCSB meetings at which the resolution that Gavin's lawsuit targets was passed.[11] Unlike my first two chapters, which considered how official institutional discourses—such as the federal government's guidance on bullying or the disciplinary policies of schools—produce racialized figurations of hetero(non)sexual youth, this chapter turns to school board meetings as very

---

6. Mock, "Gavin Grimm."
7. "30 Most Influential Teens"; and Gibbs, "100 Most Influential People."
8. Kaufman, "Laverne Cox Called Out"; and Cox and Heyman, "It's Not About Bathrooms."
9. Fischer, "Piss(ed)."
10. Staver, "Pride 2018"; and Burroughs, "Gavin Grimm Gifted."
11. Philips, "Battle over Bathrooms"; Wuest, "Scientific Gaze"; Murib, "Administering Biology"; and Eckes, "Restroom and Locker Room Wars."

narrow contexts of public democratic deliberation, or what Karen Tracy calls "ordinary democracy."[12] At school board meetings, Robert Asen argues, laypeople engage in policymaking and govern themselves, using not only rational argumentation but also emotional, rowdy, messy forms of communication and storytelling. The meetings are sites for decision-making as well as for forming opinions, sustaining community, and imagining futures.[13]

In the everyday language of parents, teachers, school administrators, and students, I contend, we can witness the vernacular rhetorical figuration of childhood (and more specifically, the racial figuration of trans youth) in process. I trace two interrelated characteristics of the figuration of trans youth that emerged across the two GCSB meetings: a skewing of the normative temporality of childhood that produces trans identity as a sexual threat, and an invocation and deferral of Blackness that makes white trans identities intelligible within a civil rights framework. First, in contrast to much of the public discourse about trans youth that emphasizes their immaturity and their inability to make important decisions about their own identities and bodies, the public comments at the school board meetings framed trans youth as unnaturally mature, precociously sexual, and threatening to the innocence of cisgender hetero(non)sexual childhood. In short, trans youth are imagined to disrupt the naturalized developmental temporality of white childhood. Second, the figuration of trans youth becomes legible by summoning up histories of racial segregation only to submerge them under the cover of discussions of trans civil rights. Thus, adult fears about the "threat" of transness—envisioned in terms of sexual precociousness and the more general anxiety that trans youth are excessive, uncontrollable, and "too much"—are displaced onto an imagined, ghostly Blackness, while anti-Black discrimination provides the framework through which the possibility for trans civil rights can be debated. Overall, then, white developmental temporalities and Black sexual excess merge in the community's figuration of trans youth as a perceived sexual provocation to the vulnerable hetero(non)sexuality of white, cisgender children.

Before I embark on my analysis of the GCSB meeting discussions, however, I begin by contextualizing Gavin's case within the legal issues at stake, the rash of "bathroom bills" proposed at local and state levels, the privileges of whiteness, and the limitations of a liberal framework of legal rights. Next, I take up each of the two aforementioned themes in turn. First, I understand the skewed temporalities of transness in relation to the white, cis-, and heteronormative expectations of chrononormativity, arguing that the community's

---

12. Tracy, *Challenges of Ordinary Democracy*.
13. Asen, *Democracy, Deliberation, and Education*, 10, 35, 5.

discourse about Gavin attempts to discipline what are perceived to be his deviations from the normative timeline of childhood development. Second, I turn to Black trans scholarship that proposes the transitivity of Blackness as a condition of possibility for the articulation of white trans identities and rights in order to suggest that the invocations of Blackness at the GCSB meetings work in the service of whiteness by strategically calling up but ultimately disavowing ongoing racial injustices. Finally, in order to further illustrate the convergence of the disruptions of trans temporality and the perpetual presence of Blackness that condition the emergence of trans identities, I offer an additional case study. Larry/Latisha King, a gender-nonconforming, mixed-race, Black-identified young person, was murdered at school at age fifteen by a white cisgender male classmate who found their feminine gender expression and flirtatiousness intolerable. In Larry/Latisha's brief life we get a glimpse of the Black trans excess, what Ricky Gutierrez-Maldonado calls the "too muchness" of queer and trans youth of color, that defies capture by modern gender identity categories, but remains as a haunting, deferred presence in the community deliberation about Gavin.[14]

This chapter argues that the surfacing of these interconnected themes—the imagined sexual threat of trans temporality and the haunting presence of Blackness as the racialized excess of trans identity—enables the intelligibility of Gavin's identity and the vernacular articulation of white trans rights for the Gloucester community. While the previous two chapters have attended to the racialized and gendered production of the category of vulnerability in the figuration of childhood, this chapter demonstrates that this figuration also insists upon a normative temporality of development—a temporality that is threatened by the excesses of transness and Blackness. The transitivity, the stubborn excess of Black transness, remains to haunt the limits of trans rights as they continue to be debated a decade later.

What is at stake for adults, therefore, is not the logistics of Gavin's bathroom use, not Larry/Latisha's compliance with the school dress code, and not even protecting the privacy and safety of cisgender students. Rather, at stake is the binary gender system, developmental temporality, and unmarked whiteness of the figuration of childhood so central to the politics of sexual morality and youth. The actual precarities of trans young people are glossed over in order to ascribe vulnerability to their white cisgender classmates, and this presumed vulnerability legitimizes adult action on their behalf. In other words, the rhetorical agency of adults in the Gloucester community hinged on this (mis)assignment of vulnerability; their decision to restrict the rights of trans

---

14. Gutierrez-Maldonado, "Lawrence 'Larry' King."

young people in their district depended on the malleability of childhood's vulnerability in their (re)production of racialized figurations of trans youth. This community's deliberation also makes clear how rhetorical figures serve as the point of contact between ideology and materiality; that is, in all their anti-Black and anti-trans entanglements, they justify policies and practices that do material harm to real young people—relatively privileged young people like Gavin, but also countless trans and gender-nonconforming youth of color like Larry/Latisha who experience this harm even more acutely.

Gavin's Case in Context: "Bathroom Bills," Trans Rights, White Privilege

While Gavin occupies a unique position in the limelight, his case is one among countless instances of trans and gender-nonconforming people—both youth and adults—having their gender identities, their rights to occupy spaces, their ability to access resources, and their opportunities for public participation policed at the intimate and embodied sites of restrooms, locker rooms, retail dressing rooms, dormitories, doctors' offices, prisons, athletic teams, single-sex schools and colleges, and many other gender-segregated institutions.[15] These restrictions on trans people's lives coincide with and constitute a backlash to what *Time* magazine called the "transgender tipping point" in 2014: the radical increase in trans visibility and consumability in mainstream media. Of course, as numerous scholars of trans studies have noted, this visibility and legal accommodation of trans subjects is also a trap; it does not necessarily amplify trans political power, produce material benefits, or foster more possibilities for livable trans lives, and it offers only a limited form of agency to the most privileged of trans subjects. Meanwhile, the most marginalized—trans people of color, trans sex workers, disabled trans people, and so on—face intensifying violences and are exposed more vividly to expanding forms of surveillance and necropolitical management by agencies of the state.[16] For example, Mia Fischer notes that "trans people continue to be discursively constructed and treated as fraudulent, deviant, and threatening both by dominant media and state institutions," while V. Jo Hsu describes how such

---

15. While Gavin's case was pending, several other cases regarding transgender students and the use of bathrooms and locker rooms at school were decided, all in favor of the transgender students' rights; see, for example, *Students v. United States Department of Education* in Illinois, *Whitaker v. Kenosha Unified School District* in Wisconsin, and *Board of Education of the Highland Local School District v. United States Department of Education* in Ohio.

16. Gossett, Stanley, and Burton, *Trap Door*; and Fischer, *Terrorizing Gender*.

anti-trans constructions also work in the service of whiteness, "tapping into racist, ableist, and heteropatriarchal logics, appealing to a pervasive sense of persecution affecting those unsettled by challenges to structural privilege."[17] Efforts to control the mobility of trans people by regulating their ability to occupy public spaces can be understood as a panicked response to a perceived viral contagion that, as Hsu argues, is a means for managing anxieties about white social and economic capital, white middle-class respectability and gender norms, and intersections of race, gender, and disability.[18]

The GCSB's attempt to enact a policy that would restrict access to multi-user facilities on the basis of gender assigned at birth is a smaller-scale version of "bathroom bills" that have been considered in over half of US state legislatures since 2013. Indeed, Gavin's series of confrontations with the school board and appearances in court coincided with the heyday of bathroom bills—at least nineteen states proposed bathroom bills in 2016 alone, and sixteen states considered them during the 2017 legislative session.[19] Many of these bills, featuring strikingly similar language, were coordinated by the Alliance Defending Freedom, a Christian Right anti-LGBTQ+ legal advocacy and training group that was designated a hate group by the Southern Poverty Law Center.[20] Legislators in Gavin's home state of Virginia introduced several such bills—including one specifically targeting schools—during 2016 and 2017, and his neighboring state of North Carolina's House Bill 2 was notorious both for being the first bathroom bill to be signed into law in 2016 and for the intense backlash from activists, corporations, and celebrities that led to its partial repeal in 2017.[21]

The question of bathroom access for trans students in schools has been especially fraught because of changing federal direction regarding the application of Title IX. In brief, Title IX is enforced by the Department of Education through the Office of Civil Rights (OCR), but these agencies have offered inconsistent interpretations of how Title IX's protections against "sex" discrimination pertain to gender identity. While the OCR under the Obama administration issued specific guidance in 2016 that the protections of Title IX apply to transgender students, the Trump administration rescinded that guidance in 2017; the Biden administration delivered a new executive order in 2021

---

17. Fischer, *Terrorizing Gender*, 9; and Hsu, "Irreducible Damage," 63.
18. Hsu, "Irreducible Damage," 63. See also Randall, "Irreversible Damage."
19. Kralik, "'Bathroom Bill' Legislative Tracking."
20. Michaels, "We Tracked Down"; and Southern Poverty Law Center, "Alliance Defending Freedom."
21. Kralik, "'Bathroom Bill' Legislative Tracking"; Ali, "Rise and Fall"; and Murib, "Administering Biology."

that suggests that the ruling in *Bostock v. Clayton County* (which addressed employment discrimination prohibited under Title VII) should be used to interpret other laws, such as Title IX, to offer a more expansive definition of "sex" that would include protections for gender identity and sexual orientation.[22] It remains unclear whether judges are required to follow the OCR's interpretations of the law and whether such interpretations of Title IX constitute a clarification to the law (which would be within the OCR's authority) or an actual change to the law (which the OCR cannot do through a guidance document).[23]

The circuitous route of Gavin's case through the courts is thus, in part, a direct consequence of these fluctuating interpretations of Title IX: although the Supreme Court was set to hear his case in 2016, once Obama's guidance was rescinded the court opted not to proceed without the support of the OCR and vacated his case in 2017, remanding it back to the Fourth Circuit Court of Appeals to reconsider. In spite of the OCR's amended guidance under the Trump administration, the court's August 2020 decision upheld its earlier opinion in Gavin's favor.[24] This ruling—the decision left in place in 2021 when the Supreme Court declined to hear the GCSB's appeal—stated plainly that at the heart of Gavin's case is the question of "whether equal protection and Title IX can protect transgender students from school bathroom policies that prohibit them from affirming their gender," and concluded, "We join a growing consensus of courts in holding that the answer is resoundingly yes."[25]

Even though Gavin's case is now settled, state legislatures continue to propose new forms of anti-trans legislation: while some states are still attempting to pass bathroom bills, others have moved on to other issues, most notably targeting trans youths' ability to access gender-affirming medical care and trans athletes' ability to participate on gender-segregated sports teams.[26] Indeed, the 2020, 2021, and 2022 legislative sessions have each, in turn, overtaken previous records for the highest number of anti-trans bills introduced in history. In 2023 anti-trans legislation skyrocketed, with six hundred anti-trans bills introduced across forty-nine states (nearly triple the number of bills in the previous year). Many of these bills are likely to fail or eventually to be determined unconstitutional, but they nonetheless endanger the safety and livelihood of

---

22. Gupta and Wilcox, "Transgender Students and Title IX."
23. Philips, "Battle over Bathrooms," 105–6.
24. Philips, "Battle over Bathrooms," 114–15; and US Dept of Justice, "Statement by Attorney General Jeff Sessions."
25. *Gavin Grimm v. Gloucester County*, 5. The decision in Gavin's case applies to public school students in the mid-Atlantic states of the Fourth US Circuit Court of Appeals. Similar decisions have been reached in the Seventh and Eleventh Circuits.
26. "How the G.O.P."

trans people everywhere. And while some anti-trans legislation affects trans people of all ages (for instance, banning drag performances or basing federal legal definitions of gender on sex assigned at birth), the majority of these bills specifically target young people.[27]

Considering this context of anti-trans sentiment and efforts to legislate trans bodies and identities, Gavin's case marks an important victory for the protection of trans rights—not just in school bathrooms but for a whole array of public spaces, activities, and institutions. But it is important to recognize that the legibility of Gavin's case both in the legal system and in popular media coverage is rooted in the privileges of whiteness and a corresponding differentiation from Blackness. Janet Mock's reference to Gavin's "cherubic face" emphasizes his childlike innocence and his vulnerability—characteristics that, as I claimed in chapter 1, are historically and presently produced through the exclusion of Blackness and, as I demonstrated in chapter 2, become available for white occupation, leaving youth of color less eligible for the protections of childhood. This descriptor also connects him to Matthew Shepard, who was similarly described, in the aftermath of his murder, as possessing a "cherubic face." Gavin's and Matthew's racialized (but unmarked as such) angelic countenances became "national symbol[s]" for queer advocacy precisely because of their ability to summon up the vulnerabilities associated with whiteness that we saw in the previous chapter.[28] Meanwhile, Gavin's positioning as the "Rosa Parks of the trans bathroom debate" installs a white trans boy as the proper object of contemporary civil rights struggles, not only drawing on racial segregation and the policing of Black bodies' movement in public spaces to make sense of Gavin's plight but also displacing the singularity of Parks's Black womanhood.

Gavin's story was undoubtedly attractive to the ACLU as a test case with a path to the Supreme Court not only due to his whiteness but also because his unambiguous assertions and appearance of masculinity (which is to say, he identifies and passes as male) can be easily accommodated into hetero- and cisnormative institutions.[29] Gavin's gender, that is, may have challenged the fixity of gender assignment but not its male/female logic. Unlike trans and gender-nonconforming youth of color whose gender passing is also always a

---

27. Ronan, "BREAKING"; Lang, "2022 Was the Worst Year"; and Trans Legislation Tracker.

28. Ott and Aoki, "Politics of Negotiating," 488.

29. The Fourth Circuit court's August 2020 opinion overtly recognizes the range of "gender-expansive youth" who are nonbinary, intersex, or whose identities do not conform to gender norms in other ways. However, it notes that the current decision only attends to "transgender students who 'consistently, persistently, and insistently' express a binary gender." *Gavin Grimm v. Gloucester County*, 11–12.

form of racial passing within categories defined by whiteness, Gavin's white masculinity appeases neoliberalism's preference for "single-issue" problems.[30] During the years his case was under consideration, Gavin presented his trans identity as an adversity to be tolerated—not as a source of pride, and certainly not as a form of resistance to the dominance of the gender binary. At the first school board meeting, for example, he analogized being trans to having cancer, suggesting that if a parent had a child with cancer, they would do everything they could to cut the cancer out and help their child. Troubling in many ways, this statement not only pathologizes transness and elides the systemic sources of cissexism, but also undercuts the possibilities for agency and political consciousness of trans youths themselves. In a later interview, when asked what LGBTQ+ youth have to feel proud about these days, he responded, "I guess I'm not the best person to ask that, because I'm not proud of being trans. I hate being trans. I would give anything not to be trans."[31]

It is also noteworthy that Gavin's complaint—being barred from the boys' bathroom even though single-stall unisex bathrooms were provided—is at odds with much of the advocacy for accessible bathrooms in public venues and on school campuses. Single-occupant, all-gender bathrooms are generally considered best suited for a range of needs, including nonbinary and trans folks, people with disabilities, parents, caregivers, and so on. In fact, some trans activists suggest that the mainstream visibility of the fight over trans bathroom access is itself a marker of privilege which relies on a biodeterministic discourse of trans identity and distracts attention from other sources of violence that trans people—especially trans feminine people of color—face: incarceration, physical and sexual assault, murder, deportation, and homelessness, to name just a few.[32] As Yve Laris Cohen explains, the issue of bathrooms puts trans people in a neoliberal trap of making defensive rights-based claims within existing gender-segregated and binary options, rather than pursuing more radical strategies of trans liberation that would demand institutional changes that are not just "about reforming or upgrading or lessening the pain" but "about freeing everyone, cis and trans alike, from the oppressive architecture of gendered facilities."[33] In short, Gavin's narrative fits neatly into what Roderick A. Ferguson has called "one-dimensional" queerness, in which the mainstreaming of queer politics—where queer demands conform to ideals

---

30. Hesford, *Violent Exceptions*, 175. For scholarship on the intersectional "passing" of Black bodies in and beyond Black communities, see McCune, *Sexual Discretion*; Snorton, *Nobody Is Supposed to Know*; and André and Chang, "'And Then You Cut Your Hair.'"
31. Riley, "Gavin's Story."
32. Spade et al., "Models of Futurity," 327; and Wuest, "Scientific Gaze."
33. Spade et al., "Models of Futurity," 327–28.

of respectability, citizenship, privacy, and consumerism—is contingent on its disavowal of earlier queer political struggles over race, class, colonialism, and capitalism.[34]

To observe Gavin's assimilation to the gender binary and the privileges of his whiteness is certainly not to criticize his own understanding or expression of his identity; nor is it to suggest that Gavin's articulation of transness, compelled within an embattled context as a fifteen-year-old, should be taken as an indelible truth about his views of trans politics. Indeed, in the aftermath of his Supreme Court victory, Gavin has begun to emphasize the multidimensionality of his experiences, describing himself on social media as "trans, bisexual, autistic, and fat," and urging other trans youth to embrace their identities and fight back against systems designed to exclude them.[35] Rather, it is to note that Gavin's white and male-passing privileges cooperate with the surveillance and policing of trans bodies, and that the legal and cultural questions he presents are more easily intelligible within white supremacist cis-heteropatriarchal systems.[36]

Gavin is thus recognizable as what Snorton and Haritaworn have labeled a "transnormative subject," whose "universalized trajectory of coming out/transition, visibility, recognition, protection, and self-actualization" is complicit with "biomedical, neoliberal, racist, and imperialist projects."[37] This is not to say that Gavin is not marginalized for his trans identity—indeed, although he ultimately won his case, the majority of this chapter traces his community's outright rejection of his civil rights, and the anti-trans legislation in the ensuing years ensures that his victory is modest at best—but that his legibility as a trans subject is indebted to the extraction of value from racialized bodies. In contrast to Larry/Latisha's undeniable embodiment of biracial, Black-identified, queer, gender-nonconforming "too muchness," which we will see later in this chapter, Gavin's intelligibility is enabled by deferring the racialized surplus of transness that is invoked repeatedly during the school board meetings but does not cling to his white, masculine-presenting body.

But first, in the following two sections I turn careful attention to the discussion about the GCSB's resolution for gender-segregated facilities during the lengthy public-comment periods of the November 11 and December 9, 2014, school board meetings. Well over an hour at each meeting was devoted

---

34. Ferguson, *One-Dimensional Queer*.
35. Hohmann, "Please, Go On." In 2022 Gavin even published a children's book called *If You're a Kid Like Gavin* (with Kyle Lukoff and illustrated by J YangSee) that tells his story and seeks to inspire other trans kids.
36. Gossett and Huxtable, "Existing in the World," 42.
37. Snorton and Haritaworn, "Trans Necropolitics," 67.

to short statements (limited to three minutes in November, two minutes in December) from any member of the community who wished to address the GCSB. Gavin and his parents each offered brief statements, and most of the remaining speakers were parents of students who went to high school with Gavin or parents with children who were in lower grades in the school district. A few high school students also spoke (especially at the second meeting), as well as a handful of teachers and religious leaders, a young trans man who was an alumnus of Gloucester High School, and a self-identified born-again "former" lesbian from a nearby community. Emotions ran high at both meetings, but the comments at the first meeting were often tempered by acknowledgments of the difficulty of the decision facing the board; speakers frequently ended their remarks by noting that this is "a tough issue," "a complex and sensitive matter," "a huge job," or "a hell of a mess," and that as elected officials, board members were "hearing opinions from both sides" and had a responsibility "to make those hard choices."[38] By the second meeting, however, opinions had clearly polarized, with speakers less likely to empathize with other positions and more likely to advocate for the GCSB's resolution as the only appropriate response; there were even frequently repeated threats that individual board members would be voted off the board and their decision immediately overturned if they did not vote in favor of the resolution. However, in spite of the stakes of the conversation and the passionately held moral, political, and spiritual convictions of the crowd, there was only one speaker who resorted to overtly disparaging terms for Gavin (his comment garnered audible disapproval from the audience and a quick reprimand from the board), and most remained at least superficially respectful.

The meetings exemplified, in Asen's and Tracy's words, the "ordinary democracy" that is carried out routinely in school board meetings around the country: the community's deliberation utilized a variety of styles of speech and argument, featured more than a few moments of rowdy emotion, and exhibited disparate perspectives ranging from the affirming and compassionate to the transphobic, homophobic, and racist.[39] By treating the GCSB meetings as instances of ordinary democracy, I emphasize that everyday forms of talk—including the moments at which it is injurious or irrational—are not only part of the school district's local decision-making process but also constitute community understandings of whiteness, trans identity, and civil rights.[40]

---

38. GCSB meeting, November 11, 2014, 16:25, 1:05:22, 1:35:56, 45:48, 58:53.
39. Asen, *Democracy, Deliberation, and Education*; and Tracy, *Challenges of Ordinary Democracy*.
40. See also McCormick, "Arguments from Analogy," 187; and Gent, "When Homelessness Becomes a 'Luxury.'"

Trans Temporality and the Sexual Threat of Gender Expression

The Gloucester community evinces an unease with the ways that trans youth like Gavin are perceived to be at odds with the normative developmental temporality of the racial figuration of childhood. Speakers justify limiting Gavin's rights by figuring his transness as dangerously out of sync with the expectations of childhood development of gender and sexuality, framing this temporal disruption in two distinct and somewhat contradictory ways that will be explored in this section: as temporal delay and temporal acceleration. While the GCSB's resolution presumes that trans youth are too young to know their own genders (and thus delayed compared with their cisgender peers), much of the community's conversation focused on fears that Gavin is too mature or knows too much (and thus poses a sexual threat to his cisgender peers). Either way, Gavin causes temporal trouble, skewing the timelines that uphold the normativities of white, cis, hetero(non)sexual childhood.

Scholarship in trans studies and trans theory has frequently noted the ways in which trans bodies and identities disrupt the traditional linear development of gender, sexuality, and relationships assumed in "straight" and "cis" temporalities. José Esteban Muñoz describes "straight time" as a "self-naturalizing temporality" that imagines the future only through "reproductive majoritarian heterosexuality, the spectacle of the state refurbishing its ranks through overt and subsidized acts of reproduction."[41] Other authors, emphasizing the "social patterning of experiences of time" as a normative force, note that linear, chronological, reproductive temporalities may be experienced as fragmenting or invalidating for trans and queer subjects whose lives do not conform to regularizing markers of growth and progress.[42] For instance, Elizabeth Freeman conceives of time as a means for cohering a group: people are brought together into "socially meaningful embodiment through temporal regulation . . . people are bound to one another, engrouped, made to feel coherently collective, through particular orchestrations of time." She uses the term "chrononormativity" to describe the process whereby institutional forces come to be incorporated into seemingly natural and embodied tempos and routines—these rhythms feel as if they arise organically from the body rather than being applied to the body.[43]

---

41. Muñoz, *Cruising Utopia*, 25, 22.
42. Amin, "Temporality," 220.
43. Freeman, *Time Binds*, 3.

Chrononormativity is fundamental to cis- and heteronormative figurations of childhood because it suggests that life is expected to unfold along a predictable timeline of developmental markers throughout childhood, adolescence, and adulthood. These markers, unsurprisingly, privilege heterosexual reproductive relationships. As Jaclyn I. Pryor explains, "certain kinds of events and relationships get historically recorded, such as births, marriages, and deaths, while others, such as coming outs, friendships, caretaking, casual sex, separations, gender transitions, nonmonogamous relationship structures, illness, ritual, and contact with the dead, do not."[44] It is not just that queer and trans temporalities may involve different flows or markers of time, but that straight time dictates which markers are valid or which experiences count, therefore limiting the possibilities and recognition of queer and trans lives. Those experiences that do not fit the framework of straight time are either rendered invisible or perceived as a deviation or perversion of life's linearity.

Chrononormativity does not only discipline expressions of gender and sexuality but also naturalizes the whiteness of progress, civilization, and futurity. Chrononormativity enforces the temporalities of labor and productivity central to capitalism and the temporalities of racialization that substantiate imperialism and white supremacy. The "temporal containment" of white time, Logan Rae Gomez argues, is a modality of racialized capture that produces a temporal distance from racial harms of the past but also from racialized bodies.[45] As Ersula Ore and Matthew Houdek describe, the "suffocating hegemony of white national time" is founded on the negation of Blackness and "assumes linearity, closure, and a denial of responsibility." Because this sense of time appears as common sense, they explain, it "occlud[es] alternative nonlinear temporalities" that might unsettle established institutional logics.[46] Likewise, Jade Crimson Rose Da Costa argues that chrononormativity is a feature of the racialized narrative of advancement that promotes whiteness as an indicator of modernity, while nonwhite others are imagined to be backwards, uncivilized, and relegated to the past. That is, "the white liberal subject comes to embody the 'cultural imperative' of movement and change, while those considered to exist beyond/before/behind modernity are deemed out of time and place."[47] The expectations of normative temporality thus naturalize the whiteness of the future as a characteristic of the modern (trans) subject.

While trans subjectivities and experiences are constituted in relation to chrononormativity, they also exceed and disrupt normative developmental

---

44. Pryor, *Time Slips*, 11.
45. Gomez, "Temporal Containment," 184.
46. Ore and Houdek, "Lynching in Times," 444–45.
47. Da Costa, "Pride Parades," 445.

timelines in ways that Kadji Amin describes as "being out of sync," or experiencing a "rupture between past, present, and future."[48] Chen and Cárdenas refer to the "disjunct time" of gender nonconformity, in which "an assignment at birth is retroactively rejected, and a present embodiment is understood as needing to become otherwise in the future."[49] Trans youth, in particular, who may be experiencing gender transition simultaneously with a transition from childhood to adulthood, as Hesford points out, might be understood as "doubly liminal," occupying various states of becoming and awaiting transformation and recognition in multiple registers.[50]

These nonnormative and nonchronological qualities of trans temporalities draw on what Jack Halberstam has called "queer time": models of temporality that exist outside "the temporal frames of bourgeois reproduction and family, longevity, risk/safety, and inheritance."[51] Queer time, as Laura Horak suggests, might identify the experiences of being "asynchronous, out of joint" with normative life schedules, but it is also a way of recognizing queer creativity.[52] As Pryor puts it, "queer and trans people have always been at the vanguard of radical ways of working, playing, fucking, organizing, educating, parenting, making home, making art, and creating ritual that defy normative patterns of clock, biological, and nuclear family time."[53]

Trans temporalities, then, draw on queer time's disruption of chrononormativity and recognition of alternative chronologies, but arise from the lived experiences of trans and gender-nonconforming people; trans temporalities might be understood to move at different rates, to be marked by different life events, and to be configured according to alternate benchmarks. For instance, awareness of gender and sexual identities and social and physical transitions may occur at any point during one's life, and may involve a "stretched-out" or "second" adolescence during which one's sense of embodiment and desire may shift; perceptions of one's "youthful" or "mature" appearance may contradict one's chronological age as a result of hormonal or surgical interventions; changing one's name or pronouns or undergoing specific elements of medical transition may be experienced as milestones or as moments of rebirth, and one's "naming day," "coming out day," or "transition day" may supplement or replace traditional birthdays; crafting intentional relationship and community structures may put one at odds with the reproductive logics of heterosexuality;

---

48. Amin, "Temporality," 220.
49. Chen and Cárdenas, "Times to Come," 475.
50. Hesford, *Violent Exceptions*, 171, 174.
51. Halberstam, *In a Queer Time and Place*, 6.
52. Horak, "Trans on YouTube," 581.
53. Pryor, *Time Slips*, 5.

the increased likelihood of violence or suicide, the threats of HIV or substance abuse—especially for queer and trans people of color—may prompt different expectations around aging and death.[54]

The disruption of chrononormativity posed by trans temporalities can be characterized in seemingly contradictory ways: either in terms of its future orientation or in terms of its slowness and delay. On one hand, trans temporality might be understood as primarily oriented toward the future, emphasizing looking forward to the imagined life to come. For example, Ruth Pearce describes trans temporality as a "time of anticipation." Trans people's feelings of anticipation, in Pearce's account, arise from waiting for the future, whether the future imagined is desired (e.g., awaiting a surgery date) or feared (e.g., apprehension about being misgendered or facing violence). The time of anticipation reflects how understandings of time also arise from social patterns, through emotional engagements with time and relationships with others, and are "mediated by community discourse and communal identity." Thus, the time of anticipation, she explains, "emerges through a collective management of uncertainty: oriented towards the future, but shaped by many people's experiences of the past, and experienced as a liminal, never-ending present."[55] Similarly, Horak suggests the phenomenon of "hormone time," in which trans people on YouTube mark the passage of time from their first dose of hormone therapy. For Horak, hormone time is linear and teleological, "point[ing] toward a utopian future, in which the subject experiences harmony between the felt and perceived body." Thus, hormone time conforms to a chrononormative narrative of life's progress but substitutes an unexpected future goal not of marriage and procreation but of gender transformation.[56]

On the other hand, trans temporality might also be defined not in terms of its future orientation but in terms of the sense of delay or "lag" that such an orientation can produce. Hil Malatino argues that the common "transnormative" progress narrative, in which one continuously evolves toward the ideal gendered body, can leave many trans people feeling "out of temporal sync, left behind." This sense of "lag" shapes the experiences of those trans subjects who do not have access to or cannot easily afford transition-related technologies, but it also characterizes the experience of transition itself, which might unfold slowly and haltingly over weeks, months, and years, and does not necessarily offer a clear moment of completion. Malatino emphasizes the negative affects of lag, asserting that "lag often comes coupled with an experience of repeated,

---

54. Pryor, *Time Slips*, 5; and Pearce, *Understanding Trans Health*, 124.
55. Pearce, *Understanding Trans Health*, 121.
56. Horak, "Trans on YouTube," 580–81.

persistent, and dogged misrecognition and allied forms of transphobic hostility," which can lead to feelings of fatigue.[57]

Whether trans temporality is characterized by a sense of lag or identified by its future orientation—a temporal delay or a temporal acceleration, respectively—the point is not that trans people uniformly experience temporality differently than cis people, or that there is a particular kind of "trans time" that contrasts with "cis time." Some trans lives, especially with the increased availability of hormone blockers for pre-pubertal trans children, do hew closely to the normative markers of childhood and adolescent development and adult accomplishments. Rather, it is key that the trans disruptions to chrononormativity described here challenge the naturalness and inevitability of such a developmental schedule, thus opening the possibility to envision temporality differently. As Chen and Cárdenas explain, "if we imagine transness to be not about a crossing from one location to another but about a multidirectional movement in an open field of possibility, then time and its direction become more fluid."[58] Such movement, which might include "pockets of slowness, dead-end diversions, and the openness of multiplicity," can be a source of creativity and possibility, but it can also create anxiety about maintaining what is perceived to be the proper timing of chrononormativity.[59]

The Gloucester community's debates exhibit anxiety about both of these ways that transness is perceived to skew the developmental temporality of white hetero(non)sexual childhood. First, the resolution itself, along with some of the subsequent discussion, frames Gavin in terms of a temporal lag, suggesting that Gavin is not old enough to be sure of his own gender identity, that it is a fleeting status that does not merit structural recognition in the form of access to sex-segregated bathroom facilities. However, this framing of Gavin is overtaken by a second, overriding temporal anxiety, in which Gavin's trans identity appears as a marker of precocious maturity: his gender identity is conflated with sexuality, such that his supposedly adultlike gender expression is read as a sexual advance, and even as sexual aggression. Gavin's developmental temporality is thus out of sync with his peers: he is simultaneously *delayed*, too childlike to make an authentic claim to gender, and *accelerated*, too adultlike to share the intimate space of the restroom with other young people. The few voices arguing on Gavin's behalf attempt to reorient his young trans identity within the dominant temporality of childhood, asserting that he is old enough to know his own gender and that he is innocent of the sexual maturity that hovers around him.

---

57. Malatino, "Future Fatigue," 639–41.
58. Chen and Cárdenas, "Times to Come," 473.
59. Chen and Cárdenas, "Times to Come," 478.

Transness as Temporal Delay

The GCSB's resolution in response to Gavin's use of the boys' bathroom asserts that Gloucester County Public Schools "recognizes that some students question their gender identities" and "encourages such students to seek support, advice, and guidance from parents, professionals and other trusted adults," while also striving to provide a safe learning environment and protect the privacy of all students. It proposes that male and female restroom and locker-room facilities "shall be limited to the corresponding biological genders, and students with gender identity issues shall be provided an alternative appropriate private facility."[60] On its face, this resolution seems to acknowledge the possibility of trans, nonbinary, or gender-nonconforming students, and to make certain accommodations for them (even as its awkward and nonsensical phrase, "biological genders," suggests little grasp of the matters at stake). However, it imagines these students to be "questioning" their genders or having "gender identity issues," relegating them to a state of perpetual unknowingness, uncertainty, and distress. It advises these students to turn to adults for "support, advice, and guidance," implying that unlike cisgender students—who are trusted to know their genders without adult help—gender-nonconforming students do not possess the maturity to understand and express their genders on their own and should defer to grownups who can set them on the right path. The resolution therefore limits the freedoms of trans students—by dictating which restrooms they can use at school—under the guise of assisting them with their presumably troubling gender identities. In short, even though Gavin had been confidently and consistently asserting his male gender identity since childhood and was already pursuing social and physical transition, the resolution imagines gender-nonconforming students to be lagging behind their classmates, not yet able to properly identify their own genders. Put differently, cisgender students' identities are assumed to be settled and persuasive in the present, while gender-nonconforming students exist in a temporal delay, where they are not yet believed to be who they say they are.

According to Jules Gill-Peterson, this framing of trans youth has been a persistent feature of transgender medical discourse since at least the beginning of the twentieth century. Gill-Peterson analyzes letters between trans young people and their doctors in which children try to convince the doctors of their claims to genuine trans experience, while the doctors put them off until they are older. For instance, Gill-Peterson quotes boilerplate replies from the well-known endocrinologist Harry Benjamin and his colleagues in the 1960s: "You are very young yet and must give yourself a chance to mature.

---

60. GCSB meeting minutes, November 11, 2014.

... In 2 or 3 years, life may look differently to you," or "Be patient, finish your education, and see how you feel once you are matured." Responses might also suggest that the child should confide in their parents, their family doctor, or a psychiatrist.[61] Thus, trans children have been silenced by this kind of infantilizing developmental discourse for more than half a century, being told that they are too young to know the truth of their genders and that they should seek out the guidance of adults. This pattern of denial prevents gender-nonconforming young people from learning about their trans ancestors and trans histories, communities, and activism, and it undermines their awareness of their own embodied experiences.[62]

Gill-Peterson also argues that continually disqualifying and distrusting trans kids' knowledge about themselves until they reach adulthood creates the illusion that transgender young people are a perpetually recent phenomenon, one without precedent or history. Refusing to recognize them and reserving legitimate trans identity only for adults effectively ensures that trans children are always "new," surprising, and controversial. Not only does this prevent trans young people from speaking or exercising agency on their own behalf, but it also treats contemporary trans youth like Gavin as a novelty, and the policies developed to accommodate or exclude them as experimental. The resolution passed by the GCSB emerges from precisely this logic, assuming that trans youth have not always been part of the student population: Gavin is imagined as the first of his kind, posing an unforeseen and urgent crisis, and requiring accommodations never previously considered.

Although the school board's resolution frames trans kids as lacking the maturity and the competence to know their genders, the public discussion demonstrated that many people present did, in fact, recognize Gavin's assertion and presentation of masculinity. In a surprising and rather amusing inversion of the expected misgendering of Gavin (which was still upsettingly common throughout both meetings), a fair number of parents and community members referred to Gavin with he/him pronouns and masculine terms, only to quickly "correct" themselves. One woman, for example, began her comments referring to Gavin as "he," asserting that "he has no right, or *she* has no right" to use the boys' bathroom, hastily adjusting her language on the fly as she realized the contradiction she was about to express. And one father blundered through all of his comments about Gavin, first using masculine language and then immediately and uncomfortably revising it repeatedly: "this fellow . . . er, er, lady . . . young person," "this young fellow . . . or

---

61. Gill-Peterson, *Histories of the Transgender Child*, 152, 154.
62. Page, "One from the Vaults."

young person," and "whether he likes it . . . or the child likes it or not, as a parent [you] have a responsibility to protect that child from himself . . . from themselves."[63] In both of these instances, the adults are arguing that Gavin does not, as a child, have the authority to claim his own gender, but their language demonstrates that they too perceive Gavin to be male. In spite of their best efforts to prove him wrong, they confirm Gavin's capacity to know and declare his gender.

Transness as Temporal Acceleration

In contrast to the immaturity and uncertainty suggested by the language of the resolution, much of the discussion at the two meetings imagined trans kids in a second sort of skewed temporality: introducing an inappropriately adult-like sexuality to their hetero(non)sexual and vulnerable peers. Most speakers did not directly indict Gavin of potential sexual impropriety in school restrooms but rather imagined hypothetical older trans students who would share bathrooms with their children. For example, at the November meeting one father asks, "Is my six-year-old daughter going to go into the restroom in elementary school with a[n] eleven-year-old boy who identifies as the opposite gender?" and a mother inquires, "Is my elementary age girl going to be in the bathroom with an older boy? She doesn't understand. And at age eight, she certainly shouldn't have to."[64] These comments are interesting because the parents are conjuring not just the possibility of their daughters encountering a boy in the girl's bathroom (ironically, precisely the result that the GCSB's policy would produce, if Gavin were to use the bathroom corresponding to his assigned or "biological" gender) but also the prospect of an *older* boy sharing the space with their younger daughters. The hypothetical trans child's age is inflated to greater than that of their peers, and they bring the threat not just of gender nonconformity but also of advanced and improper knowledge, which young children "shouldn't have to understand." This move is already familiar from chapter 1, where Black youth are perceived to be older than they are, therefore imbuing them with the stereotypical violence and hypersexuality of adult Black men and women and excluding them from the category of vulnerability. The mandates of chrononormativity, then, function intersectionally to discipline children into white, cisgender, and heterosexual standards of development.

---

63. GCSB meeting, November 11, 2014, 1:08:08; December 9, 2014, 58:33.
64. GCSB meeting, November 11, 2014, 42:53, 47:29.

This adultification of trans youth becomes more entrenched by the December meeting, where it functions not just hypothetically but in direct reference to Gavin. One grandmother who speaks up suggests that it would be more appropriate for Gavin to use the men's bathroom designated for school staff than the boys' bathroom. She dares the school board members, "If you feel comfortable enough, you male men, that you want to put him in the boys' room, let him go to the bathroom with *you*. Don't allow him to be with the underage children who do not have a voice."[65] Here, it is not actually Gavin's gender that is being challenged as inappropriate for the bathroom—after all, she is suggesting that he use the *men's* room—but his age; in contrast to the voiceless "underage children" (who are actually Gavin's teenage peers and contemporaries), Gavin is envisioned as more suitably belonging in the company of adult men. In other words, while his cisgender peers are suffused with voiceless vulnerability, Gavin's transness seems to put him on an accelerated path to a dangerous and untimely maturity.

In contrast to the aging-up of gender-nonconforming kids, speakers frequently emphasized the youthful innocence, vulnerable hetero(non)sexuality, and potential for corruption of their cisgender children, effectively downplaying their maturity. According to sociologist Sinikka Elliott, it is common for parents to view their own children as "young, immature, and naïve," regardless of their actual behaviors, and to preserve their illusions about their children by projecting their anxieties about sexuality onto their children's peers—especially those who are othered by racial, class, or gender differences.[66] Parents at both school board meetings frequently characterized their children as exceptionally helpless and imperiled and worried about their vulnerability to "safety" and "privacy" violations. Almost always, the safety and privacy of cisgender children was assumed to be ensured by maintaining sex-segregated facilities (based on gender assigned at birth) and was assumed to be put at risk by the possibility of trans children entering those facilities. Indeed, in Gavin's and similar disputes, cisgender students' "right to privacy" seems to mean, as Gayle Salamon points out, the ability "to move through sex-segregated public spaces without any trans students present," or "a right to public space purged of transpeople [sic]."[67] Although Gavin maintains that no students seemed bothered by his use of the boys' bathrooms, adults spoke on behalf of their children to assert that they are, in fact, uncomfortable; they describe their children as "very upset," "worried," and "scared" to use the bathroom at school, and one man notes that cisgender boys will experience the restroom

---

65. GCSB meeting, December 9, 2014, 59:03.
66. Elliott, *Not My Kid*, 23, 97–98.
67. Salamon, *Life and Death*, 164.

as a "hostile," "negative and disruptive environment" if Gavin is allowed to use the facilities alongside them.[68] Furthermore, several parents alluded to their children's unwillingness or inability to express their discomfort because of fears of "retaliation" or that they would be called bullies.[69] Of course, this is a direct reversal of the actual site of vulnerability: while there is no evidence that trans people harass or assault cisgender people in public bathrooms, trans people are frequently the targets of such violence from cisgender hands.[70]

Cisgender students—especially cisgender white boys—are even imagined to be too frightened or intimidated to speak on their own behalf, so saturated in vulnerability that they require their parents to speak for them. For example, two different fathers at the November meeting, when voicing the concerns of their children, do so by ventriloquizing their sons, speaking not just *for* their kids, but *as* their kids. One father recounts asking his eight-year-old son how he would feel about using the restroom "with a little girl in the bathroom with [him]," and reports his son's answer: "Oh no, Daddy, that is just totally wrong. . . . I would be scared she was lookin' at me." Another father says that his opinion is based on his son's discomfort, which he illustrates with "Hey Dad, why should I have to put up with this?"[71] Supposedly speaking the truths that their sons are too frightened or embarrassed to voice to anyone other than "Daddy," these fathers thus emphasize their sons' vulnerable need for paternalistic protection. When a couple of cisgender students do speak up at the December meeting, they describe themselves in similarly youthful and disempowered terms: a freshman boy, for example, explains that he and his friends felt afraid to come to these meetings and afraid that they would be "bullied in school and in the community . . . being labeled hateful or intolerant or sexist." This "intolerance" from his peers, he continues, is a "disgraceful" public attitude that would "attack children who are uncomfortable with pure and simple public indecency."[72]

The emphasis on the youthful vulnerability and hetero(non)sexuality of cisgender kids is driven home at the end of the December meeting, after the citizens' comment period has closed, when school board member Carla Hook, who originally brought the resolution to table, offered some final thoughts prior to the vote. In spite of Gavin being in high school, she reminds the

---

68. GCSB meeting, November 11, 2014, 36:43, 19:14; and GCSB meeting, December 9, 2014, 1:04:15.
69. GCSB meeting, November 11, 2014, 1:10:31; and GCSB meeting, December 9, 2014, 58:50.
70. Castagnaro, "Nonsense and Dangers."
71. GCSB meeting, November 11, 2014, 37:07, 52:16.
72. GCSB meeting, December 9, 2014, 37:44.

audience that the policy would apply to all public schools in Gloucester County, and therefore would include children in grades K–12. She speaks very eloquently about the ways in which social mechanisms are put into place to protect children: "These are young people that we, as a society, have decided are too young to drink. By and large, they are too young to vote, too young to smoke, too young to get a tattoo, too young to serve in the armed forces. And many of them are too young to even drive a car." Hook then contrasts this societal protectionism with expecting children to share a bathroom with Gavin or other trans youth: "But yet we want to thrust them into some very adult situations right now, and I also think that is pretty unfair to do that."[73] Cisgender youth, in other words, are understood to be forced into a dangerous and age-inappropriate "adult situation"—akin to smoking, driving a car, or joining the military—simply by sharing a restroom with a gender-nonconforming peer, whose gender expression renders him precociously mature.

But it is not just that trans youth are imagined by speakers at the GCSB meetings to be older than they are; it is also that their gender-nonconforming identities are figured as "adultlike" through invocations of sexual maturity, specifically through conflations of sexuality and gender. A nonconforming gender identity is read as a violation of the demand for the hetero(non)sexuality of childhood. In countless instances, adults' comments demonstrate that they either do not understand or choose to disregard the difference between sexual attraction and trans identity, such that Gavin's expression of his gender is read as a form of sexual orientation, and even more, as a form of sexual invitation or aggression. No evidence of specific sexual improprieties at the hands of trans youth are mentioned, but the presence of transness is feared to invite a parade of sexual horribles upon the gentle sensibilities of cisgender children. One mother imagined a string of "disastrous" consequences, such as "future sex violations, future rapes, sex in bathrooms, our pregnancy rates go up, STD rates are gonna go up." She continues, "It may not happen right away, but it will happen. That's a guarantee."[74] Another man frets that under the influence of "medical treatments" Gavin may "become more masculine and maybe sexually interested in women," making his continued use of the girls' bathroom inappropriate.[75] Although he ultimately concludes in favor of Gavin's prerogative to choose which bathroom to use, his statement misunderstands the relationship between gender and sexuality, imagining heterosexual attraction as a necessary consequence of masculinity (and oblivious to Gavin's already established interest in girls, or the possibility of queer attraction

---

73. GCSB meeting, December 9, 2014, 1:51:33.
74. GCSB meeting, November 11, 2014, 34:48.
75. GCSB meeting, December 9, 2014, 55:20.

among cisgender girls), and figuring Gavin's presence in a gendered space as a sexual provocation.

The looming sexual menace posed by exposure to transness does not depend on a realistic threat; instead, adults' distress seems to multiply in inverse relationship to the credibility of perils they envision. One father worried no fewer than eight times, "where does it end?," demonstrating the fear that the slippery slope provides its own momentum, leading from trans bathroom rights to increasingly dreadful and implausible concerns. A particularly unkind man invoked a litany of outlandish moral panics—everything from polygamy, rape, pedophilia, and bestiality to Sharia law and honor killings—that would ensue from Gavin's use of the boys' bathroom, and then doubled down on his own absurdity by comparing Gavin to a dog and wondering if tax dollars would be used to install fire hydrants where he could publicly relieve himself.[76] Most other speakers were less overtly hostile but nonetheless preoccupied with unfounded fears. For instance, many noted that permitting Gavin to use the boys' bathroom could lead to cisgender boys pretending to be trans in order to gain access with "ill intent" to the girls' bathroom, putting "someone's daughter or sister or teacher" at risk; none seemed to recognize that this unlikely threat, a commonplace in transphobic panics over bathrooms, actually implicates cisgender boys, not trans youth.

Others sexualized the space and function of restrooms, imagining their children "being exposed to . . . somebody else's sexual organs" in the bathroom or locker room. For instance, one mother suggested that since her son would be punished if he were caught sexting ("If he had a picture of a girl's vagina right up in his phone, the school would expel him!"), it is contradictory that the school would permit a trans student to "drop [his] pants" in the restroom.[77] Here, the basic act of relieving oneself in the privacy of a bathroom stall is equated to flagrant sexual indecency, revealing the shame and discomfort that talking about public bathrooms can produce. Advocacy groups such as People in Search of Safe and Accessible Restrooms (PISSAR), a coalition of gender-nonconforming people and people with disabilities, have long identified this shame—shame about the particularities of bodies, shame about the needs of disabled and trans bodies in bathrooms, shame about the realities of excretion, shame about speaking of private matters publicly—as one of the stumbling blocks to open and serious consideration of restroom

---

76. GCSB meeting, December 9, 2014, 1:22:47.
77. GCSB meeting, November 11, 2014, 1:04:05; and GCSB meeting, December 9, 2014, 1:05:38.

access as a political issue.[78] Adults who are unaccustomed to thinking and speaking about their children's activities in school bathrooms thus attempt to redirect that shame onto Gavin, characterizing his gender in terms of sexual indecency. Gavin seems to recognize and refute the strategy of this claim, stating flatly in a news story about his case, "I'm not a freak—my very existence is not a perversion." And he correctly notes that there should, of course, be rules about appropriate behaviors in shared bathrooms, but that these do not depend on the presence or absence of trans people: "You don't see other people's genitals in the bathroom unless you're looking, which is inappropriate in and of itself. . . . If an individual was to behave incorrectly in the bathroom, their crime would be misconduct in a bathroom, it would not be existing while transgender."[79]

It is clear from the wide and unrealistic variety of threats imagined that the community's concern is not with Gavin himself (who had, of course, been using the boys' bathroom for nearly two months with none of the feared consequences transpiring), or even with other specific gender-nonconforming students. Rather, their panicked responses emerge from their sense that gender expression is a kind of sexual provocation, opening the door for cisgender kids to be exposed to a whole host of age-inappropriate sexual deviations. When trans identity is associated with adultlike knowledge and when it is further conflated with sexuality, it becomes possible to articulate it to anxieties as diverse as bestiality, public urination, sexting, rape, increased teen pregnancy, and STIs, such that the simple gender expression of a young person becomes the catalyst for the moral degradation of youth. In other words, it is not necessarily Gavin's particular embodiment that causes trouble—although there is an inordinate amount of public discussion of the state of Gavin's genitals and his menstrual cycle, even as parents assert the importance of privacy for their own cisgender children—but the skewed temporality of transness that threatens to denaturalize the chrononormativity and hetero(non)sexuality of childhood innocence.

Given how Gavin is associated with adultlike knowledge and sexual non-normativities, it is no surprise that those who speak on his behalf—only a handful of people, including himself, his parents, and a few friends and community members—respond by reframing him in terms of youthful innocence and by insisting that his experiences fit within the confines of a white, hetero-, and cisnormative developmental rhetoric. One of the ways they do so is by deliberately referring to Gavin with language that reverses his aging-up,

---

78. West, "PISSAR's Critically Queer"; Chess et al., "Calling All Restroom Revolutionaries"; and Slater, Jones, and Procter, "School Toilets."
79. de Vogue, "Meet Gavin Grimm."

casting him clearly as a child. For example, at the November meeting, the first few speakers tended to call Gavin a "young lady" or "a young lady who identifies herself as a man"; this is a deliberate misgendering, of course, but the phrase "young lady" also ostensibly grants a certain degree of maturity ("lady" rather than "girl") that veils its condescending message that Gavin's gender identification should not be taken seriously. In response, Gavin's mother, Deidre Grimm, accentuates his youthfulness by introducing herself as "the mother of the *child* in question," before turning the floor over to her son.[80] Gavin begins his remarks by addressing the misgendering, but he avoids the adultlike "lady" and "man" of the previous speakers, stating instead that he is "not a girl." He goes on to say, "All I want to do is be a normal child and use the restroom in peace," and uses the word "child" to label himself at least three more times in his short speech. He ends his comments with the statement, "I'm just a boy." Gavin's mother then returns to the microphone to say with pride, "that's my boy." In the remainder of her comments she refers to him repeatedly as a "child," a "kid," and a "boy." Later in the meeting, Gavin's father, Dave Grimm, follows the same model, calling him a "boy" and "my child." This pattern is continued at the second meeting, where Gavin's mother, quoting a previous speaker who called Gavin's situation a "political hot potato" dropped into the new superintendent's lap, introduces herself as "the mom of that hot potato, that awesome, awesome kid," simultaneously reasserting his youth and reminding the audience that the "political" issue facing them is, in fact, also a mother's child.

The Grimms' insistent use of the words "boy," "kid," and "child" thus pushes back against the tendency to view Gavin as more mature than his peers because of his gender identity, and summons instead all the innocence, vulnerability, and need for protection associated with the figure of the child. This language is especially striking when used by Gavin himself because he is exceptionally well-spoken and poised in such a difficult context, presenting himself with an admirably calm and mature demeanor that contrasts with his claims to childhood; furthermore, since fifteen-year-olds are more likely to disdain than claim the markers of childhood for themselves, the impact of a well-spoken adolescent referring to himself as a child is even greater.

Another speaker, unrelated to the family, but one of the few who makes an unambiguous statement in support of Gavin, also participates in disassociating him from adulthood and specifically from adult sexuality. She asserts that the issue at hand "has absolutely nothing to do with sexuality" and then (over)emphasizes this point by stating, "he hasn't even gotten there yet in his

---

80. GCSB meeting, November 11, 2014, 14:12, 18:07, 23:09; emphasis added.

life." Seeming to recognize that perhaps she has gone too far in this childlike characterization—after all, most teenagers have "gotten there," at least identifying if not acting upon their sexual attractions—she backtracks a bit, saying "I don't know, maybe . . . I shouldn't assume," but then reiterates that this "has nothing to do with sexual identity. This is just who he is." Trying to refute the claims that Gavin's gender identity violates the mandate for childhood hetero(non)sexuality, in other words, this speaker ends up reifying the division between gender and sexuality in ways that Gill-Peterson and Stockton both contend can be harmful: attempting to stave off the sexualizing discourses of others, well-meaning allies inadvertently limit the trans child's sexual agency and ability to define their own identity.[81] Furthermore, just as the parents at the meeting cast Gavin as being too sexually mature, she winds up infantilizing him, framing him as much less sexually aware than would be expected of a teenager; in both cases, whether because he progresses too quickly or too slowly, Gavin is out of step with cis- and heteronormative developmental time.

Gavin's trans disruptions of temporality—and the development of binary gender and sexuality proper to whiteness—demonstrate the arbitrariness and fragility of this timeline, leading to the community's redoubling of efforts to assert and naturalize the racialized mandates of chrononormativity. As Chen and Cárdenas emphasize, regulating and assimilating trans lives into the "times and spaces of the state, society, and nation" requires that trans temporalities be chastened and diminished through institutional structures, policies, architectures, and norms.[82] The temporal excessiveness of transness they seek to restrain is compounded by the excessiveness of youth which, as Bess Collins Van Asselt puts it, is "consistently framed as out of control," and might be best understood in terms of a fundamental queerness.[83] As a trans young person, Gavin queerly confounds the white developmental temporality of childhood by asserting a truth about himself that he is not yet authorized to make; caught in the delay of childhood that dictates he may not yet know his own mind, he also introduces a supposedly precocious and inappropriate sexual knowledge to that time of suspension. However, given chrononormativity's imbrication with what Chen and Cárdenas aptly describe as "the linear and universal times of settler colonialism, white supremacy, and heteropatriarchy," such challenges to straight and cis time do not necessarily defy chrononormativity's whiteness; in fact, as I show in the next section, as the Gloucester community grapples with the anxieties generated by trans

---

81. Gill-Peterson, *Histories of the Transgender Child*, 188–89; and Stockton, "Queer Child Now," 531n8.
82. Chen and Cárdenas, "Times to Come," 474.
83. Van Asselt, "Imagining Otherwise," 608.

temporality, its invocation of racial segregation as an explanatory framework for Gavin's rights reproduces the subjection of Blackness.[84]

Trans Rights / Civil Rights: The Perpetual Presence of Blackness

Gavin and his family are white, and Gloucester County is approximately 85 percent white; this majority is roughly reflected in the parents and students who attended the November and December GCSB meetings, as well as in the makeup of the school board members and administrators present (one GCSB member and the superintendent are Black).[85] The controversy over Gavin's use of the boys' bathroom and the GCSB's resolution do not, either explicitly or implicitly, refer to questions of race, and given Gavin's whiteness in a majority white town and school, his race remains unspoken and unmarked, presumably irrelevant to the debate over trans youth and sex-specific facilities. It is remarkable, then, the extent to which race nonetheless emerges as a refrain across the public comments during the two meetings; race, especially in relation to definitions of civil rights, provides the framework of difference through which speakers attempt to grapple with gender's politics.

Underlying both the direct and indirect invocations of race in the meetings, I suggest, is the racialization—specifically, the Blackness—of trans identities and embodiment. As the previous section demonstrated, the normative developmental temporality of childhood is one means of reinforcing the whiteness and imperialism of chrononormativity. But in addition to serving as the foil to progress and civilization, as many queer of color critiques and Black and trans scholars illustrate, racial differentiation has always been a central component in the production of modern gender identities. Amber L. Johnson and Lore/tta LeMaster understand gender as a "colonial refrain" rooted in a white supremacist project of selectively recognizing humanity in white performances of gender while relegating racialized forms of embodiment to the category of the nonhuman. Gender's colonial refrain, they argue, illuminates violence against trans and gender-nonconforming Black, Indigenous, and other people of color as "an ongoing effect of the socio-historical dehumanization of those who fall outside of White Western criteria for 'appropriate' gender performance, comportment, embodiment, and identity."[86] The gender-segregated bathroom, Che Gossett argues, has never been racially neutral but

---

84. Chen and Cárdenas, "Times to Come," 478.
85. "Gloucester County, VA."
86. Johnson and LeMaster, *Gender Futurity*, 3–4.

is "one of the signatures . . . of the afterlife of slavery." The kind of neoliberal politics of inclusion that we see in the fight over trans bathroom access "cannot account for the ways that Blackness ghosts and haunts the normative, the way it exceeds representational fixity."[87]

Blackness, therefore, might be better thought as a historical and contemporary foundation of transness than as a separable and secondary identity category. For example, Marquis Bey presents Blackness and transness as "primordial kin," asserting that "trans* is black and black is trans*." Like many scholars of Black trans studies, Bey affixes the asterisk to trans to "highlight its own dehiscence" and "fundamental openness."[88] As Omi Salas-SantaCruz further explains, the asterisk signals a critique of whiteness and an investment in decoloniality, emphasizing that Black, Indigenous, and other trans scholars of color have constituted "foundational trans articulations of being within coloniality."[89] For Bey, Black and trans* are "disruptive orientations" that are manifested in but ultimately exceed capture by Black and trans* bodies. In other words, although they may be embodied in the world as race and gender fugitivity, Black and trans* "precede and provide the foundational condition for those fugitive identificatory demarcations."[90] Bey turns to Claire Colebrook's concept of "transitivity" to explain the "beginningness" that is antecedent to and makes possible normative assignments of or identifications with categories of race and gender.[91] In Colebrook's words, transitivity is the condition for what we come to know as human; it is "a not-yet differentiated singularity *from which* distinct genders, race, species, sexes, and sexualities are generated in a form of relative stability."[92] Understanding Blackness and trans*-ness in terms of transitivity, Bey argues that Blackness and trans*-ness are the condition of possibility for and the fugitive excesses of white transgender intelligibility; the production and legibility of white transgender identities depend upon the extraction of value from trans* bodies of color.[93]

C. Riley Snorton also proposes that Blackness and transness are overlapping conditions of possibility that give rise to particular raced, sexed, and gendered identities, and that certain pasts and lives have had to be "submerged and discarded" to "render blackness and transness as distinct categories of social

---

87. Gossett, "Žižek's Trans/Gender Trouble."
88. Bey, "Trans*-ness of Blackness," 284.
89. Salas-SantaCruz, "Decoloniality & Trans* of Color." My own use of the asterisk follows the lead of the individual scholars I cite, including the asterisk when the authors do so in their work.
90. Bey, "Trans*-ness of Blackness," 276, 278.
91. Bey, "Trans*-ness of Blackness," 285.
92. Colebrook, "What Is It Like," 228.
93. Bey, "Trans*-ness of Blackness," 287.

valuation." Snorton expands on Colebrook's transitivity, not only describing a quality of changeability or transitoriness, but also drawing from the grammatical meaning of the term, where it refers to an action that "requires a direct object to complete its sense of meaning." In Snorton's work, transitivity functions materially and rhetorically, as a condition of possibility for subjectivity and as a means of exchange within racial capitalism.[94] For example, he describes how Black bodies and their perceived fungibility—in contexts ranging from medical procedures performed without consent on enslaved Black women to cross-dressing and cross-gender modes of escape from slavery—served as "malleable matter for mediating and remaking sex and gender." In other words, the plasticity of gender that enables modern trans identities depends upon the forced "ungendering" of Blackness. "Captive flesh," Snorton argues, "figures a critical genealogy for modern transness, as chattel persons gave rise to an understanding of gender as mutable and as an amendable form of being."[95] The "freedom" of self-invention and expression that white trans people like Gavin are imagined to exercise, then, comes at the expense of the unfreedoms of subjugated Black bodies and through the nonrecognition of gender-variant bodies surveilled for their color.[96] Trans rights and protections might be said to be built upon captive and fugitive Black bodies, and as Snorton puts it, "antitrans violence is also and always already an articulation of antiblackness."[97]

Focusing on transitivity opens the possibility for Blackness and transness to name not just categories of identity but also methods or modes of reading. Marshall Green argues that a "Trans* analytic" functions as a "decolonial demand," an "act of artfulness," that can "articulate a unique relation between two or more identity categories where one marks the limits and excess of the other, simultaneously deconstructing and reconstructing or reimagining new possible ways of being and doing." For Green, Trans* is thus in unique relation to Blackness, "not perpetual alterity but perpetual presence" that "makes different scales of movement or change legible"; to engage a Trans* analytic is to be attuned to how "black is made present or not, when, where, how, why, and, most important, in relation to what."[98] Black and trans transitivity therefore enables agency and produces material and rhetorical effects. Recalling Snorton's grammatical inflection of the transitive, which is incomplete without an object, these effects are often produced *for others*; as Ellison, Green,

---

94. Snorton, *Black on Both Sides*, 5–7.
95. Snorton, *Black on Both Sides*, 20, 57. See also Spillers, "Mama's Baby."
96. Snorton, *Black on Both Sides*, 141–42.
97. Snorton, *Black on Both Sides*, 185.
98. Green, "Troubling the Waters," 66–67, 79.

Richardson, and Snorton put it, Black trans subjects often serve "as a springboard to move toward other things, presumably white things."[99] The value of trans lives and the urgency of trans rights is secured, in other words, by "the literal and figurative capture of Blackness" and the circulation of violence against Black and other trans people of color.[100] In short, the legal recognition of (white) trans rights—or in Gavin's case, the agency of white cisgender adults to refuse to recognize trans rights—depends on and often (re)produces the scene of Blackness's subjection.

While the Black trans scholarship I have described here begins from the material realities of Black trans embodiments and knowledges, it also emphatically and consistently identifies the insidious ways that Black trans experiences are used to amplify the importance of white trans lives. For instance, Green's Trans* analytic does not describe merely the presence of Blackness but the rhetorical work of how Blackness can be "*made* present" strategically, for the benefit of non-Black others.[101] This insight is crucial to making sense of the ways white members of the Gloucester community, as we will see, call up Blackness in their debate about Gavin and his right to gender-segregated bathrooms. Blackness can be simultaneously spoken and denied as a constitutive element of the category of transgender. To be clear, my intention here is not to uncritically apply Black trans scholarship to a white trans subject (thereby absenting Black experiences from Black trans scholarship); rather, it is to emphasize Blackness's centrality, to underscore the rhetorical work that Blackness does to make sense of trans youth in relation to the racial figuration of childhood. Therefore, when Gavin is held up as a symbol of the modern-day civil rights movement, "the Rosa Parks" of trans bathroom rights, representing the plight of trans youth to the nation and to the courts, his struggle alludes to the fight for racial equality as a rhetorical device (appropriating and erasing the actual Rosa Parks), while his whiteness disavows the racialized production of transness.

Racializing Trans Rights

At the November and December 2014 school board meetings, race in general, and Blackness in particular, were invoked both to support and to oppose the GCSB's resolution on the table about gender-segregated facilities. In this

---

99. Ellison et al., "We Got Issues," 162.
100. Snorton and Haritaworn, "Trans Necropolitics," 67; and Ellison et al., "We Got Issues," 162, 164.
101. Green, "Troubling the Waters," 79; emphasis added.

section I trace the ways that Blackness was made present, both directly and obliquely, as speakers debated Gavin's rights. References to race were sometimes made through quite overt analogies between discrimination against Black people and discrimination against trans people or through struggles over the meaning of "civil rights" and "separate but equal" policies. But race also occasionally entered the discussion circuitously and apparently inadvertently, when some white speakers awkwardly used racialized language in comments ostensibly about trans inclusion and trans rights; in these instances race provided the logic through which transness could be made legible.

I begin my analysis with these ambiguous and possibly unintentional invocations of race because they reveal the transitivity of Blackness and transness: in these comments the underlying but not explicitly acknowledged racialization of transness bubbles up, taking the form of verbal stumbles and malapropisms, non sequiturs, and superfluous declarations of tolerance. For example, one white father mentioned that he had a mixed-race daughter, adding that she played co-ed sports, while another community member assured the room, "I could [sic] care less if you're gay, straight, bi, black, white, green or purple. It makes no difference to me. . . . I do not judge people by their sexual orientation or their color."[102] Both of these comments expose the ways that uncomfortable discussions about trans students seem to produce racial anxiety: grappling with gender nonconformity in their midst conjures up other kinds of boundary crossings such as mixed-race children and co-ed sports, leads to compulsive assertions about tolerance for a range of (imaginary) skin colors, and conflates racial and sexual identities in a string of signifiers of difference. Another white father, in a stunning non sequitur, perfectly demonstrated the racial anxiety that Gavin's trans identity produces when he said, "I'm not trying to say anything bad about the transgender [sic], nothing like that. I'm not racist."[103] Of course, this speaker very likely did not know the terms "cissexist" or "transphobic" and would not have thought to use them here; it is striking, however, that his attempt to shield himself from accusations of discrimination toward a trans student are couched in the language of racism. His substitution of "racist" for "cissexist" suggests that bias against trans people quickly summons unwanted hints of anti-Blackness (even though—or perhaps especially because—the trans person in question is white), and his defensive denial of racism stands in for a denial of cissexism.

Other speakers voiced support for the new Black superintendent of schools or praised the "diversity and inclusion" of the school board (apparently

---

102. GCSB meeting, November 11, 2014, 57:17; and GCSB meeting, December 9, 2014, 1:28:32.

103. GCSB meeting, November 11, 2014, 37:23.

referring to the Black superintendent and board member).[104] In these cases, noting the presence of Black members on the school leadership team seems to mitigate concerns about trans discrimination; Black representation stands in for gender-affirming policy. Finally, one white mother, asserting that students should share bathrooms and locker rooms only when they have the same "sexual organs," concluded, "And until [Gavin] has sexual organs of that race, that child needs to be not mixed with the other children."[105] This speaker's substitution of "race" for "sex" or "gender" was perhaps accidental. But regardless of intention, the fact that "race" sprang to her mind first is telling, especially since the remainder of her statement draws on the dangers of "mixing"—a term that, when used in proximity to "race," obviously alludes to the white fears of "racial mixing" that segregationist and antimiscegenation policies were meant to assuage. In suggesting that facilities must be sex-segregated, she justifies such separation by reinvigorating racist rhetorics of contamination (which, as Hsu demonstrates, already echo in trans contagion panics), thus divulging the racial construction of transness through a possible slip of the tongue.[106]

In contrast to the comments I have described so far, a few speakers deliberately crafted direct analogies between Gavin's struggle and racial discrimination, explicitly asking others to view the GCSB's proposed policy about gender and bathrooms as if it were written about race and bathrooms. For example, the white student representing the Student Advisory Committee to the school board ended her comments with an impassioned plea to consider the resolution through the lens of racial segregation: "How would you all feel if this was a question of race? How would you feel if the student in question was African American and you didn't want to let him into a restroom because he was a different race? It's the same thing." By drawing an analogy between gender segregation and racial segregation—indeed, by making a hypothetical substitution of the one for the other to drive home her point—this student's statement has at least two important rhetorical effects. First, she raises the specter of racial segregation, appealing to the mostly white audience's desire to avoid being labeled as racist and their presumed unwillingness to advocate publicly

---

104. GCSB meeting, December 9, 2014, 30:23; and GCSB meeting, November 11, 2014, 58:09.

105. GCSB meeting, November 11, 2014, 1:04:31.

106. Hsu, "Irreducible Damage." The overlapping discourses of racial contamination and queer and trans contagion are evident in numerous contexts including, for example, HIV/AIDS, terrorism, child abuse, and sex trafficking, not to mention contemporary fears about queer "groomers." For scholarship on some of these contexts see, for example, Chávez, *Borders of AIDS*; Puar, *Terrorist Assemblages*, 172–75; Barnard, *Sex Panic Rhetorics*; and Hill, "Producing the Crisis."

for racial discrimination. Second, her analogy neatly divides the question of gender from the question of race, implying that a white transgender student can be thought entirely separately from a Black (presumably cisgender) student. This latter effect sutures transness and whiteness, such that the possibility of Black trans students is unimaginable, and the violence wrought by racial segregation is erased from Black lived experience, becoming a tool to be used in support of (white) trans rights. Siobhan B. Somerville writes that using histories of discrimination against racialized groups analogically to set precedent for other groups' entitlement to rights enacts a "willful amnesia" about how racial formations have always been intertwined in legal designations of rights.[107] To do so obscures the intersectionality of racial identities, decontextualizes past advancements in racial equality, and completely disavows present struggles for racial justice. Overall, this analogy between Black and trans identities offers Blackness as a symbol of otherness, what Alison Reed describes as "an empty vessel of white fears, anxieties, and desires," that performatively aligns white trans people and their white advocates with the marginalization produced by racial injustice.[108]

The most common way that race was invoked by the speakers at the meetings, however, was not by blatantly analogizing race and gender but by debating trans' students use of sex-segregated facilities in the context of civil rights. Many of the speakers made direct claims about civil rights without expanding on what those claims entailed; one father, for instance, said "on some level this is a civil rights issue too," and later repeated, "there are issues with civil rights here," and one mother asserted vehemently, "I don't really understand what is so frightening about this prospect of change and giving someone civil rights as he deserves."[109] Others provided more historical context for their comments about civil rights, often invoking the damaging implications of "separate but equal" facilities in order to explain why the discriminatory attitudes of the day should not be institutionalized in policy.

The discussions of civil rights at the meetings had the effect of positing racism as the default mode of discrimination against which other potential inequalities might be verified, while also situating racism as a matter of history; that is, struggles for racial equality in the past offer a historical framing to support struggles for transgender equality in the present. The most striking instances of this approach to civil rights came from Black speakers who called upon their own experiences with discrimination and segregation. For

---

107. Somerville, "Queer Loving," 358.
108. Reed, "Whiter the Bread," 49–50.
109. GCSB meeting, November 11, 2014, 1:34:25, 1:36:41; and GCSB meeting, December 9, 2014, 1:00:34.

example, one man identified himself as the pastor of a local Black church that had been meeting since 1866, whose members "came out of slavery" and "tried to make a better community by working together." He then suggested that the goal is the same in the dispute about Gavin: "we're still trying to make a better community by working together." Explaining that there is no advantage to "making some poor kid feel left out," he offered his own story of racial segregation: "I remember when we went [to school] here because somebody said we were significantly different than the other kids in the community, so we couldn't go with them to *their* bathrooms, to *their* swimming pool." He concluded this anecdote by emphasizing the parallel experiences of segregation by race and gender, declaring, "The issue you're talking about now is the civil rights issue of this generation."[110] Another Black commenter began her remarks by stating, "Forty years ago [sic], somebody stood up for me. They stepped out of their comfort zone and they said, 'separate but equal is not equal.'" She went on to describe how guidance from both the state and federal departments of education instructs schools that they cannot treat students differently on the basis of gender identity or presentation and concluded that "we must do the right thing and we need to respect this young person's rights."[111]

These personal narratives draw unmistakable connections between racial and gender segregation, calling upon the audience to remember the lessons learned from past attempts to enforce separate facilities for particular groups of people. Even when the designation of Gavin's rights as "civil rights" does not explicitly name race or racism, it nonetheless connects the issue before the school board to those histories, suggesting that the consequences of the board's decision will be similarly impactful. When voiced by Black speakers, these comments do the productive work of showing how racism and cissexism depend on similar rhetorics of dehumanization and take the form of eerily parallel policies and practices of segregation, thus potentially "calling in" members of their own communities who might otherwise be hesitant to support trans rights. However, in the setting of the majority white GCSB meetings, this framing of Gavin's civil rights is easily absorbed into a liberal narrative of progress in which, as David Eng argues, racial equality is "deemed a completed project and consigned to a prior historical moment," while queer and trans rights become thinkable "precisely because racial equality has been settled and achieved."[112]

As I have been describing, framing Gavin's case in relation to racialized histories of civil rights was a pervasive feature of the discussions at the GCSB

---

110. GCSB meeting, December 9, 2014, 30:01.
111. GCSB meeting, December 9, 2014, 46:27.
112. Eng, *Feeling of Kinship*, 38.

meetings. Surprisingly, even speakers arguing in favor of the school board's bathroom-segregation resolution also frequently turned to civil rights as a touchstone. Their claims tended to uphold the importance of civil rights but assert a more limited interpretation of its protections. That is, unlike Gavin's supporters, they imagined the scope of civil rights to be coterminous with rights for nonwhite people, or even more specifically, Black people; thus, they refused to view trans rights through this lens.

This narrow perspective of civil rights does, in fact, have historical precedent and contemporary relevance. The first civil rights law in the US, the Civil Rights Act of 1866, was crafted specifically in relation to race in the aftermath of the Civil War, offering citizenship and equal applications of the law to people "of every race and color" and regardless of histories of enslavement (but explicitly excluding Indigenous people).[113] Widely regarded as a failure, this law had little political power and no social authority, and thus had a negligible effect on practices of racial discrimination; it was nullified by the Supreme Court in 1883. Kirt H. Wilson argues that Southern Democrats who opposed civil rights protections for Black Americans at this time depicted the Civil War as an "epochal rupture" that separated the era of slavery from the "new sensibility" that guided their behavior in the present.[114] This temporal distancing is a precursor to the contemporary liberal narrative of progress that I describe here, which also locates racial segregation and discrimination in the past.

Current civil rights law is determined by the 1964 Civil Rights Act, passed nearly a century later, which offers a much wider scope of protection: it prohibits discrimination on the basis of multiple categorizations—including race, color, religion, sex, national origin, and now, after the 2020 *Bostock* decision, sexual orientation and gender identity as well. But given the range of applications of the language of "civil rights" in legal contexts as well as in popular speech (for instance, it is commonplace to refer to the specific struggle for racial equality for Black Americans in the mid-twentieth century as the "Civil Rights movement"), it is easy to see how some speakers could confidently define civil rights narrowly in terms of race and refuse its implications for gender identity. Acknowledging the civil rights narratives of racial segregation from earlier testimonials, in other words, they asserted that this legal protection was being incorrectly deployed in Gavin's case, and that the question on the table was not, in fact, a civil rights issue at all. For instance, one student said that he would like to "face the argument about separate but equal is not equal. That would [apply] for something like race but I feel like [applying] that

---

113. Library of Congress, "Century of Lawmaking."
114. Wilson, "Contested Space," 135.

to gender would say that all guys and girls can use any bathroom they would like. And I do not believe that that is accurate."[115]

Advocates for the GCSB's resolution thus offered a limited version of civil rights that hinged on racial overdetermination, allowing speakers to evade entirely the question of the policy's infringement on Gavin's civil rights. Carla Hook, the school board member who brought the resolution to the table, used this tactic to emphatically deny the civil rights framing of trans students' access to gender-segregated bathrooms: "I don't think that's a civil rights issue," and "I can assure you that I don't believe this implicates anyone's civil rights." She expanded, "I don't think what we're talking about tonight implicates anyone's civil rights because, let me be clear, I don't think we get to vote on each other's civil rights. That's how important they are." Instead, she offered a reframing, suggesting that the discussion is "about one thing and one thing only," namely, "respecting . . . everyone's privacy and everyone's dignity."[116] Leaving aside the laughable falsehood that we do not vote on each other's civil rights—a falsehood felt keenly by immigrants, poor people, people of color, disabled people, people with uteruses, religious minorities, not to mention queer and trans people, among others—her claims shift the focus from the protected rights of a minority to the imagined comfort of the majority. That is, to acknowledge Gavin's claim within the framework of civil rights would be to recognize the importance of safeguarding the rights of protected groups, even if those rights may be discomfiting or inconvenient to the majority; to reframe Gavin's claim as an affront to individual privacy and dignity, on the other hand, is to narrow the legal protections of civil rights legislation in such a way that they do not apply to Gavin and to recast cisgender privacy as the "right" supposedly being violated. Furthermore, this dismissal of the relevance of civil rights also disavows the lurking worries about racism and racial segregation: if civil rights are not the topic of discussion, then members of the community can feel free to vote against Gavin's freedom to use the bathroom of his choice without being encumbered with the historical baggage of anti-Black separate but equal policies.

Responding to these attempts to dodge the civil rights implications of the GCSB's resolution, Kim Hensley, the only school board member to speak unequivocally against the policy, made an extensive statement that reminded all parents, students, and community members that civil rights are not merely an empty phrase that can be redefined at will but are delineated and guaranteed by a federal law and enforced by a federal agency. Hensley pointed to a

---

115. GCSB meeting, December 9, 2014, 1:39:34.
116. GCSB meeting, December 9, 2014, 1:46:53.

number of guidance communications from state and federal officials, as well as several previous lawsuits in other states, all of which suggest that schools are expected to affirm trans students' gender identities. She argued plainly that it is not up to the school board or individual community members to interpret Title IX, and that their resolution, if passed, would be in violation of the law. Hensley also made clear that it is none other than the Department of Education's Office of Civil Rights that enforces Title IX, drawing the obvious conclusion that, in spite of Hook's protests to the contrary, the resolution most certainly implicates civil rights.

However, even as Hensley accurately describes the significant legal issues at stake and affirms trans rights as civil rights, her words nonetheless demonstrate the deferral of Blackness that I have been describing thus far. Reminding listeners of the pastor who spoke earlier about his own experience with segregated facilities, she repeated his statement that "This is a civil rights issue of this time."[117] Here, when the words of a Black speaker are reiterated in a white voice, their potential for recognizing coalitional possibilities in the shared experiences of anti-Blackness and anti-transness fall away, leaving only the suggestion of the narrative of liberal progress in place. In other words, the civil rights of trans students like Gavin, "the Rosa Parks" for trans bathroom access, are the modern, timely version of civil rights—a civil rights that draws its rhetorical urgency from anti-Black discrimination but conveniently leaves Blackness and racial inequality in the past and out of view.

Ultimately, no matter how well Hensley's speech predicted the GCSB's eventual loss in court when Gavin later sued, it failed to achieve its purpose: not a single member of the school board was swayed by her argument, and she remained the solitary "nay" vote against the resolution.[118] Her version of trans rights as civil rights, in other words, was roundly rejected by the community and the GCSB's resolution for segregated facilities was implemented. But as I have demonstrated in this analysis, the implications of the community's discussion exceed the outcome of the GCSB's vote and the legal decisions rendered. The vernacular deliberation at the school board meetings—by those arguing on behalf of and in opposition to Gavin's freedom to use the restroom of his choice—produced an understanding of civil rights that depended on the invocation and submersion of Blackness as the condition of possibility for contemporary trans identities and trans rights. This move, as Reed explains, aligns white queerness with "a racialized 'otherness'" and not only disavows the privilege of whiteness but also "override[s] a long

---

117. GCSB meeting, December 9, 2014, 2:06:09.
118. Not only did the GCSB lose the case, but it was ordered to pay $1.3 million to cover the ACLU's legal costs in representing Gavin. "School Board."

history of racial injustices . . . that erases the specific experiences of queer and trans people of color." She asserts, "Neoliberal progress narratives easily let race slide into sexuality, as current demands for legal rights presume that the civil rights movement marked an end to racial injustice, making way for 'colorblind' rhetorics that focus centrally on gender and sexuality."[119] As Gavin stands in as today's Rosa Parks, Blackness is displaced from the present and figured only as historical precedent for current concerns. Therefore, Blackness plays a crucial role, if only through its foundational disavowal; it is "rendered ghostly" in the critical genealogy of modern trans identities like Gavin's and his rights to gender-segregated bathrooms.[120]

A Short Story of Queer Possibilities: Larry/Latisha's Black Trans Excess

In the Gloucester community's debate about the trouble with trans youth like Gavin, Blackness is pressed into the service of white trans identities and rights. But to consider the racialization of transness only through the strategic disavowal of Blackness is to risk perpetuating this foundational lacuna, so before I end this chapter I turn to the life of another young person, Larry/Latisha King, as a means both to make plain Blackness's deferral and to try to illuminate, no matter how partially, the Black trans excess that defies capture.

Larry/Latisha, a gender-nonconforming, biracial fifteen-year-old in Oxnard, California, was murdered at school by a fourteen-year-old, white, cisgender male classmate named Brandon McInerney in 2008. At Brandon's trial, his defense attested that the shooting was a response to Larry/Latisha's feminine gender presentation, their use of the name "Latisha," and their flirtatious behavior toward Brandon. Like Gavin's story, Larry/Latisha's death was reported widely in local and national media (including a cover story in *Newsweek*), but those media accounts offered a limited view of Larry/Latisha's life: news writers used he/him pronouns, did not typically mention race, and described Larry/Latisha as "gay." What remained unspoken—what was "too much" to say—was Larry/Latisha's biracial, Black-identified embodiment of nonbinary gender and their use of gender transgression and sexual expression as a means of pushing back against the taunting they received at school. In my account, I use they/them pronouns and the intentionally awkward amalgamation "Larry/Latisha," which conjoins their given and chosen first names,

---

119. Alison Reed, "Whiter the Bread," 50.
120. Eng, *Feeling of Kinship*, 11; and Snorton, *Black on Both Sides*, 57.

in order to preserve in written form the ways that they were "too much" for binary categories of existence.[121]

Ricky Gutierrez-Maldonado offers the term "too muchness" to describe the "unstructured flow" of the racialized histories of trans identities, or the surplus that cannot be contained by neat categories of gender and sexuality. Gutierrez-Maldonado points to the raced, gendered, and sexual identities and behaviors among Black and Brown queer and trans youth that are frequently viewed as "disruptive," "over-the-top," "disobedient and unruly," or "overflowing." Too muchness does not indicate a shared essence or an intentional performance but rather "a mode of being that pushes against the discursive and material boundaries" that regulate young people's lives.[122] Gutierrez-Maldonado intentionally repurposes the racist stereotypes of Black sexuality as wild, uncivilized, and undisciplined—stereotypes at work in other places in this book, including the differential punishments for teen sexting, gender nonconformity, and queer sexual behavior that we saw in chapter 1, and the eugenic history of sex education coming up in chapter 4—in order to emphasize the capacity for agency, joy, defiance, and pleasure that too muchness affords.[123]

I offer this brief sketch of Larry/Latisha's racialized and gendered embodiment as an example of the "perpetual presence" of Blackness that conditions the emergence of transness. It would be easy to understand Larry/Latisha's death in direct contrast to Gavin's life. Gavin's whiteness and the legibility of his gender presentation granted him a national stage and celebrity support, a shot at having his case heard by the Supreme Court, and the chance to be remembered as an important and official part of the history of trans rights. Meanwhile, Larry/Latisha's blurring of gender and racial lines, their assertion of Blackness, and their refusal to mute their youthful sexuality were so unintelligible and intolerable to binary structures of homophobia, racism, sexism, and cissexism that they died for those transgressions.

However, I resist the "spectacular fetishization" of the suffering and dying Black body as evidence for the impossibility of life at the intersections of transphobia, homophobia, and racism and take seriously Reed's indictment of white queer scholarship's uncritical use of racialized bodies to promote "color-blind" queer communities while ignoring and perpetuating racial injustices.[124]

---

121. Other scholars make different choices about how best to refer to Larry/Latisha King. Salamon chooses to call them a "girl" and "Latisha" and uses she/her pronouns, while Gutierrez-Maldonado primarily uses the name Larry (except when referring specifically to their Black femininity, when he uses a combination of feminine names such as "Leticia and Latonya"), and alternates he/him, she/her, and they/them pronouns.

122. Gutierrez-Maldonado, "Lawrence 'Larry' King," 58, 60, 64.

123. Gutierrez-Maldonado, "Lawrence 'Larry' King," 60.

124. Reed, "Whiter the Bread," 50.

Comparing Gavin's legal victory to Larry/Latisha's death may be a stark representation of white privilege and gender privilege, but it also participates in what Snorton and Haritaworn refer to as the necropolitical extraction of value from trans of color deaths, in which the "corporeal excesses" of dead transfeminine people of color are used "as raw material for the generation of respectable trans subjects."[125] The violence of transmisogyny, in other words, becomes a literal and metaphorical resource for "the articulation and visibility of a more privileged transgender subject," the deaths of Black and Brown trans women establishing the urgency of the fight for (white) trans lives.[126]

Instead of focusing on Larry/Latisha's death as a scene of the subjection of Blackness, then, I want to take a moment to concentrate on Larry/Latisha's life as a site of possibility for envisioning race, gender, and sexuality differently. Like Gutierrez-Maldonado, I view too muchness as an opportunity for agency, pleasure, joy, and creativity, a troublesome queerness that exceeds the narrow constraints of tolerance and vulnerability. Larry/Latisha's too muchness, I want to propose, reveals the inadequacy of binary categories of race, gender, and sexuality; it is an illustration of reimagining, as Green suggests, "new possible ways of being and doing."[127]

The media coverage of Larry/Latisha's murder and the discourse in Brandon's trial characterized Larry/Latisha's too muchness through the two themes that are already familiar from the Gloucester community's discussion about Gavin: the fear that trans youth are misaligned with the normative temporality of childhood, and the invocation and denial of race. For Larry/Latisha, however, the skewed temporality of transness coupled with the sexual excesses implied by Blackness produces a third prominent theme: that Larry/Latisha poses a threat of precocious sexual impropriety, where gender expression is tantamount to sexual aggression. Although such sexual threats circulated in the conversation about Gavin, they did not directly indict Gavin as a potential offender, instead imagining hypothetical trans and cis perpetrators in the future. That is, while Gavin's whiteness and clear male identification deflected the racial, temporal, and sexual excesses of transness, for Larry/Latisha they remain an uncontainable and threatening surplus that Brandon attempted to extinguish.

First, Larry/Latisha's short life demonstrates the anxieties produced by the skewed temporality of transness. Like the Gloucester parents who imagined transness to represent an inappropriately accelerated maturity and trans students in bathrooms to be older than their own children, Larry/Latisha's

---

125. Snorton and Haritaworn, "Trans Necropolitics," 67–68, 74.
126. Snorton and Haritaworn, "Trans Necropolitics," 71.
127. Green, "Troubling the Waters," 66.

teachers also depicted their body, comportment, and behavior as being precociously grownup and "out of sync" with their peers. For example, in Gayle Salamon's monograph about Larry/Latisha's case, one teacher described Larry/Latisha's style of feminine dress as being too "sexy" for junior high, "more like a high school or college student," while another commented that Larry/Latisha ran around in three- or four-inch high-heeled boots that "most women [would] have to adjust to."[128] Yet another teacher characterized Larry/Latisha as "emotionally immature" but also described their interests and activities (such as crocheting scarves for soldiers) as more appropriate for an older age group: "This is junior high not junior college and this is not the time." Salamon offers an insightful analysis of this teacher's comments, musing that Larry/Latisha

> is thus immature, delayed, too early, at the same time that she is too mature, too far ahead, too enmeshed in something—a way of speaking? a way of being? a way of presenting?—that should more properly emerge in "junior college." Latisha's strangeness, her wrongness, becomes a temporal problem as well as a gender problem.[129]

In all of these teachers' accounts, there is nothing objectively inappropriate with the particular styles of dress or activities themselves—they are only troubling in their perceived disjointedness with Larry/Latisha's chronological age and gender presentation. Indeed, the teacher who said Larry/Latisha was too sexy recalled seeing a "pretty little girl" in "nice earrings and cute jeans"; the outfit only became too mature when the teacher realized she was looking at Larry/Latisha, not a cisgender girl.[130]

Second, Larry/Latisha's temporal disruptions are intimately connected to their Blackness and all the accompanying stereotypes of Black sexual excess. Gutierrez-Maldonado explains that Larry/Latisha's chosen names, including Latisha but also Leticia, Laquisha, Latonya, and Latoya, signaled a specifically Black feminine persona, and were a means for Larry/Latisha to face the bullying at school with confidence and defiance. According to Salamon, just moments after Larry/Latisha typed the name "Latisha King" on their computer to begin an essay in their English composition class, Brandon shot them twice in the back of the head with a handgun. The naming of Black femininity in the gender-nonconforming and biracial body of Larry/Latisha, in other words, was their final act—an act of speaking that Brandon silenced. But

---

128. Salamon, *Life and Death*, 154, 73.
129. Salamon, *Life and Death*, 118–19.
130. Salamon, *Life and Death*, 154.

remarkably, a pretrial hearing determined that Larry/Latisha's killing was not motivated by race (rather, it was deemed a hate crime because Larry/Latisha was "gay"), so in spite of the prosecution demonstrating Brandon's multiple ties to white supremacy, they were barred from suggesting that racial animus motivated his crime. As Salamon puts it, to talk about race in the courtroom was "literally disallowed," with the result that "Latisha, a black trans girl, was never named as such, was instead always named in court as Larry, a gay boy whose race was not speakable."[131] Race, therefore, was both central to and absented from Larry/Latisha's memory. Their creative performance of "wild Black femininity," a survival strategy at school, was invoked during the court proceedings to demonstrate the threat to Brandon's "innocent whiteness" and to "authorize[ ] the violence of white masculinity," but was simultaneously disavowed as a site of injury.[132] This suppression of race, as Salamon contends, alongside the substitution of gayness for transness, makes Larry/Latisha's narrative more legible as a story of (racially unmarked) homophobia; Black transness is rendered illegible in court records and written out of Larry/Latisha's body, life, and death.[133]

Therefore, Larry/Latisha's skewing of temporality, unlike Gavin's, is always already inflected by Blackness. Larry/Latisha's version of femininity was an intentional expression of Blackness, prompting the adultification that many cis and trans girls face; as we saw in the first chapter, racialized girls are often perceived to be older and more sexually mature than they are, and less deserving of care and protection than their white peers. What made Larry/Latisha's identity so disruptive to chrononormativity, then, was its multiplicity and intersectionality; as Gutierrez-Maldonado describes, "Larry was boy, girl, trans, genderqueer, Black, white, etc. all of the above, and none of the above. Larry's multiplicity resists the consolidation towards a singularity and allows for identity to remain open."[134] Larry/Latisha does not conform to the developmental temporality of childhood (which precludes gender nonconformity and sexual agency and presumes whiteness and innocence), but they also do not conform to an identifiable trans temporality, in which they might transition linearly from one gender to another. Instead, Larry/Latisha's performance of biracial, gender-nonconforming, Black femininity renders them "out of time," too much for and uncontained by normative markers of temporality.

Third, the too muchness of Blackness and trans temporalities thus converge in the perception that Larry/Latisha causes trouble as a sexual provocateur

---

131. Salamon, *Life and Death*, 19, 22.
132. Gutierrez-Maldonado, "Lawrence 'Larry' King," 63.
133. Salamon, *Life and Death*, 40.
134. Gutierrez-Maldonado, "Lawrence 'Larry' King," 65.

who poses a threat to their classmates. This is painfully evident in the ways that Brandon's trial positioned Larry/Latisha as accountable for their own death because of their "flamboyant" demeanor and style of dress. As Gutierrez-Maldonado describes, Larry/Latisha's "hair, use of makeup and femininity were viewed as excessive," leading both Larry/Latisha's classmates and teachers to view them as an "instigator."[135] While Gavin's gender identity was imagined to represent a *hypothetical* sexual threat to his peers in the restroom, Larry/Latisha's gender was interpreted as having *already committed* an aggressive sexual act. Larry/Latisha's femininity, in other words, was understood to constitute harassment of the cisgender boys around them. Salamon puts it this way: "Here we see one of the dangers of conflating gender identity and sexual identity; in this case, gender presentation becomes interpreted as a form of sexual behavior, and that 'behavior' is marked and read as aggressive in order to legitimate the violence that is visited upon the gender-transgressive person."[136] Even though Larry/Latisha lost their life at Brandon's hands, then, it was Larry/Latisha who was cast as a perpetrator, and Brandon and the other cisgender boys who were understood as the victims of Larry/Latisha's advances. One of the jurors at Brandon's trial makes this reversal of roles stark when they imagine Larry/Latisha's style of dress to violate Brandon's civil rights: "Where are the civil rights of the one being taunted by another person who is cross dressing?"[137] This question resonates with Gloucester citizens' concerns for the privacy of cisgender students; in both cases, the too muchness of transness is figured as an infringement on the "rights" of cisgender students to exist in spaces without trans people.

The undecidability and too muchness that Larry/Latisha's life exemplifies—their temporal, racial, and sexual excesses—might therefore be understood as the condition of possibility for claiming trans identities; to the extent that those excesses can be deferred, denied, or disavowed, transnormative identities can become more intelligible in schools and in the law. Of course, the disavowal of these excesses is always imperfect at best, resulting in the kinds of invocations and denials of race (as well as the discomfort with trans temporality and youth sexuality) that were present in the public comments about Gavin and the GCSB's resolution. Gavin's whiteness provides an opportunity to see how Blackness persists as the founding but destabilizing feature of transness, the "invisible-visible racial matter" that haunts the borders of white trans identity.[138] Figured only through its denial, Blackness is, as

---

135. Gutierrez-Maldonado, "Lawrence 'Larry' King," 61.
136. Salamon, *Life and Death*, 30–31.
137. Gutierrez-Maldonado, "Lawrence 'Larry' King," 63.
138. Da Costa, "Pride Parades," 449.

Snorton puts it, "somehow always out of time, out of place, wrong anyplace and anytime."[139] But as a founding yet destabilizing feature of transness, Blackness always haunts the borders of white trans identity, perpetually present, perpetually timely.

The Skewed Temporality of Black Trans Futures

The Fourth Circuit Court of Appeals, in its August 2020 decision in Gavin's case (the decision in Gavin's favor that the Supreme Court upheld in 2021), recognizes the legal, social, and democratic implications of its ruling and congratulates itself for being at the forefront of a progressive expansion of rights: "The proudest moments of the federal judiciary have been when we affirm the burgeoning values of our bright youth, rather than preserve the prejudices of the past.... How shallow a promise of equal protection that would not protect Gavin from the fantastical fears and unfounded prejudices of his adult community. It is time to move forward."[140] This statement from the court positions Gavin's suit as part of the vanguard for trans rights, while also acknowledging the school administrators and other adults in Gavin's community as an impediment to progress. Trans youth, in other words, are caught up in an interconnecting web of adult institutions that attempt to enforce naturalized chrononormative sensibilities and discipline those young people who deviate from them.

When trans youth like Gavin are imagined to be a "new" phenomenon, leading the charge into a novel and unforeseen expansion of inclusion and equality—standing in as the Rosa Parks of the contemporary version of civil rights—this progress is made possible by the transitivity of Black transness, by calling up and then denying the presence of Blackness and consigning racial inequality to history. As I have shown through this chapter's analysis of the public discourse at the two GCSB meetings, the social and legal recognition of white trans rights is predicated on citations of a Blackness that can never be current or present—a ghosting of race that reproduces the subjection of Blackness.

The racial figurations of trans youth that emerge from the ordinary democratic deliberation at the GCSB meetings and from the media treatments of Larry/Latisha's case thus seek to control trans distortions of chrononormativity's developmental timeline by imagining gender identity as sexual threat to

---

139. Snorton, *Black on Both Sides*, 181.
140. *Gavin Grimm v. Gloucester County*, 59–60.

vulnerable cisgender hetero(non)sexual youth and by displacing the racialized excesses of transness onto a Blackness that is never fully present or current. Imagining trans youth in this way produces rhetorical agency for adults: they are able to make sense of white trans identities through the framework offered by racial segregation, but to simultaneously deny Gavin's claims to those rights. While the members of the school board and the Gloucester community may have been acting genuinely in what they thought were the best interests of children, and may not have harbored ill will toward Gavin, the (re)production of racial figurations of childhood does, in fact, do significant harm—to Gavin, to other trans and gender-nonconforming youth, and especially to Black and other trans youth of color like Larry/Latisha. In other words, in the GCSB's decision we can see how racial figurations of childhood come into contact with the lives and bodies of real trans youth through policy decisions, producing effects that exceed the intentions of any individual speaker.

One of these effects, for Gavin, has been a temporal suspension of his own adolescence. Produced and enforced by institutions that determine markers of progress on his behalf, this lengthy suspension, as Caterina Nirta notes, "encapsulates relations of power and dominance between the vulnerable subject and social practice."[141] Consider, for example, the months and years Gavin waited to bring his transition to his school's attention, the seven weeks during which he used the boys' bathroom, the month between the first and the second GCSB meetings at which the resolution was debated and his dignity hung in limbo, the humiliating months of school between the GCSB's decision and the filing of his lawsuit, and of course, the subsequent seven years of legal battles punctuated by rulings and appeals. The length and quality of each of these intervals has been determined by school administrators, the school board, and the courts, whose rhetorical agency has been enabled, in part, by their strategic and racialized figurations of trans youth. But the effects of their decisions are felt most acutely—and nearly exclusively—by Gavin and other trans youth. Indeed, the 2021 Supreme Court's decision to let his earlier win stand is its own sort of temporal jumble: as an adult man Gavin learned that his victory a year earlier could now be enforced, that his past teenage self is legally allowed to use the boys' bathroom from which he was barred, at a high school from which he has long since graduated.

The future effects of Gavin's case are also undetermined. Other circuit courts are not bound by the decision in *Grimm v. Gloucester County School Board*, leaving the rights of trans students up to individual states and regions to determine. In December 2022, for example, the 11th US Circuit Court of

---

141. Nirta, *Marginal Bodies*, 66.

Appeals, in a case otherwise remarkably similar to Gavin's, upheld a Florida high school's policy forbidding trans students from using bathrooms that correspond to their gender identities. One of the lawyers from Lambda Legal who was representing Andrew Adams, the white trans boy who filed the lawsuit, called the decision "an aberrant ruling" that contradicts every other circuit court's rulings on similar questions—including Gavin's.[142] Given the heavily right-leaning Supreme Court, it is unclear whether Adams will pursue an appeal.[143]

But at least one thing is certain: the maelstrom of proposed anti-trans legislation in recent years, now focused primarily on restricting trans youths' access to gender-affirming medical care and preventing trans youth from playing on sports teams that conform to their gender identities, disproportionately impact Black trans youth and other trans youth of color. As I described in the introduction, empirical research provides a wealth of data showing that gender-affirming healthcare improves the quality of life of trans youth on multiple measures; because Black youth already experience more barriers to obtaining health care than their white peers, they are likely to see even more detrimental effects when they are prohibited from accessing such care.[144] Likewise, research suggests that trans-inclusive policies in athletics have multiple benefits for trans students, including improved mental health, lower risk of suicide, less harassment by peers, and higher grades. Legislation targeting trans athletes is often "brimming with anti-Blackness," reproducing patterns of discrimination and body policing born from attempts to establish differences in embodiment for the purposes of racial segregation.[145] Thus, Black trans athletes—and Black transfeminine athletes in particular, since the sponsors of these bills claim to be motivated by preserving the "fairness" of sports for cisgender girls—find themselves at the intersections of racism, sexism, and transphobia, offered up as scapegoats for imagined threats to the purity of white, cisgender, hetero(non)sexual femininity.

In the end, the skewed temporality and racialized surplus of trans youth are interruptions to the institutionalization of whiteness and gender normativity (re)produced in the racial figuration of childhood. In spite of Gavin's victory, the hopes represented by his case are dishearteningly modest: the right to perform a limited role in maintaining a restrictive and damaging binary gender system, a system within which the excesses of Blackness, gender, and sexuality embodied by Larry/Latisha can never be accommodated. To understand

---

142. Stempel, "U.S. Appeals Court."
143. Riedel, "Florida School's."
144. "Outlawing Trans Youth"; and Goldenberg et al., "Stigma, Gender Affirmation."
145. Center for American Progress, "Fact Sheet"; and Clifton, "Anti-Trans Sports Bills."

trans bathroom policies in schools through this lens is to notice that concerns for "safety" have a long history in the maintenance of white supremacy and that anxieties about ensuring "privacy" or determining "biological sex" are, as Gill-Peterson puts it, "convenient displacements for naked political violence against trans life."[146] That is, trans and gender-nonconforming youth like Gavin and Larry/Latisha are pressed into the service of the racial figuration of childhood that defers trans temporalities and racialized excesses; they enable moral and political projects much larger than themselves, pursued in the name of children while narrowing the possible futures for trans youth and adults.

But as the next chapter shows, it is possible to figure young people's sexuality otherwise. Describing how the history of sex education is a pedagogy of white supremacy, cis- and heteronormativity, and sex-negativity, I demonstrate how one innovative sexual-wellness organization cultivates sexual agency for Black girls, women, and femmes.

---

146. Spade et al., "Models of Futurity," 328; and Gill-Peterson, *Histories of the Transgender Child*, 196.

CHAPTER 4

From Reticence to Abundance

Talking Back to the History of Sex Education

Brittany Brathwaite and Kimberly Huggins never met when they were both growing up in the early 2000s in Brooklyn, New York, but they later learned that they had similar experiences as Black girls who wanted to learn about sex and sexuality: namely, they both found that good information was hard to come by. Brittany was a sexually active teen who never received any formal sex education and who never learned even the basics about how to prevent STIs, let alone more empowering messages about sexual decision-making, consent, or pleasure. She recalls coming home from school one day and seeing a mobile HIV-testing unit on the corner of her block. Brittany was attracted by the free metro cards they were offering as an incentive, so she went in and received an HIV test and counseling session and, for the first time, learned about what she should do to protect herself. Her test was negative, but she reports leaving the testing unit being angry and terrified that no one had ever provided her this crucial information before, and she vowed that she would start teaching her peers about safer sex. Meanwhile, Kimberly recollects asking her doctor about gonorrhea when she was fourteen or fifteen years old and being told not to worry about it because "only nasty girls get gonorrhea." Kimberly also remembers the secrecy and shame that surrounded HIV/AIDS in the 1990s and early 2000s; she describes how when she lost an uncle to HIV-related complications, the nature of his illness remained unspoken until the end. She was devastated to realize that in his last days he was unable to talk to his family about what he was going through, and she laments that his loved ones could not fully express their grief at his loss because of the stigma against speaking openly about HIV/AIDS. As a result of this personal trauma, Kimberly felt compelled to make sure that other people had access to the HIV/AIDS facts and support they needed.[1]

The lack of information about healthy sexual practices that Brittany and Kimberly both experienced is representative of the landscape of sex education for many Black girls, demonstrating how material vulnerabilities and constraints on agency are produced disproportionately in particular populations of youth. These limited resources result in Black girls' increased exposure to numerous sexual and reproductive dangers and their sexual precarity in multiple registers. For example, Black adolescent girls are at heightened risk of contracting a variety of STIs: they are nearly nine times as likely to contract gonorrhea as their white peers, and rates of chlamydia among adolescent girls are highest for those who are Black.[2] In spite of a recent overall decline in unintended teen pregnancy, the birth rates for Black teens are still more than twice the rate for white teens, and the maternal mortality rate for Black women is four times that of white women.[3] As many as 60 percent of Black girls experience coerced sexual contact before their eighteenth birthdays.[4] And of course, in the aftermath of the Supreme Court's overturning of *Roe v. Wade*, Black girls and women—who have the highest abortion rate of any racial or ethnic group and whose access to reproductive health care is already limited—are seeing their sexual health even further jeopardized.[5] These material dangers are, in part, the overdetermined result of the figurations of racialized female sexuality that I have already discussed in chapter 1, which position Black female bodies as exotic, promiscuous, and animalistic, that view Black girls as older, in less need of care, and more worldly than their white peers, and that hypersexualize and objectify girls and women of color while alienating them from their own sexual agency and desires.[6] While chapter 1 demonstrated how the *rhetorical ascription* of vulnerability is founded in the exclusion of Black queer female sexual agency, here we see how the

---

1. Bezalel, "KIMBRITIVE"; and Reed, "How Black Women."
2. Crooks and Wise, "What We Risk"; and CDC, "Sexually Transmitted Disease Surveillance."
3. CDC, "Reproductive Health"; and Brinkman et al., "Black Girls and Sexuality Education."
4. National Center on Violence against Women in the Black Community, "Black Women and Sexual Assault."
5. Artiga et al., "What Are the Implications."
6. Crooks et al., "Process of Becoming."

material effects of vulnerability bear down most cruelly on precisely those bodies precluded from vulnerability's privileges and protections.

Sex education programs in schools, which might be in the position to challenge these figurations of Black female sexuality, address these discrepancies in vulnerability, and promote sexual agency and decision-making, are unfortunately more likely to be one of the sources of the problem than its solution. From their inception in the early twentieth century, American sex education programs have worked in the names of nationalism, citizenship, and civilization to cultivate white supremacy, reinforce binary heteronormative gender roles and the nuclear family, stifle female sexual desire and agency, and promote abstinence until marriage. In this sense, sex education works alongside other historical and contemporary institutional forms of control of Black female sexuality, including using enslaved Black women for experimental gynecological surgeries, manipulating reproduction and child-rearing for the benefit of enslavers, coercing sterilization or contraception under the guise of social welfare, and so on. It is not an accident, then, that Black girls (especially those who are queer and/or gender-nonconforming) look like trouble for sex education programs. It is not merely that they are excluded or overlooked, but that—because the disavowal of Blackness founds the category of vulnerability—the whole civilizing and nationalizing pedagogical project of hetero(non)sexual sex education depends upon the vilification of Black female sexuality.

Sharing in common their early experiences with the deficiencies of sex education for Black girls, Brittany Brathwaite and Kimberly Huggins set out to normalize healthy conversations about sexuality for young people and adults—to create the resource they wished they had as teenagers. After completing graduate education in social work, public health, and human sexuality education, they developed a social startup called KIMBRITIVE, designed specifically to teach Black girls, women, and femmes about sexual wellness and reproductive justice. KIMBRITIVE brings a sex-positive, queer and trans-inclusive, youth-centered, and intersectional approach to its work. In this business, Brathwaite and Huggins hold up a mirror to the gaps and disparities of traditional programs, but they also reconfigure the entire enterprise of sexuality education itself. KIMBRITIVE encourages young women of color like themselves to be active participants in reframing conversations about sex and sexuality, refusing to be characterized exclusively by vulnerability, and as Brathwaite and Huggins put it, "reimagining and reclaiming our bodies and minds as sites of resistance, rather than places of inadequacy." This means helping young people develop self-love and autonomy, offering alternatives to narratives that frame the desires of women of color as "dangerous," and refusing to understand sexual wellness solely in terms of the "absence of disease."[7]

This chapter focuses on the work of KIMBRITIVE as an instance of what Jennifer Nash calls a "black feminist love-politics," inventing rhetorical modes of survival for Black girls and gender-nonconforming youth as sexual agents in a racist, misogynist, queerphobic, sex-negative culture. KIMBRITIVE's Black feminist epistemology refuses narrow and limiting figurations of racialized female sexuality, crafting instead an affirming and abundant rhetorical style of speech about sex. They challenge us to think queerly about claiming erotic pleasure and agency for Black girls and women whose bodies, sexualities, relationships, and lives have been defined by racist discourses and claimed as property in white supremacist institutions, arguing that sexual wellness for Black girls, women, and femmes is a key component of any comprehensive movement for racial justice. Heeding Hester and Squires's appeal to "center Black feminist thought" in rhetorical theory, I suggest KIMBRITIVE's defiant speech draws on Black feminist legacies of the power of the erotic and the revolutionary potential of loving oneself as a woman of color in order to "talk back" to the white supremacist, heteronormative, and sex-negative traditions of American sex education.[8] KIMBRITIVE thus not only reimagines sexuality education but also queerly reconfigures the rhetorical figuration of childhood by centering the lives and agency of Black, queer, trans, female, and gender-nonconforming youth, facilitating Black female relationality, and envisioning racial, reproductive, gender, and sexual justice.

While previous chapters have traced the ways adults (re)produce racial figurations of childhood that center the vulnerability of the most privileged young people, that demand whiteness, hetero(non)sexuality, and chrononormativity, and that enable the agency of adults, KIMBRITIVE demonstrates that this is not the only way to think about young people. That is, this chapter showcases a different relationship between adults and children—one where adult accomplices cultivate knowledge and agency in young people through a Black feminist rhetorical style of "affirming abundance," and where vulnerability appears as a means for intergenerational and community connections. If the first three chapters have illustrated how childhood's malleability can be used to produce policies that shore up privilege and dominant modes of thought, in other words, this chapter emphasizes the processes of rhetorical invention through which the racial figuration of childhood and its associated vulnerabilities can be imagined otherwise, as a site of agency and abundance.

---

7. Brathwaite and Huggins, "In Our Own Image."
8. Hester and Squires, "Who Are We Working For?," 343; and hooks, *Talking Back*.

I develop these claims across three parts: first, I sketch some of the discourses shaping traditional American sex education programs, noting in particular the anti-pleasure and disinformation stranglehold of present-day abstinence-only education, the promotion of the white, heteropatriarchal, nuclear family, and the elision of female desire and agency that informed the first iterations of sex education in the early 1900s. Second, I describe KIMBRITIVE's work, emphasizing the ways its programming talks back to traditional sex education by centering the lives and bodies of Black girls and women, transforming the style of speech used to talk to young people about sex, and reconfiguring the mission of sexuality education and wellness. Finally, I turn to Black feminist love-politics as a theory of justice to understand KIMBRITIVE's intervention in terms of its possibilities for Black self-care, erotic power, and intergenerational relationality.

I begin with a critical rhetorical history of sex education's insidious racist, eugenic, and heteropatriarchal aims because it shapes but does not fully determine the possibilities for present intervention. I view KIMBRITIVE as a reparative supplement to that history, one that seeks a different kind of legibility—based in agency rather than injury—for Black girls in particular, and for youth of color more generally. My reading strategy in this chapter begins from Sedgwick's characterization of the reparative impulse as "additive and accretive" (as opposed to the paranoid desire for demystification and exposure), a practice of conferring plenitude that enables contingency and queer possibilities. Reading reparatively directs critical attention to creative tactics of persistence, to "the many ways selves and communities succeed in extracting sustenance from the objects of a culture—even of a culture whose avowed desire has often been not to sustain them."[9]

I follow the lead of queer and trans of color scholars who argue that settler colonial and white supremacist scholarly practices that privilege narratives of violence through racism, cis- and heterosexism, ableism, nationalism, and so on, risk not only reproducing those violences but also centering trauma and woundedness as markers of authenticity. Scholars are conditioned, as Michael Tristano Jr. puts it, "to understand minoritarian subjects only as bodies who experience and carry trauma with them."[10] Likewise, V. Jo Hsu elaborates on Eve Tuck's work on desire to suggest that minoritized subjects are often objectified by researchers and treated as if they have no desires of their own. Hsu argues that narratives centering damage tend to view subjects as "hopelessly tragic, without self-determination," and fail to recognize the ways in which

---

9. Sedgwick, *Touching Feeling*, 149–51.
10. Tristano, "Performing Queer of Color Joy," 277.

their hopes and dreams, their "creativity, stubbornness, and experiential insights" may exceed dominating scripts.[11] Therefore, I strive in this chapter to not rest with merely describing the damages wrought in the name of the racial figuration of childhood, but also to amplify the ways that such violence is being refused and resisted. I focus on how KIMBRITIVE foregrounds agency, pleasure, and abundance, reading their work reparatively in order to center queer Black joy as a survival mechanism, as a conduit for curiosity and desire, and as a vital component of queer of color world-making.[12] KIMBRITIVE is an example of how it is possible to reimagine the kinds of sexual and rhetorical agency that exist "in the wake" of sex education's anti-Black, misogynist, and cisnormative pedagogy, and how it is still possible to queer the racial figuration of childhood.[13]

The Race/ist Problems of Sex Education: A Rhetorical History

Part of the purpose of sex education programs in schools, like other kinds of citizenship and vocational education, is to instill hegemonic cultural and community values, to teach students to become citizens, workers, and family members. It is therefore no surprise that sex education programs, even when they are supposed to be based in medicine and science, tend to reproduce not only the overt values of a particular culture but also its covert assumptions, prejudices, and inequalities. Specifically, throughout their history in American schools, sex education programs have promoted abstinence as the preferred mode of youth sexuality, cultivated white supremacy, reinforced binary heteronormative gender roles, and shamed and stifled female sexual desire. In this section I trace the way each of these pernicious sex education lessons arose historically and continue to flourish in the present day. My goal is not to offer a thorough chronology of the development of sex education but rather to thematize some of the ways this history has entrenched the agencies of whiteness, sexual restraint, and heterosexuality, while rendering marginalized young people—youth of color, girls, queer and trans youth, poor youth—vulnerable to censure for their sexual behaviors and to sexuality's material risks. In these national pedagogies of sexuality we can see the characteristics of the racial figuration of childhood made explicit in the training of both young people and adults. It is these detrimental traditions of sex education

---

11. Hsu, *Constellating Home*, 145.
12. Tristano, "Performing Queer of Color Joy," 279.
13. Sharpe, *In the Wake*.

to which KIMBRITIVE talks back; by asserting the worth of young women of color, empowering them to claim sexual agency and desire, and educating them about reproductive justice and pleasure, they directly confront the foundational assumptions of traditional American sex education programs.

The Disinformation Campaign of Abstinence-Only Sex Education

Experts in sexuality education and adolescence, including the American Academy of Pediatrics and the American College of Obstetricians and Gynecologists, recommend what is often called a "comprehensive" approach to sexuality education.[14] This perspective emerged as a reflection of changing popular sentiments about sex wrought by the sexual revolution and feminist movement of the 1960s, and was first defined with the founding of the Sexuality Information and Education Council of the United States (SIECUS) in 1963.[15] Comprehensive programs are considered the "gold standard" of sexuality education because they offer medically accurate information about anatomy, reproduction, safer sex, contraception, and condoms, but they also address healthy sexual development, gender identity, sexual orientation, consent, relationships, communication, body image, pleasure, and intimacy.[16] They recognize the needs of adolescents with disabilities and chronic health conditions, and understand that sexuality develops within specific ethnic, racial, cultural, and religious contexts.[17] Comprehensive sex education has measurable positive effects: adolescents who participate in these programs are more likely to use protection during sex, to have lower rates of STIs and unwanted pregnancies, to limit their number of sexual partners, and even to remain abstinent.[18]

The goal of comprehensive programs is not to suppress or control adolescent sexuality but rather to provide the information and skills young people need to make and communicate their sexual decisions. Comprehensive sex education, in other words, treats sexual desire and sexual expression as normal, morally neutral parts of human development. However, the vast majority of sexuality education in the US today offers instead "abstinence-only" or "sexual risk avoidance" curricula, which posit abstinence as the only appropriate sexual choice for teens and accentuate the physical, psychological, and

---

14. Breuner et al., "Sexuality Education"; and American College of Obstetricians and Gynecologists, "Committee Opinion."
15. Moran, *Teaching Sex*, 161–66.
16. Moore and Reynolds, *Childhood and Sexuality*, 9.
17. Breuner et al., "Sexuality Education," 2.
18. Santelli et al., "Abstinence-Only-Until-Marriage," 276.

moral dangers of sexual activity outside of marriage. As the remainder of this section shows, abstinence-only sex education is detrimental to all young people because it withholds important information and hampers sexual agency, but as a mechanism of enforcing white conservative values, it has particularly damaging effects for youth of color and other marginalized youth.

The current preeminence of abstinence-only sex education is due in large part to the white religious right and conservative movement's response to the transformations of racialized power structures and gendered and sexual norms that occurred in the 1960s. The founding of SIECUS and the scientifically based, morally neutral sexuality education programs it supported met with immediate conservative backlash, with increasingly polarized conservative and liberal positions on sex education developing throughout the 1970s. By the end of the 1970s, due to the spending and lobbying efforts of the evangelical Christian and Republican coalition, conservatives succeeded not only in making abstinence the dominant frame through which discussions of sex education were filtered but also in reasserting the civic virtue of self-denial and discipline as opposed to protest, rebellion, and experimentation. Indeed, controversies over sex education—coupled with opposition to civil rights legislation, women's liberation, and the gay and lesbian rights movement—proved to be a convenient platform through which the religious right attracted supporters and solidified its power among white voters.[19]

Sex education's white evangelical influence was written into law in 1981 with the passage of the Adolescent Family Life Act (AFLA). The AFLA, often called the "chastity law," was the first federal law that specifically funded sex education, but rather than supporting education about contraception, STIs, or reproductive health, it promoted "self-discipline and other prudent approaches" to teen sex.[20] Additional federal funding was made available in 1996 through the Title V Abstinence Only Until Marriage (AOUM) program, part of President Clinton's Personal Responsibility and Work Opportunity Act, known as his "welfare reform" bill. Based on the assumption that poverty was caused by the promiscuity and insufficient personal responsibility of poor Black women, this money was extended to states whose sex education programs would teach *exclusively* "the social, psychological, and health gains to be realized by abstaining from sexual activity."[21] To qualify for Title V AOUM funding, programs had to conform to a strict set of pedagogical guidelines based in religious justifications for sexual activity in the context of marriage and reproduction; they were not allowed to discuss contraception or safer sex

---

19. Kelly, "Chastity for Democracy," 354; and Moran, *Teaching Sex*, 187.
20. Levine, *Harmful to Minors*, 90–91.
21. Levine, *Harmful to Minors*, 91–92.

practices, except in order to emphasize their failure rates.[22] The promotion of abstinence-only sex education thus not only provides federal funding to uphold the religious values of powerful coalitions of white conservatives but is authorized by the specter of unrestrained Black female sexuality as a threat to the public good.

The funding sources and program requirements of abstinence education have shifted multiple times since the AFLA in 1981 (often with strategic rebrandings that co-opt the language of public health in order to mask their religious undertones and make broader ideological appeals), but the dominance of abstinence-only education remains consistent.[23] Currently, the federal government spends over $100 million per year through two funding streams on abstinence education.[24] There are two additional federal sex education programs—the Teen Pregnancy Prevention Program (TPPP) and the Personal Responsibility Education Program (PREP)—which, unlike the abstinence-only curricula, are medically accurate and evidence-based. While these programs do at least provide correct information about contraception in order to reduce teen pregnancy and STI infection rates, they do not meet the rest of the standards of comprehensive sexuality education. To be clear, there is *no* federal funding for truly comprehensive sexuality education.[25] In spite of some states' efforts to the contrary (for instance, the California Healthy Youth Act, which mandates comprehensive sex education for students in grades seven through twelve), then, abstinence is the dominant message of most American programs: when sex education is taught, thirty-nine states require that abstinence be included, and twenty-nine states require that it be stressed. In contrast, only twenty states require that sex education must include information on contraception, and even fewer require that the information taught in sex education classes be medically accurate. Only ten states and Washington, DC, require inclusive content with regard to sexual orientation.[26]

---

22. KFF, "Abstinence Education Programs."
23. Boyer, "New Name, Same Harm."
24. Guttmacher Institute, "Federally Funded Abstinence-Only." The federal funding for sexuality education programs fluctuates as control of the White House and Congress changes; these fluctuations predictably reflect, to some extent, political party affiliation, with Democratic presidents providing more funding for sexuality education that is evidence-based and medically accurate. However, abstinence-only education maintains its dominance regardless of the president's political affiliation; in fact, the Title V AOUM program, which expired in 2009, was resurrected in Obama's Affordable Care Act in 2010.
25. Guttmacher Institute, "Federally Funded Sex Education."
26. KFF, "Abstinence Education Programs"; and Guttmacher Institute, "Sex and HIV Education."

In spite of the federal funding and moral presumption that AOUM curricula enjoy, studies consistently show that abstinence-only sex education does not actually produce any of its desired outcomes (refraining from sexual activity, lowering rates of unplanned pregnancies, decreasing STIs). On the contrary, some researchers find a positive correlation between abstinence education and teen pregnancy: the more strongly abstinence is emphasized in states' sex education policies, the higher the average rates of unwanted teen pregnancies and births.[27] The problem, of course, is that although abstinence is 100 percent effective at preventing pregnancy and STIs, young people are far from 100 percent effective at practicing abstinence. For instance, one study of students who took "virginity pledges" found that although they delayed sexual initiation an average of eighteen months longer than students who had not taken the pledge, eventually a whopping 88 percent of the "pledgers" did have premarital sex. And, of much more concern, when they did have sex they were less likely to use protection or seek medical testing and treatment, and more likely to become pregnant or infected with certain STIs. As Santelli et al. conclude, "user failure with abstinence is high"; consequently, "in actual practice the efficacy of AOUM interventions may approach zero."[28]

Predictably, since the prominence of abstinence-only education in the US has been driven by white evangelical values, the detrimental impacts of these programs are not equally distributed—their effects vary depending on the relative degree of socioeconomic and racial privilege of the students they target. The most impoverished areas of the country are the most likely to have no choice but to accept federal funding with abstinence-only strings attached. This means that rural students, poor urban students, and students in communities of color are more likely than their racially and economically privileged peers to receive no information or disinformation about sexual health, contraception, or disease prevention. Thus, marginalized young people who are already sexually active and have the most immediate need for practical lessons to guide their sexual decision-making are offered only moralizing messages about their behavior.[29] As Fine and McClelland stress, "young people are being educated to mistrust condoms and contraception, to feel shame about their premarital sexuality, and to remain silent about their own sexual development. By insisting that a pledge of abstinence is enough to guarantee subsequent sexual decision-making—by condemning premarital sexual activity, contraception, and condoms—educators, policymakers, and families are

---

27. Stanger-Hall and Hall, "Abstinence-Only Education."
28. Santelli et al., "Abstinence-Only-Until-Marriage," 276.
29. Fine and McClelland, "Sexuality Education and Desire," 307; see also Stanger-Hall and Hall, "Abstinence-Only Education."

placing young people at risk."[30] This unequal access to accurate information about sexuality rings true with Kimberly and Brittany's experiences; it is not surprising, then, that Black girls and queer youth of color experience higher rates of STI infections, unwanted pregnancies, and contact with the juvenile justice system as a result of their sexual activity.

The dominance of abstinence-only education in American schools and federal policy has thus resulted in curtailing adolescent sexual agency and making youth of color and other marginalized youth vulnerable to unequally distributed sexual health risks. It also produces a markedly limited space for deliberation about sexuality education for young people, such that the question up for public debate is no longer *whether* young people should be taught to abstain from sex—that conclusion is essentially foregone—but whether abstinence should be the *only* thing they are taught. As Judith Levine asserts, "The idea that sex is a normative—and, heaven forfend, positive—part of adolescent life is unutterable in America's public forum."[31] The terrain of public-school sex education is currently even more embattled as conservatives and conspiracy theorists envisage any discussion of gender identity, sexuality, or LGBTQ+ lives as tantamount to pedophilic "grooming"—in spite of abundant evidence that comprehensive sex education, with lessons in consent and bodily autonomy, is an excellent defense against child sexual abuse.[32] Even progressive advocates for adolescent sexuality education, in other words, find themselves backed into a conservative corner where they must first concede that abstaining from sexual pleasure and exploration is the preferred form of adolescent sexuality and that even the most basic facts about healthy sexual development, identity, hygiene, and risk-reduction practices are controversial forms of knowledge for young people.

The Supremacy of the White Family

The religious right's influence on sex education policy in the US is an undeniable factor in depriving young people of sexual agency and contributing to the material precarities of youth of color. However, the racism, heterosexism, and sex negativity of American sex education certainly did not originate in the 1970s; rather, these biases were part of the core values of the very first sex education programs, which explicitly framed the promotion of the white nuclear

---

30. Fine and McClelland, "Sexuality Education and Desire," 311–12; and Santelli et al., "Abstinence-Only-Until-Marriage," 276.
31. Levine, *Harmful to Minors*, 93.
32. Riedel, "Why Are Republicans"; and Wong, "Worried about Grooming?"

family as the reason for sexual continence. Indeed, the earliest efforts at sex education in the late nineteenth through mid-twentieth centuries were a site at which the "normal" came to be defined in terms of whiteness, reproductive marital heterosexuality, and modern civilization. In order to understand the racist, heterosexist, and anti-pleasure agendas of contemporary sex education, then—the agendas that are radically reformulated in KIMBRITIVE's work— it is crucial to examine the rhetorical project in which sex education of the early twentieth century participated: delineating the values of whiteness in reproduction and sexual conduct, and establishing the language of whiteness through which sex education was delivered.

Sex education during this period was a eugenic endeavor that helped to distinguish whiteness as a category and inculcated in young people the sexual self-control needed to transmit to future generations not just the essence of whiteness, but more specifically whiteness's self-discipline. As Julian Carter explains, "sex education was a major cultural site for articulating the bourgeois familial and social patterns that helped to define ideal whiteness, and for training young people of varied backgrounds to reproduce those normative patterns in their sexual behavior."[33]

The cultivation of white sexual normality was distinctly rhetorical: the appropriate sexual self could be exhibited through the style of one's sexual communication, which should model what Carter calls "frank reticence." This was a racially coded mode of expression that, on the one hand, displayed a modern view of sexuality as normal and healthy and deserving of direct speech but, on the other hand, avoided explicit or "uncivilized" discussions of eroticism, thereby demonstrating the restraint and reticence of whiteness.[34] Importantly, "frank reticence" was presented as evolutionarily superior to other ways of communicating about sex, such that learning to speak the proper language of sex was also to learn the natural supremacy of white ideals.[35]

Thus, the desired "reticence" of sexual expression, working through indirection, euphemism, and metaphor, obscured sexual desires and experiences outside the realm of normal reproductive heterosexuality while also masking the racism it encoded: as Carter explains, "just as normal heterosexuality was, by definition, reticent about sexual desire and practice, normal whiteness was inarticulate about racial politics and power."[36] The strategic use of "ambiguous" language for instruction about sexual health during this period, Robin

---

33. Carter, *Heart of Whiteness*, 120–21.
34. Carter, *Heart of Whiteness*, 122–25.
35. Carter, *Heart of Whiteness*, 126.
36. Carter, *Heart of Whiteness*, 126.

E. Jensen notes, not only cloaked racism, sexism, classism, and xenophobia, but such equivocation also hindered those with the fewest health resources—women, immigrants, racial minorities, and the poor—from accessing the sexual information they needed.[37]

The style of "frank reticence" was deployed through two specific tactics of sex education that were popular throughout the first half of the twentieth century: the "venereal contagion" model and the "zoological" model. The venereal contagion model shaped the earliest efforts at national sex education, which targeted American military troops during World War I. Spurred by fears about the "corrupt" sexual culture of military camps, mandatory sex education for soldiers emphasized the self-control expected of middle-class white men and presented venereal infection and prostitution as threats to individuals, families, American society, and white civilization. These educational campaigns had to counter the prevailing belief that white male soldiers' performance on the battlefield was associated with their sexual virility, so some pamphlets distributed to soldiers counseled that it was actually the mental strength of chastity that demonstrated manliness and strength. Thus, early sex education discursively linked masculinity and national military might with sexual continence, as well as with whiteness.[38] Meanwhile, Black male soldiers, who served in segregated units, were not offered equivalent information about sexual health because they were assumed to be "natural" carriers of venereal diseases due to their lack of sexual restraint and inability to learn to control their desires. Instead, Black soldiers were often forced to undergo chemical prophylaxis treatments for venereal diseases (regardless of their reported sexual activity) and faced stricter rules and harsher punishments for sexual misconduct than white soldiers.[39]

However, this model of sex education drew public criticism because discussion of venereal disease, no matter how delicately or reticently phrased, necessarily made reference to—and, it was feared, may even encourage—erotic activities outside of monogamous heterosexual marriage.[40] Thus, by the mid-1920s a new "zoological" narrative of the evolution of the family, thought to be more suited to civilian and mixed-gender audiences, had replaced the venereal contagion model of sex education. The zoological model framed its lessons through analogies to the reproductive processes of flowers, insects, and animals: that is, young people were quite literally taught about the birds and the bees. Describing human procreation in terms of the pollination of

---

37. Jensen, *Dirty Words*, 2–3.
38. Jensen, *Dirty Words*, 73–74; and Carter, *Heart of Whiteness*, 127–29.
39. Jensen, *Dirty Words*, 84–85.
40. Carter, *Heart of Whiteness*, 134.

flowers allowed instructors to teach sex education without ever mentioning human bodies, sexual activities, or eroticism (all of which would violate the demand for reticence in sexual speech) and to render sexuality scientific and mechanical. One of the innovations of this model of sex education, according to Carter, was its ability to capture the potentially vulgar or perverse variations of sexual desire within the civilizing structure of the loving white family, positing this family structure—with the sexually monogamous couple at its core—as an ideal form that had been refined through centuries of evolution.[41] As Carter explains, "Through nature study . . . white children and adolescents were taught that evolution culminated in their rational ability to contain their sexuality inside emotionally and erotically charged monogamous marriage."[42] The white family was the ideal container within which to carry out the eugenicist goal of cultivating a genetically exceptional race of people through prolific reproduction: the evolutionary fitness of white people required powerful sexual urges and vigorous reproduction, but their racial superiority was also demonstrated through the sublimation of their carnal appetites and their preference for the sexual modesty and restraint of monogamous marriage and family life.[43]

The connection between sexual restraint and whiteness was at times rendered quite literally, as in the Women's Christian Temperance Union's (WCTU's) turn-of-the-century White Cross Campaign, which was designed to teach men to resist sexual temptation outside of marriage.[44] Frances Willard, the WCTU's president and an advocate for women's rights and suffrage, described this campaign with the slogan "a white life for two," suggesting that women could achieve equality only when men were held to the same strict standards of sexual continence that were expected of white women. The "whiteness" of "a white life" ostensibly referred to purity: abstaining from alcohol, avoiding premarital sex, and remaining monogamous within marriage. However, given the racialized story of evolution that supports such sexual restraint—and given Willard's own belief in a racialized hierarchy of civilization in which white Christians demonstrate their superiority through the emancipation of white women—the White Cross Campaign must also be understood as a clear statement on the white supremacy of morality and "purity" discourses.[45]

---

41. Carter, *Heart of Whiteness*, 140–41, 146.
42. Carter, *Heart of Whiteness*, 149.
43. Carter, *Heart of Whiteness*, 147; and Jensen, *Dirty Words*, 19.
44. Jensen, *Dirty Words*, 10–11.
45. Newman, *White Women's Rights*, 66; and D'Emilio and Freedman, *Intimate Matters*, 153.

The contours of whiteness and its supposedly naturally ordained superiority, then, were packaged into the earliest iterations of American sex education for young people and linked to specific modes of sexual expression and behavior. And this evolutionary story of the white family has had remarkable staying power. For example, Kelly's analysis of congressional testimony on the AFLA (the 1981 "chastity law" described in the previous section that provided federal funding for abstinence-only education) demonstrates the extent to which the eugenicist language of white sexual fitness shapes more contemporary conservative views of sex education. Testimony in support of the law claimed that the mind must be trained to overcome the animalistic, irrational desires of the "uncivilized natural body." Sexual abstinence, Kelly suggests, was "extrapolated as a civic ideal" whereby carnal physical desires are restricted to the confines of marriage and thus embody "the civilizing force of culture over nature."[46] Additional testimony by one of the AFLA's sponsors contrasted a "breeding society," governed only by animalistic impulses and marked by civilizational decline, with a "rearing society," which elevated reproduction and protection of the young as a primary civic duty. The AFLA's emphasis on chastity and self-discipline was meant to recover an American rearing society in which the family is a site of sexuality directed not toward pleasure but toward the productivity of future generations.[47] Such discourses of "civilized minds" and "uncivilized bodies," "the civilizing force of culture over nature," and the distinction between "breeding" and "rearing" are not-so-secretly racially coded, drawing the eugenic logics of the early twentieth century into the present-day insistence on abstinence.

In sum, the demand for abstinence is entwined with the promotion of whiteness, such that sexual self-discipline is imagined as the apotheosis of evolution. To violate the demand for frank reticence or to acknowledge sexual desires that exceed the reproductive bounds of the white nuclear family—let alone desires for queer, cross-racial, nonreproductive, or otherwise nonnormative erotic acts—invites individual shame, but also suggests a betrayal of race and nation. These narratives of the superiority of the white nuclear family thus not only disregard Black women's sexual health and negate any role for Black female pleasure, but they also reveal the racist and eugenicist constructions of civilization that shore up mainstream pedagogies of abstinence in US sex education.

---

46. Kelly, "Chastity for Democracy," 364–65.
47. Kelly, "Chastity for Democracy," 367–68.

The Disappearance of Female Sexual Agency

As early twentieth-century sex education advocated for the supremacy of the white family, it also designated distinct but complementary binary gender roles for white men and women within that family. Contributing to the future of the nation through a reproductive heterosexual union, that is, demanded chastity of both men and women, but only highlighted the sexual choices made by men. While women might pose a threat to men's sexual self-discipline, they were not imagined to be sexual agents pursuing pleasures of their own. In other words, female sexual agency was elided; this tendency to overlook girls and women as erotic agents, to neglect their desires and to discourage sexual self-knowledge, persists into sex education in the present.

The sexual choices of men, both within and outside the confines of the nuclear family, were perceived to have national consequences during World War I. For instance, the venereal contagion model, described in the previous section, framed men as potential sources of harm or safety to their families while framing women as, respectively, their innocent victims or as objects to be protected. Lessons for white male soldiers figured women only in terms of a dichotomy of sexual object choice: while "the temptress" was vilified as the origin of immorality and carrier of disease, "the sweetheart" represented the purity of family life at home. Black women, excluded from the role of the sweetheart, were grouped together as "active or impending" temptresses. Sexual contact with the temptress posed a direct threat to a white soldier's patriotic future with the sweetheart at home; as Jensen explains, "A temptress might offer soldiers temporary pleasure, but she also forced soldiers to risk their health, victory on the battlefield, self-respect, and happiness after the war's end. An American sweetheart, however, offered enduring love, safety, respectability, and a family that would grow to support the nation in the future."[48] Achieving a middle-class nuclear family and marital monogamy with a white sweetheart, then, was depicted as a continuation of the white soldier's mission on behalf of the nation—a national mission that could be "consummated" only after his service abroad ended.

These racialized lessons in military sexual continence and social hygiene were later translated into sex education for young white civilians by conflating the protection of the nation with the protection of the white American family.[49] The consequences of white boys' sexual choices were thus imagined

---

48. Jensen, *Dirty Words*, 79.
49. Jensen, *Dirty Words*, 79–80.

to be personal, national, and racial: the self-discipline of white masculinity protected the white family from Blackened sexual threats, whether by bravely fighting a war abroad or by exercising sexual restraint at home. But white girls, depicted only as the objects of male attention—whether as temptresses or sweethearts—were not imagined to make similarly consequential sexual decisions, and therefore did not receive information about sexual health.

The zoological narrative, or "birds and bees" approach, when it eventually replaced the venereal contagion model, upheld this distinction between men as active sexual beings and women as passive objects. Leaving behind the more explicit language of the temptress and the sweetheart, however, this model described human procreation in terms of the pollination of flowers. Carter paints a vivid picture of these lessons: "The blossom, with its ovary, sweet fragrance, and showy petals, stood for feminine white womanhood, alluring and passively receptive. . . . The bees (or wasps or moths) bumbled and pushed their pollen-laden way into the heart of the flower."[50] This model thus taught children not only a racist interpretation of human evolution and a sexist depiction of sexuality but also a wildly inaccurate representation of natural science. (In fact, there is a remarkable amount of scientifically incorrect labor done by this single analogy: it flattens the variety of ways that plants reproduce, it erroneously suggests that the bee is mating with the flower instead of merely transporting the pollen of one flower to another, and it rather hilariously ignores the fact that the foraging bees who pollinate flowers are actually female![51])

The zoological narrative also had the effect of removing all hints of eroticism and sexual desire from sex education (both for girls and for boys); indeed, as Jeffrey Moran contends, rendering sex "boring" was precisely what recommended this model. One such program foregrounding botany and zoology was praised "for how *seldom* it referred to sex and how effective it was in *quashing* curiosity."[52] The analogies to plant and animal reproduction, in spite of their obvious flaws as teaching tools, thus persisted precisely because they seemed to teach children about the science of sex without arousing interest in the pleasures of sex, and because they sustained what was already understood to be the truth about the masculine pursuit of sex and feminine submission to it.

Sex educators who resisted this disappearance of female sexual agency and desire were often met with ridicule and censorship. For example, Margaret Sanger argued that working-class girls and women deserved to learn

---

50. Carter, *Heart of Whiteness*, 142.
51. "Exploring the Process of Pollination."
52. Moran, *Teaching Sex*, 57–58.

about their sexual anatomy, the processes of menstruation, pregnancy, and menopause, and possibilities for birth control, all in straightforward language that avoided euphemism and moralism. She also recognized that girls develop sexual impulses at puberty, an assertion of female desire that was anathema to early twentieth-century sex education discourses. Although some of Sanger's radical ideas about sexuality emerged from her connections to anarchist and socialist thinkers, she later aligned herself with eugenicist beliefs about "racial betterment" that promoted racist, ableist, and classist practices of contraception. While Sanger's work offers a counterpoint to the erasure of female sexual desire, then, it is striking that women's sexual agency is afforded here—much as it also was in the eugenicist work of Frances Willard—only through the privileging of whiteness. Not only is such female erotic agency available exclusively to white women, but it also comes at the cost of further entrenching the deep racial injustices of women's reproductive and sexual health.[53]

Just as the race politics of early sexuality education have created a cramped space for discourses of comprehensive sexuality education today, so too are contemporary programs' contours shaped by the racial stereotyping and elision of female desire evident in the venereal contagion and zoological models of the early twentieth century. For instance, Michelle Fine describes the messages girls receive about sexuality in sex education and school-based health clinics in terms of a "missing discourse of desire." She notes that sex education programs tend to dichotomize female sexual agency and female sexual victimhood, couching discussions of female sexuality in discussions of the latter, understanding adolescent sexuality in terms of danger and violence, and foreclosing any possibility of discussions of the former. In other words, adolescent girls are taught to understand themselves only in relation to (and usually as the victims of) male sexuality, not as sexual subjects or initiators themselves.[54]

In conversations and interviews with Black and Latina young women, Fine notes that girls themselves articulate much more complicated understandings of desires, pleasures, needs, and experiences with sex—not in opposition to questions of victimization but in relation to them.[55] However, the young women's discourse of desire enters the "official discourse" of school sex education programs only as "interruptions," when girls interject comments about bodies or pleasures that are silenced or redirected by the adult instructors. For example, in response to a teacher's question about why it is important to look at one's genitals in the mirror, one girl frames her response in terms

---

53. Jensen, *Dirty Words*, 26–32; and Planned Parenthood, "Our History"; see also Gandy, "How False Narratives."
54. Fine, "Sexuality, Schooling," 30.
55. Fine, "Sexuality, Schooling," 35–36.

of pleasure, asserting that "you should like your body." The teacher, however, quickly reframes the conversation in terms of danger and disease, suggesting that you should know what your healthy genitals look like, "so you can recognize problems like vaginal warts."[56] In other words, a young woman's attempt to affirm her body as a source of enjoyment is squelched in order to reassert, instead, its imminent risks.

Casting female sexuality only in terms of vulnerability and without agency of its own coincides with the representations of white hetero(non)sexual girls that we have seen in the sexting panic and the sexualization discourse. Coupled with the shame-based messaging and disinformation of abstinence-only programs and their legacies of racialized discourses of gender, sexual behavior, family, and nation, contemporary sex education programs do an incredible disservice to all the young people they are meant to instruct. But Black girls, in particular, are framed in terms of an especially disempowering dichotomy: either they are the object of another's desire and therefore vulnerable to coercion and in need of protection from sexual knowledge and contact, or they pose a threat of contagion, promiscuity, and temptation and are therefore deserving of censure and restriction. Such a figuration of Black adolescent female sexuality assuages cultural anxieties about girls and sex by espousing abstinence under the guise of protectionism, while also derogating any version of female sexuality that exceeds monogamous heterosexual marriage.[57] It leaves no possibility to explore or articulate emerging sexual desire or identity and compels teenage girls to be complicit in denying their own sexual agency.

The model of American sex education that I have described throughout this rhetorical history has proven extraordinarily adaptable over more than a hundred years. It has expanded, for instance, into the "Family Life Education" programs of the 1940s and 1950s that focused on the domestic scene of the monogamous heterosexual couple and their offspring, and the HIV-prevention programs of the late 1980s that reinvigorated the discourse of sexual responsibility in the face of the infectious threat posed by the external other.[58] But while its content shifts with the cultural tides, its founding assumptions—its eugenic view of the white nuclear family, its heteropatriarchal gender roles, its preference for sexual continence over sexual expression, and its frank reticence—have been remarkably resilient.

I have lingered with this history in some depth, then, in order to demonstrate that the traditions of sex education are one site at which the racial figuration of youth—as hetero(non)sexual, developing along a chrononormative

---

56. Fine, "Sexuality, Schooling," 37–38.
57. Fine, "Sexuality, Schooling," 41–42.
58. SIECUS, "History of Sex Education."

timeline, and with specifically racialized access to the protections afforded by the conferral of innocence—is produced and reproduced as a site of national sexual pedagogy. Sex education in this country has always been a project designed to inculcate hegemonic values and cultivate the well-being of certain populations at the expense of others. Across this history we can observe how whiteness, masculinity, heterosexuality, and sexual continence have been promoted through the denigration of racialized, feminized, and queer desires. Although mainstream sex education in the US does not serve any young people particularly well, it does confer limited forms of sexual agency on the most privileged populations of youth (who are imagined to be evolutionarily equipped to control sexual desire) while figuring marginalized others as driven by and vulnerable to their sexual appetites. The version of vulnerability that emerges in this context does not function, as it did for the figuration of the white, cis, gay boys at risk for bullying and suicide in chapter 2, as a form of privileged weakness or fragility that compels protection. Rather, here certain young people—youth of color, queer and trans youth, girls—are *made* vulnerable to material sexual risks, as illuminated by Brittany's and Kimberly's lack of access to sexual health information and the prevalence of STI infections and unintended pregnancies among Black adolescent girls. This legacy of vulnerability and disempowerment, where Black girls and queer and gender-nonconforming youth of color are deprived of vital sexual information and offered messages of shame instead of sexual agency, shapes the context within which KIMBRITIVE, founded a century after the earliest sex education programs in the US, attempts to intervene.

Trading Continence for Confidence: KIMBRITIVE's Sexual-Wellness Platform

The historical and present troubles with mainstream sex education—the racism, ableism, sexism, cis- and heteronormativity, sex negativity, and cultural insensitivity—are well recognized and documented by educators, therapists, pediatricians, school counselors, and other youth service providers. Experts recommend "culturally responsive" programs, policies, and practices for all youth-serving organizations, an important component of which is recognizing how culture shapes sexual attitudes and behaviors. For example, Advocates for Youth, an organization that works alongside youth and adult allies to secure sexual health and equity for all youth, understands cultural responsiveness as recognizing and taking action in response to "different backgrounds, worldviews, and lived realities," while acknowledging one's own biases and limitations. For Advocates for Youth, cultural responsiveness takes into account a wide array of potential differences including, for instance, personal identities like gender expression, race and ethnicity, sexuality, and physical and cognitive abilities, as well as social or familial characteristics like socioeconomic status, language, religious beliefs, family composition, and traditional health and hygiene practices.[59] In recent years organizations like SIECUS, which has been advocating for comprehensive sex education since the early 1960s, have also published calls to action and guidelines for best practices related to the specific contexts of, for example, addressing racial justice in sex education, creating LGBTQ+-inclusive sex education, crafting shame-free messaging about teen pregnancy in sexual health curricula, promoting disability competency in sex education, and so on.[60]

The growing resources and support for culturally responsive and inclusive sex education has also led to a proposed federal bill, the Real Education and Access for Healthy Youth Act (REAHYA), first introduced in Congress in 2021 and reintroduced in 2023. If passed, this bill would allocate $100 million of federal funds to grants for institutions providing sex education to minors and would be the first to offer federal money specifically earmarked for comprehensive, medically accurate, evidence-informed, culturally responsive sexual health information. Furthermore, the bill promotes programs that recognize and seek to redress the adverse impacts created by other health policies and practices on marginalized groups, including Black, Indigenous, and other people of color, LGBTQ+ people, people with disabilities, immigrants, and incarcerated people, among others. REAHYA would repeal the AOUM program and appropriate its funds, directly repudiating the guidelines that the AOUM program used to promote abstinence until heterosexual marriage. REAHYA states plainly, for example, that the federal dollars it provides cannot be used for sex education or sexual health services that withhold vital information about HIV and other sexuality-related topics; that are not medically accurate; that are unresponsive to racial and gender inequalities; that do not address the needs of sexually active young people; that do not account for different physical, developmental, and mental abilities; or that are not inclusive of all gender identities, gender expressions, and sexual orientations.[61] REAHYA is, of course, unlikely to become law without a strong Democratic majority in both houses of Congress, but it has more co-sponsors than any other

---

59. Advocates for Youth, "Building Cultural Responsiveness."
60. Gary-Smith et al., "Sex, Race, and Politics"; SIECUS, "Call to Action"; Vianna and Harley, "Long Overdue"; and Holmes and Doyle, "Comprehensive Sex Education for Youth with Disabilities."
61. "S.1689"; and SIECUS, "The Real Education."

previous comprehensive sex education bill, suggesting that the tireless efforts of national sex education advocates have at least begun to make some inroads in the national conversation about sex education.[62]

KIMBRITIVE is therefore clearly not alone in demanding that young people, and especially the most marginalized young people, deserve more autonomy and better information about sexual health. Indeed, numerous social justice–oriented sex education programs, independent of school systems and the strictures of state and federal funding, have developed novel approaches to sex education that foreground some of the identities that mainstream programs overlook or have been designed to exclude. For example, to name just a few, Daughters of the Diaspora educates young women about reproductive health throughout the African diaspora, A Queer Endeavor helps schools and educators learn about gender and sexual diversity and develop LGBTQ+-inclusive environments and practices, RespectAbility offers numerous resources and sex education curricula centering the needs of youth with cognitive and physical disabilities, and Heart has developed a toolkit for talking to Muslim American youth about sexual and reproductive health that emphasizes both scientific accuracy and Islamic values.[63]

In the context of the many advocates fighting to improve sex education, then, I showcase KIMBRITIVE in this chapter as one example of a productive and defiant response to the legacy of American sex education. KIMBRITIVE complements the efforts of other alternative sex education programs for youth, as well as sex-positive sexual-wellness programs for adult Black women and other women and femmes of color. I focus on KIMBRITIVE in particular not only because they are overt in their opposition to the racist, cis- and heteronormative, and sex-negative assumptions built into sex education that I have described in the previous section's rhetorical history, but also because their manner of addressing youth is infused with Black feminist theories of self-care and the erotic that refuse the demand for frank reticence. That is, KIMBRITIVE simultaneously presents a challenge to the content of sex education, to the whiteness of its rhetorical style, and to the racial figuration of hetero(non)sexual youth that it (re)produces.

In order to best highlight KIMBRITIVE's multidimensional interventions in the second half of this chapter, I draw on their publicly available materials such as their website, social media, and news media where they are featured,

62. SIECUS, "2023 State of Sex Education."
63. Websites for the organizations can be found at the following URLS: Daughters of the Diaspora, http://www.dodiaspora.org/; A Queer Endeavor, http://aqueerendeavor.org/; RespectAbility, https://www.respectability.org/resources/sexual-education-resources/; Heart, https://hearttogrow.org/resources/sex-education-for-muslim-youth-starting-the-conversation/.

but I also engage with Brathwaite and Huggins and the work of KIMBRITIVE more directly. Because this is a departure from previous chapters, it is worth pausing for a moment to describe my methodological choices as a means of foregrounding the anti-racist ethics of this project. As a white queer scholar seeking to illuminate the reparative work of an organization run by Black women, I want to ensure that my representations of KIMBRITIVE are rooted not just in practices of critical reflexivity but also in values of amplification rather than extraction.[64]

While I could not eliminate the power dynamics of our identities or roles, I made a series of intentional choices about my interactions with Brathwaite and Huggins, my writing practices, and my material backing of their work in order to best use my racial and institutional privileges to support their project and make their agency legible to my readers. First, I sought their permission to feature them in this chapter prior to beginning my project, and then traveled to meet them for an in-person interview in their co-working space in Brooklyn, New York. During the interview I drew on what E. Patrick Johnson characterizes as a feminist approach that honors the communication practices of the interviewees: I conducted the interview in a flexible manner, asking open-ended questions that invited Brathwaite and Huggins to highlight the experiences that were most significant to them, and taking my cues for follow-up questions from their comments. I used the interview to get a sense of their attitudes and opinions as Black sex educators in order to portray them here, as Johnson puts it, "as feeling and thinking subjects," rather than merely as a source from which information can be extracted.[65] I also participated in one of their virtual workshops that was open to adult accomplices to witness their rhetorical style of affirming abundance firsthand, with a typical setting and audience. Second, the Black feminist scholarship I use as the theoretical foundation for this chapter is inspired directly by Huggins's and Brathwaite's own invocations of this body of work in KIMBRITIVE's messaging and in their own narrative of KIMBRITIVE's origins. I invited Huggins and Brathwaite to read and comment on drafts of my writing to ensure that my analysis represented them appropriately, and I made adjustments in response to their suggestions. Finally, my support of their business also takes material form: I compensated them for the time they spent with me during the interview, paid for the workshop I attended, purchased items from their online store, and donated to their IFundWomen fundraising campaign to sponsor memberships for their new digital sexual wellness space for Black women. Overall,

---

64. Alexander, *Performing Black Masculinity*, xviii–xix.
65. Johnson, "Put a Little Honey," 57–59.

I tried to ensure that I was guided by Huggins's and Brathwaite's own sense of their work and sought to present them on their own terms. I offer the following description of KIMBRITIVE's project, then, in order to underscore a specific instance of Black feminist agency that, in spite of traditional sex education's lessons in silence and shame, talks back to legacies of racism, cis- and heteronormativity, and sex negativity through Black feminist love-politics and an affirming and abundant rhetorical style.

KIMBRITIVE aims to bring Black girls, women, and femmes to the center of genuine conversations about bodies, sexual health, reproductive justice, and pleasure, and to recruit youth service providers and educators as their accomplices.[66] Brathwaite and Huggins are committed to providing information that is medically accurate, sex-positive, developmentally appropriate, empowering, and unapologetic; their materials and language are queer- and trans-inclusive, celebrating a range of femme, transfeminine, nonbinary, and gender-nonconforming identities. Their work is explicitly propelled by womanism, feminism, anti-racism, social justice movements, and intersectional analyses of power and privilege, and employs interactive practices that center the needs and experiences of youth.[67]

Brathwaite and Huggins, who had in common their firsthand girlhood experiences with being failed by sex education and recognizing the need to "talk back" to such damaging racist discourses, met when they were attending college at Syracuse University in upstate New York. They first began organizing together through the student group Sex S.Y.M.B.A.L.S. (Sexually conscious, Youthful, Mature, Black And Latino Students), which sought to promote healthy sexual decision-making and lower the risk of HIV and other STIs among students of color. They recall taking on leadership of the organization in 2011 and using the money they earned from their work-study stipends to fund Sex S.Y.M.B.A.L.S. projects, such as a safer sex party featuring a pleasure expert and games and activities. From the start, they emphasized clear and candid information about safer sex coupled with conversations about pleasure and consent, and they recognized that as young Black women speaking up about sexual health they were actively performing an alternative to the vulnerability, stigma, and shame that they had learned as teens.[68]

Therefore, by the time Brathwaite and Huggins started KIMBRITIVE in 2014, they were already extending candid advice and support around sexuality to their friends, who recognized their approachability and honesty. The KIMBRITIVE brand is an amalgamation of Brathwaite's and Huggins's first

---

66. KIMBRITIVE, "About."
67. KIMBRITIVE, "Workshops + Events."
68. Brathwaite and Huggins, interview with author; Jones, "'Black Women Deserve.'"

names, and they attribute their willingness to engage with vulnerable topics and feelings to their own relationship: as best friends who have long shared the most intimate parts of their lives, they are likewise able to share their real experiences with others. Whether referring to their struggles to find reliable sexuality information when they were younger or the process of coming out and claiming queerness, they say they "owe it to Black girls" to be honest about their lives, their mistakes, and their identities.[69]

As such, KIMBRITIVE's focus has shifted in tandem with Brathwaite's and Huggins's own personal and professional development. Brathwaite explains, "KIMBRITIVE evolves as we evolve," while Huggins jokes that KIMBRITIVE went through puberty, went to college, and is a grown woman now. Thus, although the needs of Black girls are always at the center of their efforts, their approach to sexuality education and sexual wellness is constantly being creatively reimagined. For instance, in their early years they concentrated more narrowly on sex education for young people, but they learned from some of the women who enrolled in their workshops for youth service providers that "even adults need sex ed," and later began expanding their programming for adults to fill that gap. Furthermore, as their friends and peers began having children of their own, Brathwaite and Huggins realized that parents needed to learn how to talk to their children about their bodies, the basics of consent, and sexuality and pleasure (especially given the dearth of comprehensive and sex-positive sexuality education programs in schools), so helping parents have affirming conversations about sex with their Black daughters became a vital part of their work. Thus, as KIMBRITIVE builds on its original commitment to sexuality education for youth to cultivate broader conversations about sexual wellness for Black girls, women, and femmes, Brathwaite and Huggins seek not only to enhance sexual health and embodied pleasure for adults but also to explore "intergenerational perspectives on sexual wellness."[70]

The workshops and content KIMBRITIVE offers are designed for three specific audiences: youth and young adults, adult women and femmes of color, and professionals who want to become "askable and affirming adult allies." KIMBRITIVE's signature group of ten workshops for young people, meant for

---

69. Brathwaite and Huggins, interview with author.

70. Brathwaite and Huggins, interview with author. While I focus here primarily on their sex education programming for young people, KIMBRITIVE also is in community with other platforms that provide sex-positive information on sexual and reproductive wellness to adult Black women and other women and femmes of color. Some examples of these include Reproductive Justice Initiative (formerly Decolonizing Contraception), https://reprojusticeinitiative.org/; The Triple Cripples, https://thetriplecripples.uk/; Black Girl's Guide to Surviving Menopause, https://blackgirlsguidetosurvivingmenopause.com/#Home; and Afrosexology, https://afrosexology.com/.

middle and high school aged girls and gender-nonconforming youth, provide "affirming and brave spaces" to explore identities, bodies, and relationships, and to make informed decisions and take action for sexual health. The topics of these workshops include puberty, sexual identity and gender expression, contraception, sexually transmitted infections, and relationships, as well as boundaries, consent, and body liberation. Their workshops for professionals, intended to help youth service providers be better equipped for their work, cover equity and inclusion in sex ed, sessions on reproductive justice, and four courses on "The Basics" of sexuality education and how to reduce shame and support sexual decision-making among young people. Finally, emphasizing sexual wellness as a lifelong practice, KIMBRITIVE's programming for adult women and femmes of color includes workshops on reclaiming bodies from trauma, shame, and stigma, embracing natural hair and sexual health, and exploring intimacy, boundaries, communication, and pleasure.[71]

One of the centerpieces of KIMBRITIVE's website is the downloadable "Your Sexual Wellness Regimen," which "helps you to explore different ways to care for your incredible body, deepen your self-love practice and prioritize your health." Explicitly inspired by regimens for caring for Black skin and natural hair, it suggests a similarly mindful, individualized, and habitual process of maintaining sexual wellness. Departing dramatically from civic pedagogies of sex education that work in service of whiteness and the nation, this is a model of sexual wellness that trusts Black women's, girls', and femmes' embodied knowledge and that aims to promote Black female agency and pleasure in all its forms. As such, "Your Sexual Wellness Regimen" is not a list of rules or facts but a set of self-care practices and resources, along with a series of questions to ask oneself—with space to record responses—as one's body, relationships, and desires fluctuate throughout life.

Developing a sexual-wellness regimen might include, for example, scheduling regular wellness practices such as STI testing, cervical cancer screenings, and mammograms or clinical breast/chest exams. But sexual wellness is not limited to a medical model of physical health; KIMBRITIVE also advocates knowing and asking for what one needs for their own body and well-being, urging readers to create a checklist for what is important to them in a medical provider (e.g., perhaps someone who "looks like you?" "is LGBTQIA affirming?" "is sex and kink positive?"), and to identify their "go-to" reliable and supportive person who can be trusted to discuss intimate matters and "can hold you in all of the complexity of your sexual life." A sexual-wellness regimen also involves articulating boundaries about sexual activities, bodies and

---

71. KIMBRITIVE, "Work with Us."

body parts, love and relationships, and communication, and identifying specific ways to respect and protect one's body, heart, spirit, and mind. Finally, a sexual-wellness regimen includes favorite products and routines—everything from preferred brands of lube and condoms to underwear that flatters one's body type and skin tone to favorite sexual positions or scripts. KIMBRITIVE provides links to sexual-wellness products from Black creators and books by Black authors, suggesting that readers make a list of the products they love and the products they would like to try.[72] Importantly, different kinds of self-care regimens can be complementary; for instance, Brathwaite suggests combining sexual wellness and haircare practices by doing monthly breast/chest self-exams while deep conditioning one's hair.

In addition to their workshops and sexual-wellness regimen, KIMBRITIVE curates a plethora of online content that can be accessed independently and for free. Their Instagram feed is full of rich images of Black women in all shades and sizes, including custom-made drawings that represent a wide variety of gender expressions, body and hair types, and abilities. They feature profiles of Black queer, trans, and feminist foremothers ranging from trans advocate Marsha P. Johnson to former surgeon general Joycelyn Elders to author and social justice facilitator adrienne maree brown to Southern midwife Maude Callen, and quotes from Black feminist authors like Audre Lorde and Brittany Cooper. They also frequently invoke Black feminist popular culture, for example, by creating a Beyoncé playlist "for when you need a reminder of what you deserve and when you want to get your sexy on," or using the lyrics of Cardi B. and Megan Thee Stallion's "WAP" as invitations to talk openly about the withdrawal method of birth control, oral sex, lubrication, sexual boundaries, and using drugs and alcohol during sex. These profiles and popular culture references elevate the historical and contemporary contributions of Black women and situate KIMBRITIVE's work within a long tradition of Black feminist advocacy, encouraging intergenerational awareness and relationality. By juxtaposing figures like Joycelyn Elders (famously forced to resign from her position in 1994 for acknowledging masturbation as a normal part of youth sexuality) with "WAP"'s explicit declarations of desire and embodied needs, KIMBRITIVE provides a way to imagine legacies of Black women's eroticism that are neither determined by nor particularly concerned with the limitations imposed by sex education's white traditions of frank reticence and sexual continence. The history of the denial of Black female sexual pleasure is long, but KIMBRITIVE suggests the history of Black women's and femmes' unabashed assertions of erotic agency and embodied joy is longer.

---

72. KIMBRITIVE, "How to Prep"; KIMBRITIVE, "What's Your Sexual Wellness Regimen?"; and KIMBRITIVE, "Your Sexual Wellness Regimen."

FIGURE 1. Kimberly Huggins and Brittany Brathwaite, the founders of KIMBRITIVE, wearing "Black Women Deserve Great Sex" sweatshirts. Photograph by Sade Fasanya.

Indeed, KIMBRITIVE's social media presence is overt in its emphasis on pleasure and empowerment and consistently highlights their signature statement: "Black Women Deserve Great Sex" (see figure 1). Functioning as both a challenge and a slogan, this phrase appears across many of KIMBRITIVE's materials, including tote bags, T-shirts, and pins available to purchase on their website, and it recognizes that, as Huggins puts it, "You deserve to have experiences that are pleasurable. That are great. That speak to what you need. We get to say what happens to our bodies."[73] To claim pleasure in this way is risky for Black women and girls whose desires have been pathologized in order to define the boundaries of appropriate white reproductive sexuality. Teaching Black girls to demand pleasure violates the embedded traditions of sex education that elide female desire, that frame self-denial as evidence of white evolutionary superiority, that limit sexual expression to the white heterosexual nuclear family, and that discourage explicit speech about sexuality. For Black girls, women, and femmes to speak of deserving great sex, as well as actually desiring great sex, in other words, is a layered performance of sexual agency that traditional sex education has been designed to foreclose.

Recognizing its potentially radical implications, the "Black Women Deserve Great Sex" slogan names physical satisfaction, but it also encompasses

---

73. Brathwaite and Huggins, interview with author.

the tenets of reproductive justice, in which Black women, girls, and femmes are entitled to embodied self-determination and access to the resources they need to make safe and informed decisions about sexual and reproductive wellness. For example, KIMBRITIVE's guide to contraception is not merely a list of the pros and cons of various methods of preventing pregnancy but also includes the history of how Black women's reproduction has been and continues to be coerced and controlled; reproductive agency, in other words, is contextualized in histories and current realities of reproductive vulnerability. Likewise, their commentary on abortion restrictions and the *Dobbs* decision centers their disproportionate harms to Black women, girls, and nonbinary folks.

KIMBRITIVE's emphasis on sexual wellness, erotic agency, and community-building is perhaps best exemplified in their custom-made infographic on breast/chest self-exams (see figures 2 and 3). Brathwaite and Huggins are particularly proud of this infographic because it features a Black breast—they commissioned graphic designers to make it for them after realizing that all the existing images they found were of white or supposedly "race-neutral" chests.[74] In contrast, their ten-image Instagram carousel, titled "check-in on your besties," showcases drawings of an unambiguously dark-brown-skinned and curly-haired person demonstrating the techniques of a chest self-exam. Carefully using the gender-neutral language of breast/chest throughout, KIMBRITIVE's message highlights the high incidence of breast cancer in Black communities but also emphasizes the action and connection that can emerge from that vulnerability. For example, in addition to the usual advice about monthly self-exams in the shower, they also urge "intergenerational dialogue" with mothers, grandmothers, aunties, sisters, and cousins, and "compassionately curious" check-ins about family histories of cancer; such conversations are thus an opening for building networks of Black girls', women's, and femmes' intimacy rather than just a means of managing risk. And they also encourage the erotic opportunities afforded by becoming familiar with and caring for one's body, suggesting breast/chest exams can be "incorporate[d] into foreplay with bae" or can be accompanied by a "sensual mirror selfie."

Taken as a whole, KIMBRITIVE's workshops and content deliver cohesive and radical lessons that center the specific needs and emphasize the value of Black girls and gender-nonconforming youth as well as adult Black women and femmes. They treat sexual-wellness information not as a national pedagogy in citizenship and racial betterment, or as a series of prescribed "lessons" for vulnerable young people, but as a lifelong set of practices relevant at

---

74. Brathwaite and Huggins, interview with author.

 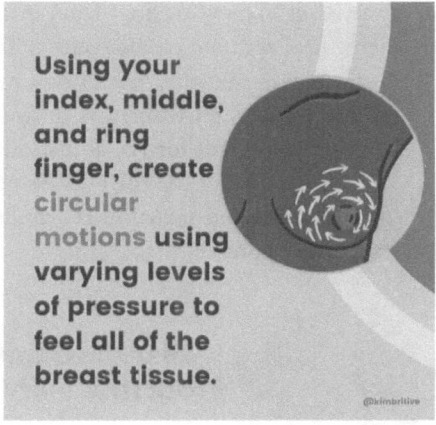

FIGURE 2, LEFT. KIMBRITIVE's custom-designed infographic for breast/chest self-exams. Art by Brittany Harris.

FIGURE 3, RIGHT. Detail from KIMBRITIVE's custom-designed infographic for breast/chest self-exams. Art by Fanesha Fabre.

any age. Their model of sexuality education refuses a fear-based or damage-centered approach and throws off the sexual shame of respectability politics. Defying the disciplining whiteness and civilizing restraint of frank reticence, they reimagine the possibilities of speaking to young people about sex through a Black feminist rhetorical style of "affirming abundance," which declines sexual continence in favor of sexual confidence. Affirming abundance includes candid and accurate language about the mechanics of sex and bodies but also affirming messages that celebrate sexual expression, pleasures, boundaries, and exploration. It emphasizes curiosity, information-gathering, and self-knowledge, teaching girls to trust what they know about their bodies and desires, and encouraging adults to become askable accomplices in young people's pursuit of answers and resources. Sexuality education in this style swaps the scientific detachment of frank speech for affirmations of the emerging sexual self, and the restrictions of reticence for lush, abundant self-care and joy.

Finally, KIMBRITIVE's style of affirming abundance draws explicit connections among sexuality, pleasure, reproductive justice, and racial justice, weaving discussions of structural oppression into every experience they provide. Recognizing that girls of color are bombarded with negative messages about their bodies' shapes and sizes, their hair and skin, their gender presentations, and their sexualities, KIMBRITIVE's work demonstrates that it is not the young people themselves who need to be "fixed" but the interlocking systems of oppression that label them "fast" or promiscuous and that deem them inappropriate or distracting. They contend that because the control of Black female sexuality has always served white supremacy, sexual wellness for Black girls and women is necessarily a key component of any comprehensive movement for racial justice, reproductive justice, and queer justice. Thus, at the core of KIMBRITIVE's rhetoric of youth sexuality is how to imagine embodied and sexual liberation in the context of systemic inequality and structural oppression.

Black Feminist Love-Politics: Eroticism, Self-Care, Relationality

If the history and most common contemporary forms of sex education in this country can teach us anything, perhaps it is that their work on behalf of white supremacy, their heteronormative, binary, sexist gender expectations, and their inaccurate, pleasure-sapping lessons are not merely accidents, oversights, failures of inclusion, or the product of old-fashioned values. Rather, these results of sex education are, in fact, precisely the educational outcomes that it is intended to produce. Furthermore, sex education programs naturalize these assumptions such that their further implications—the hypersexualization of the Black female body, the pathologization of the nonwhite or nonreproductive family, or the perversity of the pursuit of sexual pleasure in queer, digital, transactional, or nonmonogamous contexts—are also naturalized.

KIMBRITIVE "talks back" to these lessons in a Black feminist rhetorical style, not merely refuting them but offering a refiguration of the sexual agency and embodiment of Black girls, women, and femmes. To make this claim is, of course, to draw specifically on bell hooks's sense of Black women's and girls' "defiant speech" as "a courageous act—an act of risk and daring." For hooks, Black women speaking truth "is not solely an expression of creative power; it is an act of resistance, a political gesture that challenges politics of domination that would render us nameless and voiceless." Her formative experiences with talking back as a child connected her to her Black female ancestors' "legacy of defiance, of will, of courage," an alliance that would provide strength for future acts of defiant speech. Thus, talking back is both a refusal and a means for healing; part of a long tradition of Black women exercising rhetorical agency against anti-Blackness and within the context of white supremacist institutions, it "makes new life and new growth possible."[75] It is an instance of Black women's truthtelling and invention, what Ashley R. Hall calls a "fugitive act"

---

75. hooks, *Talking Back*, 5, 8, 9.

that reimagines rhetorical agency and "create[s] an elsewhere, a space beyond the now."[76]

In the context of what Ore and Houdek have named "times of suffocation" to mark the ceaseless exploitation of and violence against Black bodies, talking back is not just an individual act of breaking silence but a coordinated effort to put "ongoing legacies of trauma and grief" into motion toward political transformation.[77] The urgency of this project draws on the epistemic traditions and discursive practices of Black women's communities that emphasize that justice is long overdue and cannot be delayed any longer, or what Tamika L. Carey describes as Black women's "rhetorical impatience." Importantly, Carey's rhetorical impatience—like hooks's talking back, Hall's fugitive speech, and KIMBRITIVE's style of affirming abundance—has an eye toward the future, seeking a better quality of life for the individual and justice and advancement for communities of color.[78] To understand KIMBRITIVE's talking back in this framework of Black women's rhetorical heritage is therefore to emphasize its public and political qualities, as well as its legacies of defiance. It is also to recognize that KIMBRITIVE's work does not simply react to hegemonic whiteness but demonstrates the flourishing of Black rhetorical and cultural production in spite of whiteness's constraints, as a source of creative imagination and a means of pleasure and joy.[79]

Therefore, KIMBRITIVE intervenes in individual practices of sexual wellness and relationships, to be sure, but their project also intervenes publicly and socially, reformulating the racial figuration of childhood's characteristics of whiteness, hetero(non)sexuality, and vulnerability. They do so not just by offering affirmative abundance as an alternative rhetorical style of sex education but also by building on the work of Black feminists who see the radical potential in the love, joy, and erotics of women of color for healing and invention. Jennifer C. Nash describes this perspective as a tradition of "black feminist love-politics," which seeks to move love from the personal to the public, where it can work as a theory of justice. She identifies the rhetorical and affective trope of love-politics across a range of second wave and contemporary Black feminist thinkers, including June Jordan, the Combahee River Collective, Audre Lorde, bell hooks, Patricia Hill Collins, Ntozake Shange, Alice Walker, Gwendolyn Pough, and Joan Morgan, among others. In each of these authors' hands, she asserts, "love act[s] as a doing," with a variety of intentions and implications: "a call for a labor of the self, an appeal for transcending the self, a strategy for remaking the public sphere, a plea to unleash

---

76. Hall, "Slippin' in and out of Frame," 343, 348.
77. Ore and Houdek, "Lynching in Times," 448, 456.
78. Carey, "Necessary Adjustments," 270, 273.
79. Sobande and Osei, "African City"; and Lu and Steele, "'Joy Is Resistance.'"

the radical imagination, and a critique of the state's blindness to the violence it inflicts and enables."[80]

Black feminist love-politics advocates for "love as a resistant ethic of self-care" that remakes and transcends the self and energizes Black feminist relations.[81] This sentiment, which Barbara Ransby calls "self-determination," is at the heart of the Combahee River Collective Statement: the authors share the conviction that "Black women are inherently valuable," and explain that their politics "evolve from a healthy love for ourselves, our sisters and our community which allows us to continue our struggle and work."[82] This sense of love does not arise casually—it is an intentional relationality, a set of joyous, life-affirming practices and attachments that affirms marginalized bodies.[83]

Love in its erotic form is also central to Black feminist love-politics as a creative resource and mode of relation. As Audre Lorde maintains, the erotics of Black women are a means of experiencing embodied joy and of sharing joy with others, but they are also an avenue toward agency—not just in the narrow sense of erotic fulfillment but in an expansive sense of political empowerment. Claiming the erotic power of Black women—a capacity systemically debased and shamed in the construction of racial difference—is one means, for Lorde, of refusing to be resigned to suffering. She writes, "In touch with the erotic, I become less willing to accept powerlessness, or those other supplied states of being which are not native to me, such as resignation, despair, self-effacement, depression, self-denial."[84]

Accessing the power of the erotic means also coming to terms with the anger and self-loathing wrought by internalizing racism, sexism, and homophobia, or what Lorde likens to "metabolizing hatred like a daily bread."[85] She describes, for example, the "horizontal hostility" that can be experienced between Black women and Black men, and between Black lesbians and Black heterosexual women, when they view one another as competitors or "as the visible face of our own self-rejection."[86] Thus, the possibilities of the erotic, in tension with this animosity, must exceed the narrowly imposed bounds of the sexual or romantic. Brittney Cooper, who insists that Black feminism is a fundamentally queer project, argues that in a context where Black women are consistently devalued, feminism means loving Black women and investing in

---

80. Nash, "Practicing Love," 2–3, 19.
81. Nash, "Practicing Love," 3.
82. "Comments by Barbara Ransby," 180; and "Combahee River Collective Statement," 18.
83. Mason, "Embracing," 275.
84. Lorde, *Sister Outsider*, 58.
85. Lorde, *Sister Outsider*, 145–75, 152.
86. Lorde, *Sister Outsider*, 48–49.

their pleasure regardless of categories of sexual orientation: "Deep and abiding love can be sisterly and it can be erotic, and sometimes it can be and needs to be all these things at the same damn time."[87] Neither Lorde nor Cooper idealizes the erotics of Black feminism as a panacea: the possibilities of pleasure and joy always coexist with pain, loss, shame, and rage, as resources for resisting and surviving anti-Blackness.[88]

KIMBRITIVE's materials exemplify Lorde's sense of the erotic as a creative source, speaking clearly to the relationship between sexuality and politics and affirming the kinds of self-loving practices that are fundamental to Black girls' and femmes' embrace of erotic potential. In this sense, their messaging may seem to coincide with the contemporary popularity of self-care practices that have been heavily commodified by the beauty, fitness, and diet industries and that have found even wider circulation through social media. Pooja Lakshmin refers to these wellness practices and products that are sold as a remedy for women's problems as "faux self-care." Faux self-care suggests that there is something lacking in women that needs to be fixed—by purchasing the best smoothie, by cultivating the right multistep skincare regimen, or by going to the latest trendy yoga class—while preserving the structures of inequality and social systems that leave them craving relief in the first place.[89]

Brathwaite and Huggins laughingly acknowledge their association with social media wellness culture, including "yoga, green tea, matcha, meditation, CBD oil."[90] Indeed, they embrace this connection through the recognizable aesthetics of their website and Instagram presence, as well as through their liberal use of the language of wellness and self-care. In contrast to faux self-care, however, KIMBRITIVE's self-care practices are rooted in Black feminism's much more radical version of self-care, which refuses the expectation that Black women's care work must only be directed toward others, rather than the self. As Lorde famously wrote in reference to living with cancer, "Caring for myself is not self-indulgence, it is self-preservation, and that is an act of political warfare."[91] Sara Ahmed takes up Lorde's words in support of the political force of self-care, placing them against the indictment that self-care is simply a disguised form of self-indulgence, a selfish, individual practice with-

---

87. Cooper, *Eloquent Rage*, 22.
88. This is also true for the racialization of other women of color, whose sexualities have been exaggerated, commodified, and lampooned in the service of white supremacy, limiting their opportunities to enjoy their own bodies and desires on their own terms. On queer Brown women, Latinx femmes, and Filipina women see, for instance, Musser, *Sensual Excess*; Rodríguez, *Sexual Futures*; and Velasco, *Queering the Global*.
89. Lakshmin, *Real Self-Care*.
90. Brathwaite and Huggins, interview with author.
91. Lorde, *Burst of Light*, 130.

out communal import. She argues that for those whose bodies and lives have been determined to not matter, "self-care is about the creation of community, fragile communities, assembled out of the experiences of being shattered." Ahmed explains that when women of color redirect care away from its "proper objects," insisting on self-care rather than care for "the bodies deemed worth caring about," they are "transforming what matters," making a claim that they too are precious.[92]

Redirecting care in this way refuses the capitalist logic that views Black women and girls only as they can be possessed by or contribute to the prosperity of others, as a source of wealth or as objects to be used.[93] Indeed, KIMBRITIVE is careful to mark their rejection of the drive toward optimization assumed in wellness culture (the guilt-inducing message that one should always aspire toward—and work harder for—externally imposed goals), as well as its prioritization of whiteness, thinness, and a narrow version of traditional heteronormative femininity. KIMBRITIVE's Black feminist version of self-care substitutes instead affirmations of self-knowledge and conviction, such as "I trust my embodied wisdom," and their own nonaspirational declaration: "You *are* goals."[94]

For Black girls and gender-nonconforming youth to treasure their lives that have been viewed as disposable and find beauty and delight in their bodies that have been made expendable is also to recognize the value in one another; thus, KIMBRITIVE's Black feminist love-politics cultivates generous relationality among Black girls, women, and femmes. As Shanesha Brooks-Tatum asserts, "when sisters unite in self-care . . . when we support our sisters and admonish that they too take care of themselves, we engage in radical feminist praxis."[95] Self-care, in other words, functions both individually and collectively, "not just good for the self but also generative for others."[96] Just as the Combahee River Collective understood love for themselves as the source of their politics, then, so too is KIMBRITIVE's emphasis on self-care and a collective investment in sexual wellness central to their vision for liberation.

Importantly, this relationality plays out in the specific context of adult Black women educating, mentoring, and serving as role models for girls of color. Thus, the relationships forged are intergenerational, but not confined to the structure of the reproductive family unit. In this sense, KIMBRITIVE draws on traditions of Black community-based child-rearing practices that

---

92. Ahmed, "Selfcare as Warfare"; and Lorde, *Sister Outsider*, 146.
93. Green and Bey, "Self-Love," 108.
94. KIMBRITIVE, "I trust"; Brathwaite and Huggins, interview with author.
95. Brooks-Tatum, "Subversive Self-Care."
96. Green and Bey, "Self-Love," 109.

Patricia Hill Collins calls "othermothering." For Hill Collins, othermothers serve the practical purpose of ensuring that Black children survive when they are separated from their birth mothers (due to enslavement, incarceration, poverty, state intervention, drug addiction, etc.), but they also challenge capitalism's assumptions of individualism and the status of children as the "private property" of independent families.[97] Thus, she understands othermothering as revolutionary, both in terms of property relations and in terms of the nonhierarchical accountability that it encourages within communities. She explains, "Community othermothers' actions demonstrate a clear rejection of separateness and individual interest as the basis of either community organization or individual self-actualization. Instead, the connectedness with others and common interest expressed by community othermothers models a very different value system, one whereby Afrocentric feminist ethics of caring and personal accountability move communities forward."[98] The emphasis on community care and intergenerational but nonfamilial relationships also poses a direct challenge to the supremacy of the white nuclear family model as a container for sexuality, in which children are the property and achievement of individual parents, that traditional sexuality education promotes.

Although KIMBRITIVE does not position itself in an explicitly maternal role toward the girls it serves, the community ethics of child-raising in Black traditions is nonetheless evident in their project. KIMBRITIVE does not just provide information or attempt to inculcate a particular set of values (as more traditional sex education curricula might be said to do) but also fosters relationships among young and adult women of color. This effort resonates with how Alexis Pauline Gumbs describes mothering: as "an emergent strategy" of collaboration across difference that can potentially sustain scales of care beyond gendered familial roles and forms of intimacy not limited by obligation and duty.[99] As I described at the start of this chapter, Brathwaite's and Huggins's shared adolescent frustrations with finding information about sexuality was one of their motivating factors in developing KIMBRITIVE; now, as adults, they hope to provide resources to future generations of Black girls and gender-nonconforming youth that were unavailable to themselves.

Furthermore, Hill Collins's and Gumbs's reclaiming of collaborative mothering is a particularly fitting framework through which to understand the complexities of Black women's and femmes' sexual wellness because motherhood is a key site at which Black women's sexuality, desire, bodily autonomy, and reproductive choices have been systematically constrained and surveilled;

---

97. Hill Collins, *Black Feminist Thought*, 119–22.
98. Hill Collins, *Black Feminist Thought*, 131–32.
99. Gumbs, *Undrowned*, 51–56.

motherhood, in other words, is a relation through which racism and sexism are materialized and the corporeality of Black female sexuality is politicized and policed. Supporting Black youth in the tradition of community mothering thus offers an excellent example of how love-politics functions as a "public theory of justice": it reconfigures both the emergent Black female/femme sexual self and the power relations of the family. It also rejects the instrumentalization of the idea of childhood, in which the vulnerability associated with the child is exploited to adults' benefit. Working outside of the sanctioned sources of sexuality information (parents, doctors, churches, schools), then, KIMBRITIVE centers the needs and realities of Black girls, expanding the progressive, intergenerational, nonhierarchical, women-oriented networks through which they can access knowledge and support about their bodies and desires.

Affirming Abundance in the Wake

KIMBRITIVE demonstrates that it is possible to re-envision the hegemonic discourses of sex education, to make room for other options; as Ore and Houdek describe it, to "create[e] time and space to breathe, take stock, and imagine other futures and different forms of justice."[100] Drawing on Black feminist traditions of rebellious speech, KIMBRITIVE talks back to the troubling legacies of American sex education, calling into question the dominant figurations of childhood and sexuality, in which Black girls are sacrificed to preserve the fantasy of vulnerability associated with white childhood. In KIMBRITIVE's hands, "love act[s] as a doing," inviting Black girls and trans and gender-nonconforming youth to speak the truths of their bodies and desires and opening up breathing room for the delights of sexuality, the communal joy of self-care, and the urgency of defiant speech.

As we have seen, contemporary sex education (re)produces the characteristics of the racial figuration of childhood that are already familiar from previous chapters: its whiteness, its refusal of queerness, its insistence on normative temporalities, and crucially, its assumption of an essential vulnerability. In the context of sex education, this figuration suggests that children are endangered by the health and social risks of sex, that they require adult protection from sexual information, and of course, that their hetero(non)sexuality is circumscribed by the future expectations of the white, heterosexual, nuclear family. Sustaining the *rhetorical* vulnerability of the racial figuration of childhood produces *material* vulnerabilities for those youth who are not

---

100. Ore and Houdek, "Lynching in Times," 448.

granted the privileges of protection—namely, the Black girls and gender-nonconforming youth who are the focus of this chapter and the targets of KIMBRITIVE's programming. Of course, the operations of white supremacy and cis- and heteronormativity are not easily interrupted; the racial figuration of childhood cannot simply be turned on its head by one organization. However, KIMBRITIVE does provide a chance to think about what it might mean to figure childhood queerly: to take childhood's excesses and strangeness not as a source of trouble to be corrected but as a source of inquisitiveness, knowledge, and self-determination. KIMBRITIVE's Black feminist rhetorical style of affirming abundance challenges both the content and the mode of address of sex education, and thus understands the child as an emerging sexual and social actor whose self-knowledge is already embodied, and whose incipient pleasures, curiosities, and joys are their own to explore and cultivate with the support of adult accomplices. This queer refiguration of childhood sustains youthful agency and affirms Black self-care, recognizing that both are carved out in contexts of oppression and constraint.

This is not to deny the vulnerable qualities of childhood but to recognize in them an opportunity for intergenerational connection rather than paternalistic and infantilizing protection. It is to view learning about sexual wellness as a lifelong practice in which young people and adults can be engaged cooperatively, where vulnerability might be a shared orientation instead of a politically designated sympathetic status of disenfranchisement. But most importantly, it is also to emphasize that the distribution of material vulnerabilities is unequal, and that the racial figuration of childhood binds those vulnerabilities tightly to the bodies and lives of particular young people. To understand the racial figuration of childhood as a conduit between the symbolic work of language and the material conditions of real young people is to view the consequences of sex education as manifestations of the insidious anti-Blackness, misogyny, and coloniality at the heart of national values. That is, the difficulties Black girls face in accessing sexual health information, and their disproportionate risks for certain STIs, for unintended teen pregnancies, and for coerced sexual contact, are not evidence of sex education's flaws but rather of its unfortunate success in producing precisely the material results that it intends.

In this context, KIMBRITIVE's queer intervention, its Black feminist love-politics carried out through the rhetorical style of affirming abundance, is not just to offer a different model of sex education. Instead, it hints at a means for imagining otherwise, for the enduring possibilities of invention within contexts of subjection. KIMBRITIVE, that is, engages in what Christina Sharpe calls "wake work." In the wake of slavery, Black life occupies and is occupied by the "continuous and changing present of slavery's as yet unresolved unfolding," existing "as, and in, the wake of the unfinished project of emancipation."[101] For Sharpe, "wakefulness" refers to a consciousness of experiencing and recognizing subjection without "*simply* or *only* liv[ing] *in* subjection and *as* the subjected," and to creating lateral relations of care and livable, even joyful moments in the midst of the quotidian and extraordinary violences that define Black life.[102] Sharpe names one such practice of care "aspiration," pointing to the urgent need to keep breath in the Black body and to the audible breath of speech sounds.[103] Likewise, Gumbs identifies breath as a "practice of presence," a reminder of evolution and the potential for growth, a representation of the permeability of strength.[104] Aspiration, both as basic function of living and as metaphor for rhetorical agency, is an apt descriptor of KIMBRITIVE's mission, since it is simultaneously embodied and expressive, drawing attention to physical safety and corporeal care, as well as to the breathy articulation of bodily desire and pleasure.

By reading KIMBRITIVE's work as a reparative supplement to existing forms of sex education, I have endeavored, as Tristano and Hsu urge, to focus on their creative insights and self-determination in the wake of the trauma and woundedness wrought by sex education's national pedagogy of white supremacy and sexual shame. Black queer joy, in other words, appears in KIMBRITIVE's concentration on the sexual wellness of Black girls, women, and femmes as a resistant ethics of care and survival, and as an undeniable part of the struggle for racial, reproductive, and queer justice. The youthful agency inspired and nurtured in KIMBRITIVE's project will be the centerpiece of my concluding chapter—not as a repudiation of vulnerability, but in delicate and contingent relation to it, as an affective resource for queerly imagined survivals and futures.

---

101. Sharpe, *In the Wake*, 13–14, 5.
102. Sharpe, *In the Wake*, 4.
103. Sharpe, *In the Wake*, 5, 109.
104. Gumbs, *Undrowned*, 21–27.

CONCLUSION

Refiguring Futures

Youth Innovations in Agency and Vulnerability

> Being queer saved my life. Often we see queerness as deprivation. But when I look at my life, I [see] that queerness demanded an alternative innovation from me, I had to make alternative routes. It made me curious; it made me ask, "Is this enough for me?"
> —Ocean Vuong, "All the Ways"

On September 9, 2020, Netflix released *Cuties* (originally *Mignonnes*, in French), a film that tells the story of eleven-year-old Amy, the daughter of Senegalese immigrants living in present-day Paris, as she navigates the conflicting messages about womanhood she receives from her traditional Muslim family and her peers, and tries to imitate the forms of adult female sexuality she sees on the internet and on social media. Amy, who is Black, joins a dance troupe called the Cuties, composed of a racially diverse group of popular and seemingly more worldly girls of the same age; as they rehearse for an upcoming competition, both their dance moves and their social activities reflect their burgeoning sexual awareness and their yearning for maturity. The debut feature film by French Senegalese filmmaker Maïmouna Doucouré, *Cuties* is alternatingly sweet, sad, and funny, offering a nuanced look at the confusing pressures contemporary girls face as they grow up. Doucouré earned the Directing Award at the Sundance Film Festival, actress Fathia Youssouf won Most Promising Actress at the César Awards in France for her portrayal of Amy, and the film, director, and actors were nominated for numerous other accolades internationally.

In spite of its positive reception by critics, however, the distribution of *Cuties* on Netflix prompted an immediate backlash, with #CancelNetflix trending on Twitter and the number of Netflix subscription cancellations spiking to eight times their usual rate in the days following its release.¹ The controversy over the film actually began even before it was available, when Netflix used a promotional poster and trailers that presented the Cuties in a sexualized fashion that was inconsistent with the substance of the film. Opposition to *Cuties* was a rare bipartisan alliance in 2020, with politicians from both parties, as well as celebrities, social media influencers, and private citizens, calling out the film for sexualizing children, accusing it of violating laws against child pornography, suggesting that it would "whet the appetite of pedophiles & help fuel the child sex trafficking trade," and demanding that Netflix remove it.² Public outcry was also fueled by supporters of QAnon's #SaveTheChildren conspiracy theory (which imagines a vast underground human trafficking network controlled by a secret cabal of pedophiles) and resulted in personal attacks and even death threats to Doucouré.³

It is true that the film does feature several scenes in which the camera lingers on the bodies of Amy and the other young dancers, zooming in on their buttocks as they twerk and their barely covered crotches as they squat and thrust their hips provocatively. There is no question, in other words, that the girls in the film perform explicitly sexual dance moves, or that watching them do so is a discomfiting experience. Indeed, according to Doucouré, who describes her film as a feminist and activist critique of the sexualization and objectification of girls, the unease that adults feel is part of the point: "Some people have found certain scenes in my film uncomfortable to watch. But if one really listens to 11-year-old girls, their lives are uncomfortable." She argues that adults do not provide young people the tools they need to navigate cultural pressures, and that she made *Cuties* in the hopes of stimulating debate about how to "give the most beautiful space" for children to have the freedom to "grow up safely and become the best version of themselves."⁴

What is striking about the most sexualized moments of *Cuties*, however, is that they are also moments in which the girls are performing by and for themselves. Most of the dance scenes take place during their rehearsals, where they are alone (indeed, adults play only small parts in the film, and adult men are conspicuously absent) and where their experimentation with sexual expression, accompanied by joyful laughter, represents freedom and the bonds of friendship. In fact, nearly without exception, when the girls' sexualized performances reach wider audiences—when Amy posts a nude photo online, when she unbuttons her shirt and pants in an awkward and unsuccessful attempt to

---

1. Tinubu, "'Cuties' Director Maïmouna Doucouré"; and Spangler, "'Cuties' Controversy."
2. Knibbs, "How Cuties Got Caught"; and Cole, "Democrat Tulsi Gabbard."
3. McNeal, "Netflix Movie 'Cuties'"; and Tinubu, "'Cuties' Director Maïmouna Doucouré."
4. Doucouré, "I Directed 'Cuties'"; and Doucouré, "Why I Made Cuties."

appease her older cousin after stealing his phone, and when the Cuties perform at the dance competition to an audience of parents and families—their sexualization is met with the disapproval and condemnation of adults. Ultimately, running off the stage during this performance, Amy realizes that her approach to womanhood cannot follow either of the paths presented to her: not the explicit sexual display of the Cuties, nor the conservative traditions of her family. In other words, the film does not showcase adults' sexualization of children (as the bulk of the social media frenzy suggested), and it does not even include adults who appreciate or facilitate the sexualization of children (as, for instance, child beauty pageants and shows like *Toddlers & Tiaras* have been said to do). Instead, *Cuties* seems to do something even more shocking to American sensibilities: it presents Black and Brown tween girls embodying sexual agency, taking pleasure in their bodies as they experiment with adultlike forms of expression, testing the limits of the public and private boundaries of their emerging sexual beings, and ultimately making their own decisions about their bodies and their sexual expression. It neither insists on childhood innocence nor denounces youthful sexuality but rather showcases the conflict between the two, inviting viewers into the girls' imperfect attempts to traverse the uncertain terrain of puberty and adolescence. As Monica Hesse writes for the *Washington Post*, *Cuties* centers the experience of the girls' "betweenness," offering "a frank look at their exploration of sexuality: the influences they respond to or rebel against, the power they think they have, the things they think they understand." It juxtaposes their bravado with their naivete, and "their desire to grow up only underscores how young they are."[5]

The controversy over *Cuties* was intense but ultimately short-lived. Netflix apologized for its unfortunate choices of promotional materials, changed the photo associated with the film, and defended the filmmaker's freedom of expression. Because most of the outrage was sparked by decontextualized clips and shared by those who had not actually watched the film, the uproar died down quickly once the film was available to view, with Netflix feeling no material effects from the cancellations (presumably, many of the cancelled accounts were later quietly reactivated).[6] I showcase the brief hubbub over *Cuties*, then, not because of its lasting impact on the landscape of youth sexuality but because both the film itself and the controversy surrounding it showcase two of the most important threads that run throughout this book. First, *Cuties* offers a glimpse of the queerness of childhood—it does not depict any hint of same-sex sexual attraction, but it does deftly convey the yearning, the

---

5. Hesse, "Cuties on Netflix."
6. Spangler, "'Cuties' Controversy."

eroticism, the confusion, the ambivalence of the girls' embodiment of desire and sexual agency. Their imitation of sexual exhibitionism and their bodily development put them on an accelerated course toward adulthood that is out of sync with their childlike lack of sophistication and maturity; they illustrate, that is, the temporal disjunction, the uncertainty, the inconsistency, the *trouble* of childhood's queerness.

Second, the strong public reaction to the film exemplifies how the rhetorical figuration of childhood that circulates in public discourse serves adult interests and preserves sexual morality. Unlike the rest of the case studies I have featured up until this point, which all concern the well-being of real young people, *Cuties* is a work of fiction and does not document any harms to actual children. Indeed, Doucouré took great care with her young actors, creating a "climate of trust" with them and their parents, and providing a child psychologist to work with the youth on set and after the film wrapped to help them navigate their new notoriety.[7] She also notes that the adolescents who worked on the film had, of course, already seen on their own social media feeds all of the sexual dance moves they were asked to perform. In other words, the film makes adults uncomfortable not because it sexualizes children, as its critics claim, but because it reveals the sexuality of children—not just as it is imposed by external cultural forces but also how it emerges within and is negotiated by young people themselves. Decrying the supposed desecration of innocence that *Cuties* depicts and assuming its unlikely impact on child sex trafficking and pedophilia does nothing to protect actual children from these and other real harms; rather, it preserves adults' belief in the fiction of the pure, sexually naïve figuration of the white child against which adulthood and adult sexual normalcy is defined. Furthermore, since the film is set in Paris and Amy is a Black Muslim girl, and since all but one of the Cuties are girls of color, it is possible to displace the contamination of sexualization onto the bodies of racialized, foreign, religious others. This permits adults to maintain the fantasy of the innocence of "our" girls—white, American, hetero(non)sexual girls who grow up according to a proper chrononormative schedule—while also imagining them to be imperiled by any exposure to the bad influence of sexual awareness and performance.

In the preceding chapters, we have witnessed how the (re)production of the racial figuration of childhood depends upon the malleability of the idea of childhood and shapes the availability of and relationship between agency and vulnerability. Although each case study illuminates how the rhetorical process of figuration produces specific material implications for marginalized

---

7. Tinubu, "'Cuties' Director Maïmouna Doucouré."

youth, they all contribute to a coherent cultural message about the racialized, gendered, and sexual exclusions of childhood's protections, as well as about adults' reluctance to acknowledge childhood's queerness. In the first chapter, for instance, we saw how the boundaries of the category of vulnerability are starkly defined through the dehumanization and exclusion of Blackness, queerness, and female sexual self-determination. The teen sexting panic is thus not only an example of the adult resistance to the possibility of adolescent sexual agency—especially for girls—but also an opportunity to understand how youth of color and queer, trans, and gender-nonconforming youth disproportionately bear the burden of adult policies that disguise punishment and disenfranchisement as protections. In the second chapter, queer youth were imagined to be inherently at risk for bullying and suicide based on their sexual identities, but the frame of vulnerability through which these young people became intelligible in mainstream media, public communication, and policy discourse was built upon the assumptions of the weakness of whiteness and the precarious performativity of masculinity. Here, not only are queer youth denied agency, but the category of vulnerability is occupied by whiteness, such that the white vulnerability of childhood is further entrenched as a site of paternalistic protection and privilege. The third chapter highlighted how the chrononormativity of the category of childhood precludes trans youths' declarations of gender identity. Casting trans kids as precociously sexual and menacing both reinforces the purity and vulnerability of cisgender hetero(non)sexual kids and justifies adult agency to deny the rights of trans youth. This skewed temporality of trans youth is also racialized, such that Blackness is invoked but ultimately disavowed in the production of white trans rights, and the intersection of Blackness and transness is legible only as a site of violence. Finally, the last chapter demonstrated the role of sex education in the US as a national pedagogy of white supremacy and eugenics, heteronormativity, and traditional binary gender roles; the history of sex education provides examples of explicit lessons that shape the racial figuration of childhood. But in KIMBRITIVE's insistence on sexual wellness for Black women, girls, and femmes, we also see the possibility not only for addressing young people through a Black feminist affirming and abundant style of speech but also for figuring differently the racialization and queerness of childhood's relationship to vulnerability and agency.

In short, across the different contexts of these case studies—teen sexting, the bullying and suicides of queer youth, trans students' rights to gender-segregated spaces, and sex education—a common racial figuration of childhood emerges. This figure operates according to an exclusionary logic that constitutes an idealized and imaginary version of the child who is innocent, white, cisgender, hetero(non)sexual, growing according to a normative developmental temporality, and always already imperiled. Envisioned in this way, the privileges of childhood—protection from harm, as well as tolerance for mistakes and indiscretions—are sacrificed for knowledge and empowerment. That is, young people who know too much, who exercise sexual agency, or who are adultified by their race or gender identity become the scapegoats for the queerness of all youth. In the rhetorical figuration of youth, I argue, we can observe the rhetorical process through which these racialized discourses of childhood vulnerability (re)produce material violences, leaving the most marginalized young people in the greatest jeopardy.

Reimagining Queerness's Risk as Resource

In spite of the pervasiveness of this limited racial figuration of childhood, it does not preclude other possibilities for thinking about youth and sexuality that emphasize the agency, curiosity, ingenuity, and strangeness of childhood, rather than the innocence and vulnerability so useful to the maintenance of white privilege and cis-, hetero-, and chrononormativities. To imagine childhood differently refuses to disavow childhood's queerness but rather opens up that queerness as a resource, a well of cunning creativity, a source of eccentric innovation, and indeed, a means for imagining astonishing and unexpected futures. In the previous chapter KIMBRITIVE demonstrated how Black feminist love-politics can revise the work of sexuality education for youth of color by rooting it in the precious and desiring bodies of Black girls, women, and femmes and directly confronting the material constraints that have shaped Black women's sexual freedom. By approaching Black self-care and embodied pleasures through the rhetorical style of affirming abundance, they refuse the white supremacist framing of youthful innocence and purity. Keeping KIMBRITIVE's intervention in mind, I want to turn to another example of reframing—one that returns us to the problem of the vulnerabilization of queer youth that emerged in the second chapter. Like KIMBRITIVE's insistence that Black femme bodies not be understood as sites of inadequacy or vectors of disease, the Beyond Bullying Project (BBP) similarly rejects the assumption that queer youth are primarily defined in terms of risk and fragility, moving instead toward what Audrey Bryan describes as "a more expansive consideration of queer lived experience" that emphasizes the "sexualized, pleasurable and agentic aspects of queer identity."[8] The organizers of the BBP

---

8. Bryan, "Queer Youth and Mental Health," 74–75.

ask, "What happens when we think about LGBTQ+ gender and sexuality in schools beyond risks like bullying, poor mental health, and dropping out?"[9] By giving queer youth and adults the opportunity to tell their own stories about gender and sexuality, the BBP offers an alternative means for recognizing the struggles of queer youth without relegating them to weakness and victimhood, and takes seriously young people's queer innovations in expressing identities, desires, relationships, and communities.

The Beyond Bullying Project debuted during the 2014–15 school year, when creators Jen Gilbert, Jessica Fields, Laura Mamo, and Nancy Lesko set up booths in high schools in Minneapolis, New York, and San Francisco, where students, teachers, and administrators could privately share and record their experiences with gender and sexuality. According to the BBP's website, participants offered accounts of "school assignments, crushes, families, friendships, break-ups, coming out, harassment, bravery, and aspirations—all connected to LGBTQ+ sexuality and gender."[10] Transcripts and audio recordings of some of these stories are featured on the BBP website. In 2021 the BBP began collecting stories from Canadian high school students and staff virtually, through an online storytelling portal. Unlike other collections of video submissions from queer youth, such as It Gets Better, the BBP does not have a persuasive agenda or a suggested theme for contributions. Seeking only to represent the diversity of queer youths' lives, their call for stories is broad and open-ended:

> Tell us a story about LGBTQ+ sexuality or gender. The story you share could be about you or someone else; it can be about family, school, friends, being in love, or being uncomfortable. It can be about a celebrity or a neighbour or a cousin. It doesn't even need to be true. Any story is OK and every story is welcome. The story can be as long or as short as you'd like.[11]

The BBP's website also features blog posts and resources for queer youth, including information about community, mental health, sexuality and faith, education, social change, and storytelling.

To imagine queer youth in their vast variety of experiences and in their intersectional gendered and sexualized identities, as the BBP attempts to do, does not just replace "risk" with "resilience"—a model that produces its own limiting expectations, as I detailed in chapter 2—as the organizing narrative term. Rather, it emphasizes queer young people as agents who can and do act

---

9. Beyond Bullying Project.
10. Beyond Bullying Project, "About Us."
11. Beyond Bullying Project, "Share Your Story."

creatively, flexibly, and resistantly within contexts of precarity, demonstrating that queer youth have long been struggling, but also surviving.[12] Attending to both individual agency and community and contextual factors, we can begin to understand how the risks that queer teens face arise from dysfunctions in community relations—heterosexism and cissexism, white supremacy and racism, sexism and sex-negativity, ableism and insufficient mental health care, poverty and inequalities in school—not from weaknesses inherent in themselves. By addressing the contexts in which queer teens struggle—and recognizing that queer teens are also acting within and against those contexts—we can begin to imagine them as gendered and sexual agents in their own right.

Gilbert, Fields, Mamo, and Lesko contend that the stories they collect do not merely document the challenges or success stories of queer youth, but instead identify some of the often overlooked desires, relationships, and experiences of belonging and recognition that queerness makes possible. The stories inspire and produce what they call "intimate possibilities—the range of desires, relationships, identities, and pleasures one anticipates, pursues, and claims for oneself and others." These are stories, in other words, of "who they are, who they want to be, and social worlds they want to build." Gilbert, Fields, Mamo, and Lesko note that the intimate possibilities forged and narrated in these stories are "differently apportioned" in relation to entrenched social inequalities, and that the desires and wishes they express are not always realized—sometimes they bring disappointment, pain, and confusion in equal measures with joy, surprise, and delight. Students also articulate possibilities for reimagining their experiences at school, suggesting that they can carve out "shifting zones of refuge, exploration, and struggle" within what might otherwise be viewed as sites of unsafety or exclusion.[13]

Thus, when queer youth are invited to narrate their own lives and experiences, the intimate possibilities they describe are not necessarily mired in pain and loneliness, nor are they uniformly positive or liberating. Their stories instead reveal how they create alternate identification and relational possibilities that circulate alongside, against, and through the limited discourses of bullying and suicide prevention sanctioned by their schools. The authors say, "For storytellers, wanting more for oneself and others pointed to a world beyond what was currently available and to the disappointments and demands of what was immediately at hand."[14] Described in their own terms, the desires youth articulate are wide-ranging and imaginative, seeking sexual possibility, embracing nonnormative identities, and orienting toward the future.

---

12. Robertson, *Growing Up Queer*, 8.
13. Gilbert et al., "Intimate Possibilities," 164–66.
14. Gilbert et al., "Intimate Possibilities," 174.

Placing KIMBRITIVE and the BBP side by side as interruptions to the dominant figurations of youth sexuality traced in *Minor Troubles* provides a glimpse of the possibilities for thinking about young people and sexuality differently. These two efforts do not merely run parallel—one addressing race and one addressing sexuality—but rather each complicates the terms of the other. The BBP's challenge to the supposed innocence of youth is also a challenge to the white supremacist boundaries of the category of childhood, and KIMBRITIVE queers the potential of Black girls' and femmes' sexuality by resisting the constraints on desire and demands of respectability imposed on Black women. Recognizing the quotidian innovations of these projects requires a complex lens for understanding young people's sexualities that acknowledges the fraught cultural, political, and media environments within which desires develop. Michelle Fine and Sara McClelland posit the concept of "thick desire" to situate adolescent sexuality not only as a privately exercised right but also as functioning within "a human rights framework, allied with struggles over reproductive rights, political economy, health care, education and prison reform, structural and personal violence." Thick desire, for these authors, suggests that "young people are entitled to a broad range of desires for meaningful intellectual, political, and social engagement, the possibility of financial independence, sexual and reproductive freedom, protection from racialized and sexualized violence, and a way to imagine living in the future tense." In other words, Fine and McClelland call attention to how individual desires and private sexual acts are always articulated to and imbricated with public and social policies, and how sexual health is related to educational, economic, psychological, and social health.[15] The framework of thick desire therefore demands structural systems of support for young people's sexual health, especially for those placed most at risk not by virtue of their identities but because of systemic inequities—namely, girls, gender-nonconforming and trans youth, youth of color, youth with disabilities, queer youth, youth living with poverty or homelessness, and sexually abused youth.

Kath Albury and Paul Byron suggest that such a shift in perspective is difficult insofar as there is generally wide support for "young people's negative rights, or 'freedoms from' unwanted sexual experiences," but it is much more challenging to make a strong case for youths' "positive rights, or 'freedoms to' sexual expression and sexual experience."[16] Albury and Byron advocate for removing the "risk goggles" that often lead researchers and youth policy decision-makers to overemphasize the severity of risk while underestimating the opportunities for discovery and growth that youthful sexual expression

---

15. Fine and McClelland, "Sexuality Education and Desire," 298–301.
16. Albury and Byron, "Taking Off the Risk Goggles," 169.

entails. They argue that it is crucial to distinguish between "risk" and "harm"; not only is risk-taking with sexual and gender expression not necessarily harmful, but in fact, it is an essential aspect of gathering knowledge, developing responsibility, and actualizing sexual agency.[17]

Albury and Byron's admonition about adults' "risk goggles" is offered specifically in relation to youths' digital media practices and therefore serves as a particularly apt disruption of adults' panic about teen sexting and other technologies that can facilitate sexual interaction. But it is also a means for rethinking the apparent risks of bullying and suicide associated with queerness, the risks that trans and gender-nonconforming kids are imagined to pose to cisgender youth, and the risks of sexual activity outside the context of heterosexual marriage. Rather than framing young people of color and queer, trans, and gender-nonconforming youth exclusively in terms of their marginalization, that is, we must also focus on the ways in which they exercise agency and power. Queer and gender-nonconforming youth and youth of color do not just find ways to survive; they also generate new knowledges, new languages, and new ways of being that exceed the limiting frameworks of identity, relationships, and futures all too often offered in their schools.[18]

Therefore, as Katie Fitzpatrick and Hayley McGlashan argue, a binary model of youths' marginalization and resistance does not do justice to the ways that youth "reimagine power relations" beyond these terms. For example, Fitzpatrick and McGlashan describe a group of queer and gender-nonconforming students who proposed a presentation for teachers by students, aimed at helping adults understand the vocabularies of gender and sexuality in which the students are more fluent. The students intervened in homophobic experiences of exclusion and marginality at their school by positioning themselves as "experts" and their teachers as "ignorant." That is, rather than pointing out the ways that they were victimized or resisting the existing power hierarchy, the students instead reconfigured the power relationship, seeing themselves as "more knowledgeable than their teachers" and feeling "a responsibility to educate [teachers] about issues of sex, gender and sexuality." Fitzpatrick and McGlashan describe this as a subjectivity of leadership, in which young people understand themselves as holding vital forms of expertise and as the benevolent educators of adults: "Instead of seeing the school as a site of teacher power, they identify the lack of knowledge held by some teachers and, crucially, they take up the responsibility to address this lack."[19]

---

17. Albury and Byron, "Taking Off the Risk Goggles," 176–78.
18. Van Asselt, "Imagining Otherwise," 609.
19. Fitzpatrick and McGlashan, "'Some Teachers Are Homophobic,'" 270–71.

In each of these instances of agency I have been describing—Black girls insisting on sexuality education; queer and trans kids telling their stories, defining their desires, risking sexual and gender exploration, owning their expertise; and even the fictional Cuties experimenting with their dawning sexual awareness through dance—we can recognize young people crafting their own versions of identity in relation to and rejection of existing categories, developing sexual ethics true to their personal experiences, and cultivating thick desires informed by their individual embodied knowledges and situated within cultural structures of meaning-making. In these interventions childhood becomes troublesome—it is potentially disruptive to, rather than merely reproductive of, adult visions of sexual morality. These examples show us a future imagined from below, from the double-bind of the restricted rights and enhanced protection of the minor: it is a queer vision of the future that, like Muñoz's queer utopia, is horizonal, invokes the possibility for disappointment alongside the necessity of hope, and imagines the future as a means of troubling the present.[20]

New Survivals: Black Futures, Queer Futures

Eve Sedgwick famously summed up American sentiment toward the possibility of queer youth in a couple of pithy statements in the early 1990s: that many people would "as soon their children were dead as gay," and that "it's always open season on gay kids."[21] She notes that the injury of these claims is produced not only when such cruelty is expressed overtly but also through the preponderance of school, religious, family, and community structures that systematically invalidate, sequester, and disavow young queer lives. These are many of the same institutional settings and messages that I have explored here—the lack of genuine engagement with problems of bullying and suicide, the punitive measures that disproportionately affect queer and gender-nonconforming youth and youth of color, the policies that attempt to regulate trans kids out of existence, sex education that withholds crucial health information from the most marginalized young people—and thirty years later, her assessment still rings true. Indeed, given the relentlessness of the contemporary legislative assaults on trans youth (and queer and trans people in general)

---

20. Muñoz, *Cruising Utopia*, 11–12.
21. Sedgwick, *Tendencies*, 2, 155.

with which I opened this book, her words are now more accurate and more prescient than she could have imagined.

Sedgwick asserts that our mistreatment of queer youth is embedded in our deep ambivalence toward them: "Seemingly, this society wants its children to know nothing; wants its queer children to conform or (and this is not a figure of speech) die; and wants not to know that it is getting what it wants."[22] This stunning diagnosis of homophobia's covert operations also identifies adults' orientation toward and desire for particular kinds of futures, as well as their misidentification of those desires. In other words, it is not only that our culture denies its shameful wish for queer and trans kids, Black and Brown and Indigenous kids, and otherwise confusing or discomfiting kids to no longer exist. It also denies that we want something even more insidious from those young people: to fulfill our fantasies of saviorism, of fighting valiantly (but ultimately unsuccessfully—the failure is key) for their lives in the name of the racial figuration of childhood.

The self-perpetuating nature of this cultural phenomenon, whereby the most marginalized youth must be maintained in precarity in order to require our care for them—a care not extended when they do what they can to survive on their own—brings us back to Edelman's notion of reproductive futurism and its sacralization of the Child who is always and necessarily the white Child. Sedgwick calls upon us to ask not just how queer youth can survive, but also what they "survive into" in the complex context of queer life in the wake of the AIDS crisis: a hostile and dehumanizing environment defined by threat, stigma, violence, fear, and loss, but also "a moment of unprecedented cultural richness, cohesion, and assertiveness."[23] This framework is no less apt today, as queer and trans youth of color survive into a climate of spectacular racial violence, ascending white supremacy, escalating disinformation, and endangered democracy, but also into a time of powerful movements for racial justice and decolonization, and a proliferation of possibilities for identity construction and world-making.

To imagine a way out of the dead-end future that Edelman describes, then, requires both queer and anti-racist visions of futurity, or, as Kara Keeling would have it, "queer times and Black futures."[24] Keeling reconfigures the very notion of survival: rather than survival as endurance within the current terms of inequality and injustice, Keeling instead understands it as a "task [that] calls for its own undoing in time," and freedom as "giv[ing] way to other things." To view survival in this way "takes seriously the generative

---

22. Sedgwick, *Tendencies*, 3.
23. Sedgwick, *Tendencies*, 3.
24. Keeling, *Queer Times, Black Futures*, 16.

proposition *another world is possible,* the insistence that such a world already is here now and it listens, with others, for the poetry, the refrains, the rhythms, and the noise such a world is making."[25] Youth of color and queer, trans, and gender-nonconforming youth are making noise of their own, constantly pressing up against—or simply disregarding with youthful naivete and chutzpah—the constraints imposed by adult concerns for the sexual and social order. Although they are limited by the racial figuration of childhood that positions them as unequally eligible for the innocence, vulnerability, and protections of youthfulness, they are not, in the end, fully determined by these discourses. They invoke, as Sedgwick puts it, the not yet broken childhood promises "to make invisible possibilities and desires visible; to make the tacit things explicit; to smuggle queer representation in where it must be smuggled."[26] We might thus understand their survival not in Edelman's sense of a reproduction of the white supremacist and heteronormative status quo or even as an impossible project of persistence, but rather in Keeling's terms of a creative and imaginative process of becoming.

To think about the survival of queer, trans, and gender-nonconforming youth and youth of color in this manner is also to reevaluate the significance of vulnerability and risk—central terms to public discourse about youth and sexuality—and the importance of queerness as a resource for agency and invention. Vulnerability, that is, need not be understood as a defining quality of childhood that justifies adult intervention, nor as a necessary and debilitating characteristic of marginalized youth; instead, it might be an affective resource for queerly reimagining bodies, identities, relationships, and power. For Keeling, queerness might be "utopian or dystopian, quotidian, banal, spectacular, public, private"; felt palpably, it "carves out our relations temporally and spatially and proliferates connections within difference." And Black futures, "animated in queer times and inseparable from queer relations," she asserts, are "a way of indicating an investment in the risk that already inheres in social life—an antifragile investment in the errant, the irrational, and the unpredictable."[27] The vulnerability and risk of queerness and Black futures, in other words, are not limiting conditions that can be measured or accounted for in advance or that can be ameliorated through harm-reduction strategies. Rather, the vulnerabilities and risks of bodies made precarious are the very qualities through which new forms of survival emerge.

To forward vulnerability not in opposition to agency, but as a resource, as a site of connection and community, is itself a risky proposition. On one

---

25. Keeling, *Queer Times, Black Futures,* ix.
26. Sedgwick, *Tendencies,* 3.
27. Keeling, *Queer Times, Black Futures,* 18, 32.

hand, as Anu Koivunen, Katariina Kyrölä, and Ingrid Ryberg warn, asserting universal vulnerability as an ontological condition of humanity risks ignoring the "uneven distribution of violence and injury between bodies" that leaves certain subjects more precarious than others; on the other hand, assuming the vulnerability of certain groups on the basis of their divergence from dominant cultural norms also risks leaving uncontested the white, male, cisgender, heterosexual status of the individual subject.[28] To imagine queer and trans youth of color as heroically overcoming their inherent vulnerabilities would thus both overdetermine their identities and downplay the structural inequalities that condition their lives. Instead, I am pointing toward a more modest consideration of vulnerability that is inspired by what Lisa Flores and other feminist, queer, and anti-racist scholars call "critical vulnerability," a practice of engaging in the risky work of surviving, desiring, thriving in and against white heteropatriarchal institutions "from bodies always made inferior."[29] This perspective on vulnerability suggests that the agencies of queer and trans youth of color demonstrate the potential for individually experienced corporeal vulnerabilities to become "theories in the flesh" that both illuminate structural oppressions and generate solidarity in creative existence.

Keeling illustrates how such a perspective on survival in the present and the future emerges from the materiality of Black existence. Because Blackness has been cast as antagonistic or even antithetical to humanity, she asserts, "Black existence is a condition of possibility for moving beyond what is. At the same time, it presently anchors a set of possibilities for 'something else to be.'" She continues, "the long arc of Black existence contains vital elements that might be recombined to call forth new relations for all. . . . It carries within it alternative organizations of time in which the future, if there is such a thing, has not been promised; it has had to be created by reaching through and beyond what exists. It still does."[30] To survive, within this framework, thus may involve tenaciously withstanding painful dehumanizing and stigmatizing forces, but it also crucially requires a pliability, an exposure, a sensitivity, a yielding; to bend is to embody a novel way of being, to "reforge ourselves" in response to contexts beyond our own making.[31]

Youth of color, and queer, trans, and gender-nonconforming youth, as the sacrificed remainder produced by the racial figuration of childhood—childhood's troublemakers—exemplify what it means to survive through and into material vulnerabilities, vexing the logics of their exclusion. They reconfigure

28. Koivunen, Kyrölä, and Ryberg, *Power of Vulnerability*, 5.
29. Flores, "Towards an Insistent," 354.
30. Keeling, *Queer Times, Black Futures*, 34–36.
31. Keeling, *Queer Times, Black Futures*, ix.

the risks to which they are relegated, drawing on queerness's imaginative reserves and Blackness's possibilities for another world, practicing sometimes astonishing ways of claiming identities, expressing desires, and forging relationships in the everyday spaces of their schools and their communities. The sparks of invention they enact may not be legible within the adult discourses that understand queerness and other forms of difference only in terms of deficit or imperfection, but they are crucial to survival. As writer Ocean Vuong insists in the epigraph to this chapter, queerness is lifesaving because it activates ingenuity: "Often we see queerness as a deprivation. But when I look at my life, I [see] that queerness demanded an alternative innovation from me, I had to make alternative routes."[32] The critical vulnerability of queer and trans and gender-nonconforming youth and youth of color, in other words, is one such alternative route. It is an innovative mode of existence that leans into vulnerability as a means of agency, that neither shuns nor accepts queerness's fragility or immanent woundedness, that recognizes in Blackness a resource for other ways to be. Most importantly, it reminds us that childhood may be deployed symbolically to reconstitute the past in the future, but young people are also carving out their own desires, forms of intimacy, and relations with the self and others, generating new futures and new worlds of their own.

---

32. Vuong, "All the Ways."

BIBLIOGRAPHY

"The 30 Most Influential Teens of 2016." *Time*, October 19, 2016. https://time.com/4532104/most-influential-teens-2016/.

Acland, Charles R. *Youth, Murder, Spectacle: The Cultural Politics of Youth in Crisis*. Boulder, CO: Westview Press, 1994.

Adams, Heather Brook. "Rhetorics of Unwed Motherhood and Shame." *Women's Studies in Communication* 40, no. 1 (January 2017): 91–110.

Adkins, Brendan. "Being Aggressive about Fighting Crime, That Sounds Like a Good Thing." *Not Falling Down* blog, January 17, 2011. https://www.xorph.com/nfd/2011/01/17/zero-tolerance/.

Advocates for Youth. "Building Cultural Responsiveness: A Toolkit for Youth-Serving Professionals." June 2021. https://www.advocatesforyouth.org/resources/curricula-education/building-cultural-responsiveness-for-youth-serving-professionals/.

Ahmed, Sara. *Living a Feminist Life*. Durham, NC: Duke University Press, 2017.

———. *The Promise of Happiness*. Durham, NC: Duke University Press, 2010.

———. "Selfcare as Warfare." *Feminist Killjoys* blog, August 25, 2014. https://feministkilljoys.com/2014/08/25/selfcare-as-warfare/.

Albury, Kath, and Paul Byron. "Queering Sexting and Sexualisation." *Media International Australia* 153 (2014): 138–47.

———. "Taking Off the Risk Goggles: Exploring the Intersection of Young People's Sexual and Digital Citizenship in Sexual Health Promotion." In *Youth, Sexuality and Sexual Citizenship*, edited by Peter Aggleton, Rob Cover, Deana Leahy, Daniel Marshall, and Mary Lou Rasmussen, 168–83. New York: Routledge, 2019.

Alexander, Bryant Keith. *Performing Black Masculinity: Race, Culture, and Queer Identity*. New York: AltaMira Press, 2006.

Alexander, Elizabeth. *The Trayvon Generation*. New York: Grand Central Publishing, 2022.

Ali, Diana. "The Rise and Fall of the Bathroom Bill: State Legislation Affecting Trans & Gender Non-Binary People." *NASPA,* April 2, 2019. https://www.naspa.org/blog/the-rise-and-fall-of-the-bathroom-bill-state-legislation-affecting-trans-and-gender-non-binary-people.

Amar, Paul. "The Street, the Sponge, and the Ultra: Queer Logics of Children's Rebellion and Political Infantilization." *GLQ: A Journal of Lesbian and Gay Studies* 22, no. 4 (2016): 569–604.

The American College of Obstetricians and Gynecologists. "Committee Opinion on Comprehensive Sexuality Education." No. 678 (November 2016; reaffirmed 2018): 1–4.

American Psychological Association, Task Force on the Sexualization of Girls. "Report of the APA Task Force on the Sexualization of Girls" (2007). https://www.apa.org/pi/women/programs/girls/report-full.pdf.

Amin, Kadji. "Temporality." *TSQ: Transgender Studies Quarterly* 1, nos. 1–2 (2014): 219–22.

André, Amy, and Sandy Chang. "'And Then You Cut Your Hair': Genderfucking on the Femme Side of the Spectrum." In *Nobody Passes: Rejecting the Rules of Gender and Conformity,* edited by Mattilda Bernstein Sycamore, 254–69. Berkeley: Seal Press, 2006.

Angelides, Steven. *The Fear of Child Sexuality: Young People, Sex, and Agency.* Chicago: University of Chicago Press, 2019.

Annamma, Subini, Yolanda Anyon, Nicole Joseph, Jordan Farrar, Eldridge Greer, Barbara Downing, and John Simmons. "Black Girls and School Discipline: The Complexities of Being Overrepresented and Understudied." *Urban Education* 54, no. 2 (2016): 1–32.

Artiga, Samantha, Latoya Hill, Usha Ranji, and Ivette Gomez. "What Are the Implications of the Overturning of Roe v. Wade for Racial Disparities?" *Kaiser Family Foundation,* July 15, 2022. https://www.kff.org/racial-equity-and-health-policy/issue-brief/what-are-the-implications-of-the-overturning-of-roe-v-wade-for-racial-disparities/.

Asakura, Kenta. "Paving Pathways through the Pain: A Grounded Theory of Resilience among Lesbian, Gay, Bisexual, Trans, and Queer Youth." *Journal of Research on Adolescence* 27, no. 3 (2016): 521–36.

Asen, Robert. *Democracy, Deliberation, and Education.* University Park: Pennsylvania State University Press, 2015.

———. "Women, Work, Welfare: A Rhetorical History of Images of Poor Women in Welfare Policy Debates." *Rhetoric and Public Affairs* 6, no. 2 (2003): 285–312.

Attwood, Feona, ed. *Mainstreaming Sex: The Sexualization of Western Culture.* London: IB Tauris, 2010.

Barnard, Ian. "Rhetorical Commonsense and Child Molester Panic—A Queer Intervention." *Rhetoric Society Quarterly* 47, no. 1 (2017): 3–25.

———. *Sex Panic Rhetorics, Queer Interventions.* Tuscaloosa: University of Alabama Press, 2020.

Bernstein, Robin. *Racial Innocence: Performing American Childhood from Slavery to Civil Rights.* New York: New York University Press, 2011.

Berton, Justin. "Are Lots of Teens 'Sexting'? Experts Doubt It." *SFGate,* March 21, 2009. https://www.sfgate.com/news/article/Are-lots-of-teens-sexting-Experts-doubt-it-3167764.php.

Bey, Marquis. "The Trans*-ness of Blackness, the Blackness of Trans*-ness." *TSQ: Transgender Studies Quarterly* 4, no. 2 (2017): 275–95.

Beyond Bullying Project. https://beyondbullyingproject.com/.

———. "About Us." https://beyondbullyingproject.com/about-us/.

———. "Share Your Story." https://beyondbullyingproject.com/share-your-story/.

Bezalel, Danielle. "KIMBRITIVE with Kimberly Huggins and Brittany Brathwaite." *Sex Ed with DB* podcast, season 4, episode 6. https://soundcloud.com/user-260204496.

Block, Joshua. "'All I Want to Do Is Be a Normal Child and Use the Restroom in Peace.'" *ACLU*, October 21, 2015. https://www.aclu.org/blog/lgbtq-rights/transgender-rights/all-i-want-do-be-normal-child-and-use-restroom-peace.

Board of Education of the Highland Local School District v. United States Department of Education. United States District Court for the Southern District of Ohio Eastern Division, No. 2:16-CV-524 (2016).

Boyer, Jesseca. "New Name, Same Harm: Rebranding of Federal Abstinence-Only Programs." *Guttmacher Policy Review* 21 (2018): 11–16. https://www.guttmacher.org/gpr/2018/02/new-name-same-harm-rebranding-federal-abstinence-only-programs.

Brathwaite, Brittany, and Kimberly Huggins. "In Our Own Image[:] Sexual Expression and Violence in Popular Culture." In Women of Color Network, *Women of Color Voices*, Fall 2015, 25–26. https://online.anyflip.com/mybz/guic/#p=26.

———. Interview with author, Brooklyn, NY, February 29, 2020.

Breslow, Jacob. "Adolescent Citizenship, or Temporality and the Negation of Black Childhood in Two Eras." *American Quarterly* 71, no. 2 (June 2019): 473–94.

Breuner, Cora C., Gerri Mattson, Committee on Adolescence, Committee on Psychosocial Aspects of Child and Family Health. "Sexuality Education for Children and Adolescents." *Pediatrics* 138, no. 2 (2016): 1–11.

Brinkman, Britney G., José Garth, Katie Rose Horowitz, Samantha Marino, and Kelly Nestman Lockwood. "Black Girls and Sexuality Education: Access. Equity. Justice." The Black Girls Equity Alliance, October 2019. http://www.gwensgirls.org/wp-content/uploads/2019/10/BGEA-Report2_v4.pdf.

The Bronfenbrenner Center for Translational Research. "The Complex Consequences of Sexting for Teens." *Psychology Today*, March 18, 2022. https://www.psychologytoday.com/us/blog/evidence-based-living/202203/the-complex-consequences-sexting-teens.

Brooks-Tatum, Shanesha. "Subversive Self-Care: Centering Black Women's Wellness." *Feminist Wire*, November 9, 2012. https://thefeministwire.com/2012/11/subversive-self-care-centering-black-womens-wellness/.

Brown, Antjuanece. Interview with author, June 1, 2023.

Bruhm, Steven, and Natasha Hurley, eds. *Curiouser: On the Queerness of Children.* Minneapolis: University of Minnesota Press, 2004.

Bryan, Audrey. "Queer Youth and Mental Health: What Do Educators Need to Know?" *Irish Educational Studies* 36, no. 1 (2017): 73–89.

Bucholtz, Mary. "The Public Life of White Affects." *Journal of Sociolinguistics* 23 (2019): 485–504.

Buerkle, C. Wesley. "Adam Mansplains Everything: White-Hipster Masculinity as Covert Hegemony." *Southern Communication Journal* 84, no. 3 (July 2019): 170–82.

"'Bullycide': A Sadly New Pandemic." *The Mirror*, November 3, 2010. http://fairfieldmirror.com/news/%E2%80%9Cbullycide%E2%80%9D-a-sadly-new-pandemic/.

Burroughs, Davis. "Gavin Grimm Gifted College Scholarship." *Dogwood*, June 25, 2019. https://vadogwood.com/2019/06/25/gavin-grimm-gifted-college-scholarship/.

"Caleb R. Nolt Obituary." *D.O. McComb and Sons Funeral Homes.* https://www.legacy.com/us/obituaries/fortwayne/name/caleb-nolt-obituary?id=23083980.

Calvente, Lisa B. Y., Bernadette Marie Calafell, and Karma R. Chávez. "Here Is Something You Can't Understand: The Suffocating Whiteness of Communication Studies." *Communication and Critical/Cultural Studies* 17, no. 2 (2020): 202–9.

Canaday, Margot. *The Straight State: Sexuality and Citizenship in Twentieth-Century America*. Princeton, NJ: Princeton University Press, 2009.

Carey, Tamika L. "Necessary Adjustments: Black Women's Rhetorical Impatience." *Rhetoric Review* 39, no. 3 (2020): 269–86.

Carter, Julian B. *The Heart of Whiteness: Normal Sexuality and Race in America, 1880–1940*. Durham, NC: Duke University Press, 2007.

Castagnaro, Giulia. "The Nonsense and Dangers of the Transphobic 'Bathroom Debate.'" *GenderGP*, August 30, 2022. https://www.gendergp.com/transgender-bathrooms-discrimination-2022/.

Castañeda, Claudia. *Figurations: Child, Bodies, Worlds*. Durham, NC: Duke University Press, 2002.

Center for American Progress. "Fact Sheet: The Importance of Sports Participation for Transgender Youth." March 18, 2021. https://www.americanprogress.org/article/fact-sheet-importance-sports-participation-transgender-youth/.

Centers for Disease Control and Prevention (CDC). "The Relationship Between Bullying and Suicide: What We Know and What It Means for Schools." National Center for Injury Prevention and Control, Division of Violence Prevention, 2014. https://stacks.cdc.gov/view/cdc/34163.

———. "Reproductive Health: Teen Pregnancy." March 1, 2019. https://www.cdc.gov/reproductive-health/teen-pregnancy/.

———. "Sexually Transmitted Disease Surveillance 2018." Atlanta: U.S. Department of Health and Human Services, 2021. https://stacks.cdc.gov/view/cdc/79370/cdc_79370_DS1.pdf.

———. "Youth Risk Behavior Survey: Data Summary & Trends Report, 2009–2019." https://www.cdc.gov/healthyyouth/data/yrbs/index.htm.

———. "Youth Risk Behavior Survey: Data Summary & Trends Report, 2011–2021." https://www.cdc.gov/healthyyouth/data/yrbs/pdf/YRBS_Data-Summary-Trends_Report2023_508.pdf.

Chávez, Karma R. *The Borders of AIDS: Race, Quarantine, and Resistance*. Seattle: University of Washington Press, 2021.

Chen, Jian Neo, and Micha Cárdenas. "Times to Come: Materializing Trans Times." *TSQ: Transgender Studies Quarterly* 6, no. 4 (November 2019): 472–80.

Chess, Simone, Alison Kafer, Jessi Quizar, and Mattie Udora Richardson. "Calling All Restroom Revolutionaries." In *That's Revolting: Queer Strategies for Resisting Assimilation*, edited by Mattilda Bernstein Sycamore, 189–205. Brooklyn, NY: Soft Skull Press, 2004.

Chow, Rey. *The Protestant Ethnic and the Spirit of Capitalism*. New York: Columbia University Press, 2002.

Clifton, Derrick. "Anti-Trans Sports Bills Aren't Just Transphobic—They're Racist, Too." *them*, March 31, 2021. https://www.them.us/story/anti-trans-sports-bills-transphobic-racist.

"Cody Barker." *Chasing Rainbows*. http://chasingrainbowsuk.weebly.com/cody-barker.html.

Cole, Brendan. "Democrat Tulsi Gabbard Says Netflix Is Complicit in Child Sex Trafficking for 'Child Porn' Film 'Cuties.'" *Newsweek*, September 12, 2020. https://www.newsweek.com/tulsi-gabbard-netflix-cuties-child-trafficking-1531474.

Colebrook, Claire. "What Is It Like to Be a Human?" *TSQ: Transgender Studies Quarterly* 2, no. 2 (May 2015): 227–43.

Comartin, Erin, Roger Kernsmith, and Poco Kernsmith. "'Sexting' and Sex Offender Registration: Do Age, Gender, and Sexual Orientation Matter?" *Deviant Behavior* 34, no. 1 (2013): 38–52.

"The Combahee River Collective Statement." In *How We Get Free: Black Feminism and the Combahee River Collective,* edited by Keeanga-Yamahtta Taylor, 15–27. Chicago: Haymarket Books, 2017.

"Comments by Barbara Ransby." In *How We Get Free: Black Feminism and the Combahee River Collective,* edited by Keeanga-Yamahtta Taylor, 177–83. Chicago: Haymarket Books, 2017.

Cooper, Brittney. *Eloquent Rage: A Black Feminist Discovers Her Superpower.* New York: St. Martin's Press, 2018.

Cottom, Tressie McMillan. *Thick and Other Essays.* New York: The New Press, 2019.

Cover, Rob. "Queer Youth Resilience: Critiquing the Discourse of Hope and Hopelessness in LGBT Suicide Representation." *M/C Journal* 16, no. 5 (October 2013).

———. *Queer Youth Suicide, Culture and Identity: Unliveable Lives?* Burlington, VT: Ashgate, 2012.

Cox, Laverne, and Jessie Heyman. "It's Not about Bathrooms: Laverne Cox on the Attack against Trans Rights." *InStyle,* March 6, 2017. https://www.yahoo.com/entertainment/not-bathrooms-laverne-cox-attack-213205530.html.

Cram, Emerson. *Violent Inheritance: Sexuality, Land, and Energy in Making the North American West.* Oakland: University of California Press, 2022.

Crenshaw, Kimberlé Williams, with Priscilla Ocen and Jyoti Nanda. "Black Girls Matter: Pushed Out, Overpoliced and Underprotected." New York: African American Policy Forum and Center for Intersectionality and Social Policy Studies, 2015.

Crooks, Natasha, and Akilah Wise. "What We Risk When We Fail to Protect Black Girls." *Rewire,* February 25, 2019. https://rewire.news/article/2019/02/25/what-we-risk-when-we-fail-to-protect-black-girls/.

Crooks, Natasha, Barbara King, Audrey Tluczek, and Jessica McDermott Sales. "The Process of Becoming a Sexual Black Woman: A Grounded Theory Study." *Perspectives on Sexual and Reproductive Health* 51, no. 1 (2019): 17–25.

Curry, Tommy J. "Expendables for Whom: Terry Crews and the Erasure of Black Male Victims of Sexual Assault and Rape." *Women's Studies in Communication* 42, no. 3 (2019): 287–307.

Da Costa, Jade Crimson Rose. "Pride Parades in Queer Times: Disrupting Time, Norms, and Nationhood in Canada." *Journal of Canadian Studies* 54, nos. 2–3 (2020): 434–58.

Dancy, T. Elon. "The Adultification of Black Boys." In *Trayvon Martin, Race, and American Justice: Writing Wrong,* edited by Kenneth J. Fasching-Varner, Rema E. Reynolds, Katrice A. Albert, and Lori L. Martin, 49–55. Rotterdam: Sense Publishers, 2014.

Davis, Wendy N. "'Sext' Education: States Look for Ways to Chastise Teens for Bawdy Cellphone Shots." The National Pulse, *ABA Journal,* May 2011. https://www.abajournal.com/magazine/article/sext_education.

de Vogue, Ariane. "Meet Gavin Grimm, the Transgender Student at the Center of the Bathroom Debate." *CNN,* September 8, 2016. https://www.cnn.com/2016/09/08/politics/transgender-bathroom-issues-gavin-grimm/index.html.

de Vogue, Ariane, and Chandelis Duster. "Supreme Court Gives Victory to Transgender Student Who Sued to Use Bathroom." *CNN Politics,* June 28, 2021. https://www.cnn.com/2021/06/28/politics/gavin-grimm-supreme-court/index.html.

DeChaine, D. Robert. "Bordering the Civic Imaginary: Alienization, Fence Logic, and the Minuteman Civil Defense Corps." *Quarterly Journal of Speech* 95, no. 1 (February 2009): 43–65.

Dehnert, Marco, Daniel C. Brouwer, and Lore/tta LeMaster. "Anti-Normativity under Duress: An Intersectional Intervention in Queer Rhetoric." In *The Routledge Handbook of Queer Rhetoric,* edited by Jacqueline Rhodes and Jonathan Alexander, 319–27. New York: Routledge, 2022.

Del Rey, Rosario, et al. "Sexting among Adolescents: The Emotional Impact and Influence of the Need for Popularity." *Frontiers in Psychology* 10 (2019). https://doi.org/10.3389/fpsyg.2019.01828.

D'Emilio, John, and Estelle B. Freedman. *Intimate Matters: A History of Sexuality in America*. 2nd ed. Chicago: University of Chicago Press, 1997.

Dir, Allyson L., Ayca Coskunpinar, Jennifer L. Steiner, and Melissa A. Cyders. "Understanding Differences in Sexting Behaviors across Gender, Relationship Status, and Sexual Identity, and the Role of Expectancies in Sexting." *Cyberpsychology, Behavior, and Social Networking* 16, no. 8 (2013): 568–74.

Dixon, Travis L. "Good Guys Are Still Always in White? Positive Change and Continued Misrepresentation of Race and Crime on Local Television News." *Communication Research* 44, no. 6 (2017): 775–92.

Dobson, Amy Shields. "Sexting in Context: Understanding Gendered Sexual Media Practices Beyond Inherent 'Risk' and 'Harm.'" In *Cybercrime and Its Victims*, edited by Elena Martellozzo and Emma A. Jane, 79–93. New York: Routledge, 2019.

Doucouré, Maïmouna. "I Directed 'Cuties.' This Is What You Need to Know about Modern Girlhood: We, As Adults, Have Not Given Children the Tools to Grow Up Healthy in Our Society." *Washington Post*, September 15, 2020. https://www.washingtonpost.com/opinions/cuties-director-maimouna-doucoure-why-i-made-the-film/2020/09/15/7e0ee406-f78b-11ea-a275-1a2c2d36e1f1_story.html.

———. "Why I Made Cuties." Netflix, 2020.

Douglas, Edward. "Interview: Bully Director Lee Hirsch." *Coming Soon*, March 26, 2012. https://www.comingsoon.net/movies/features/88160-interview-bully-director-lee-hirsch.

Draper, Nora R. A. "Is Your Teen at Risk? Discourses of Adolescent Sexting in United States Television News." *Journal of Children and Media* 6, no. 2 (2012): 221–36.

Duane, Anna Mae. *Suffering Childhood in Early America: Violence, Race, and the Making of the Child Victim*. Athens: University of Georgia Press, 2010.

Durber, Dean. "The Paedophile and 'I.'" *Media International Australia* 127, no. 1 (2008): 57–70.

Durham, M. Gigi. *The Lolita Effect: The Media Sexualization of Young Girls and What We Can Do About It*. Woodstock, NY: Overlook Press, 2008.

Dyer, Hannah. "Queer Futurity and Childhood Innocence: Beyond the Injury of Development." *Global Studies of Childhood* 7, no. 3 (2017): 290–302.

Dyer, Richard. *The Matter of Images: Essays on Representations*. New York: Routledge, 2013.

Eckes, Suzanne E. "The Restroom and Locker Room Wars: Where to Pee or Not to Pee." *Journal of LGBT Youth* 14, no. 3 (2017): 247–65.

Edelman, Lee. *No Future: Queer Theory and the Death Drive*. Durham, NC: Duke University Press, 2004.

"Education Secretary Calls for Tolerance in Response to Bullying, Suicides of Gay Teens." *LGBTQ Nation*, October 1, 2010. https://www.lgbtqnation.com/2010/10/education-secretary-calls-for-tolerance-in-response-to-bullying-suicides-of-gay-teens/.

Egan, R. Danielle. *Becoming Sexual: A Critical Appraisal of the Sexualization of Girls*. Cambridge: Polity Press, 2013.

———. "Sexualizing Girl Troubles." *Contexts* 11, no. 2 (Spring 2012): 56–57.

Elliott, Sinikka. *Not My Kid: What Parents Believe about the Sex Lives of Their Teenagers*. New York: New York University Press, 2012.

Ellison, Treva, Marshall (Kai M.) Green, Matt Richardson, and C. Riley Snorton. "We Got Issues: Toward a Black Trans*/Studies." *TSQ: Transgender Studies Quarterly* 4, no. 2 (2017): 162–69.

Elman, Julie Passanante. *Chronic Youth: Disability, Sexuality, and U.S. Media Cultures of Rehabilitation.* New York: New York University Press, 2014.

Eng, David. *The Feeling of Kinship: Queer Liberalism and the Racialization of Intimacy.* Durham, NC: Duke University Press, 2010.

Epstein, Rebecca, Jamilia J. Blake, and Thalia González. "Girlhood Interrupted: The Erasure of Black Girls' Childhood." Georgetown Law Center on Poverty and Inequality.

"Exploring the Process of Pollination." *Perfect Bee: Your First Beehive and Beyond.* https://www.perfectbee.com/learn-about-bees/the-science-of-bees/exploring-the-process-of-pollination.

Fanon, Franz. *The Wretched of the Earth.* Translated by R. Philcox. New York: Grove Press, 2008 [1961].

"Federal Laws." StopBullying.gov. https://www.stopbullying.gov/resources/laws/federal.

Ferguson, Roderick A. *One-Dimensional Queer.* Cambridge: Polity Press, 2019.

Fine, Michelle. "Sexuality, Schooling, and Adolescent Females: The Missing Discourse of Desire." *Harvard Educational Review* 58, no. 1 (February 1988): 29–54.

Fine, Michelle, and Sara I. McClelland. "Sexuality Education and Desire: Still Missing after All These Years." *Harvard Educational Review* 76, no. 3 (Fall 2006): 297–338.

Fischel, Joseph J. "Transcendent Homosexuals and Dangerous Sex Offenders: Sexual Harm and Freedom in the Judicial Imaginary." *Duke Journal of Gender Law and Policy* 17 (2010): 277–311.

Fischer, Mia. "Piss(ed): The Biopolitics of the Bathroom." *Communication, Culture & Critique* 12 (2019): 397–415.

———. *Terrorizing Gender: Transgender Visibility and the Surveillance Practices of the U.S. Security State.* Lincoln: University of Nebraska Press, 2019.

Fitzpatrick, Katie, and Hayley McGlashan. "'Some Teachers Are Homophobic, You Know, Because They Just Don't Know Any Better': Students Reimagining Power Relations in Schools." In *Youth, Sexuality and Sexual Citizenship,* edited by Peter Aggleton, Rob Cover, Deana Leahy, Daniel Marshall, and Mary Lou Rasmussen, 263–77. New York: Routledge, 2019.

Flores, Lisa A. "Between Abundance and Marginalization: The Imperative of Racial Rhetorical Criticism." *Review of Communication* 16, no. 1 (2016): 4–24.

———. "Towards an Insistent and Transformative Racial Rhetorical Criticism." *Communication and Critical/Cultural Studies* 15, no. 4 (2018): 349–57.

Freeman, Elizabeth. *Time Binds: Queer Temporalities, Queer Histories.* Durham, NC: Duke University Press, 2010.

Fremon, Celeste. "Why Did So Many of Our Boys Kill Themselves Last Month?" *Witness LA,* October 10, 2010. https://witnessla.com/why-did-so-many-of-our-boys-kill-themselves-last-month/.

Galarte, Francisco J. *Brown Trans Figurations: Rethinking Race, Gender, and Sexuality in Chicanx/Latinx Studies.* Austin: University of Texas Press, 2021.

Gandy, Imani. "How False Narratives of Margaret Sanger Are Being Used to Shame Black Women." *Rewire News,* August 20, 2015. https://rewire.news/article/2015/08/20/false-narratives-margaret-sanger-used-shame-black-women/.

Garmezy, Norman. "Vulnerability Research and the Issue of Primary Prevention." *American Journal of Orthopsychiatry* 41, no. 1 (1971): 101–16.

Gary-Smith, Mariotta, Cindy Lee Alves, Christine Harley, and Gabrielle Doyle. "Sex, Race, and Politics in the U.S.: A Call to Action to Address Racial Justice in Sexuality Education." *SIECUS: Sex Ed for Social Change,* 2022. https://siecus.org/resources/2022-racial-justice-resource/.

Gavin Grimm v. Gloucester County School Board. United States Court of Appeals for the Fourth Circuit, No. 19-1952 (2020).

Gent, Whitney. "When Homelessness Becomes a 'Luxury': Neutrality as an Obstacle to Counterpublic Rights Claims." *Quarterly Journal of Speech* 103, no. 3 (2017): 230–50.

Gibbs, Nancy. "The 100 Most Influential People in the World 2017." *Time,* April 20, 2017. https://time.com/magazine/us/4748217/may-1st-2017-vol-189-no-16-u-s/.

Gilbert, Jen, Jessica Fields, Laura Mamo, and Nancy Lesko. "Intimate Possibilities: The Beyond Bullying Project and Stories of LGBTQ Sexuality and Gender in US Schools." *Harvard Educational Review* 88, no. 2 (2018): 163–83.

Gilchrist, Kristen. "'Newsworthy' Victims? Exploring Differences in Canadian Local Press Coverage of Missing/Murdered Aboriginal and White Women." *Feminist Media Studies* 10, no. 4 (2010): 373–90.

Gill-Peterson, Jules. *Histories of the Transgender Child.* Minneapolis: University of Minnesota Press, 2018.

Gladden, R. M., A. M. Vivolo-Kantor, M. E. Hamburger, and C. D. Lumpkin. "Bullying Surveillance among Youths: Uniform Definitions for Public Health and Recommended Data Elements." Version 1.0. Atlanta, GA; National Center for Injury Prevention and Control, Centers for Disease Control and Prevention and U.S. Department of Education, 2014.

Gloucester County School Board (GCSB) meeting minutes, November 11, 2014. https://pub-gloucesterva.escribemeetings.com/FileStream.ashx?DocumentId=1027.

Gloucester County School Board (GCSB) meeting, December 9, 2014. https://pub-gloucesterva.escribemeetings.com/Players/ISIStandAlonePlayer.aspx?Id=a7e4ed07-1735-2513-4f68-7b8ee03799a6. Video recording.

Gloucester County School Board (GCSB) meeting, November 11, 2014. https://pub-gloucesterva.escribemeetings.com/Players/ISIStandAlonePlayer.aspx?Id=0a771f9f-9611-5efa-487a-9d5aeob47fee.

"Gloucester County, VA." *DataUSA.* https://datausa.io/profile/geo/gloucester-county-va/#demographics.

Godsoe, Cynthia. "#MeToo and the Myth of the Juvenile Sex Offender." *Ohio State Journal of Criminal Law* 17, no. 2 (Spring 2020): 335–60.

Goff, Phillip Atiba, et al. "The Essence of Innocence: Consequences of Dehumanizing Black Children." *Journal of Personality and Social Psychology* 106, no. 4 (2014): 526–45.

Goldenberg, Tamar, Laura Jadwin-Cakmak, Elliot Popoff, Sari L. Reisner, Bré A. Campbell, and Gary W. Harper. "Stigma, Gender Affirmation, and Primary Healthcare Use among Black Transgender Youth." *Journal of Adolescent Health* 65, no. 4 (2019): 483–90.

Gomez, Logan Rae. "Temporal Containment and the Singularity of Anti-Blackness: Saying Her Name in and across Time." *Rhetoric Society Quarterly* 51, no. 3 (2021): 182–92.

Gossett, Che, and Juliana Huxtable. "Existing in the World: Blackness at the Edge of Trans Visibility." In *Trap Door: Trans Cultural Production and the Politics of Visibility,* edited by Reina Gossett, Eric A. Stanley, and Johanna Burton, 39–55. Cambridge: MIT Press, 2017.

Gossett, Che. "Žižek's Trans/Gender Trouble." *Los Angeles Review of Books,* September 13, 2016. https://www.lareviewofbooks.org/article/zizeks-transgender-trouble/.

Gossett, Reina, Eric A. Stanley, and Johanna Burton, eds. *Trap Door: Trans Cultural Production and the Politics of Visibility*. Cambridge: MIT Press, 2017.

Graves, Lucia. "Gay Teen Suicides Pervasive, a 'Hidden Problem': Expert." *HuffPost*, October 22, 2010. https://www.huffpost.com/entry/gay-teen-suicides-a-hidden-problem_n_772707.

Gray, Mary. "It Doesn't Get Better for Anyone If We Don't Make It Better for Everyone." *Queer Country*, March 4, 2011. https://web.archive.org/web/20110403235434/http://queercountry.fromthesquare.org/.

Green, Erica L., Mark Walker, and Eliza Shapiro. "'A Battle for the Souls of Black Girls.'" *New York Times*, October 1, 2020. https://www.nytimes.com/2020/10/01/us/politics/black-girls-school-discipline.html.

Green, Marshall (Kai M.). "Troubling the Waters: Mobilizing a Trans* Analytic." In *No Tea, No Shade: New Writings in Black Queer Studies*, edited by E. Patrick Johnson, 65–82. Durham, NC: Duke University Press, 2016.

Green, Marshall (Kai M.), and Marquis Bey. "Self-Love." In *Gender: Love*, edited by Jennifer C. Nash, 107–19. New York: Macmillan, 2016.

Guerrero, Lisa. "Can the Subaltern Shop? The Commodification of Difference in the *Bratz* Dolls." *Cultural Studies ↔ Critical Methodologies* 9, no. 2 (April 2009): 186–96.

Gumbs, Alexis Pauline. *Undrowned: Black Feminist Lessons from Marine Mammals*. Chico, CA: AK Press, 2020.

Gupta, Neeru "Nina," and Suzann M. Wilcox. "Transgender Students and Title IX: Biden Administration Signals Shift." *National Law Review* 11, no. 327 (November 23, 2021). https://www.natlawreview.com/article/transgender-students-and-title-ix-biden-administration-signals-shift.

Gutierrez-Maldonado, Ricky. "Lawrence 'Larry' King and Too Muchness: Complicating Sexual Citizenship through the Embodied Practices of a Queer/Trans Student of Colour." In *Youth, Sexuality and Sexual Citizenship*, edited by Peter Aggleton, Rob Cover, Deana Leahy, Daniel Marshall, and Mary Lou Rasmussen, 57–70. New York: Routledge, 2019.

Guttmacher Institute. "Federally Funded Abstinence-Only Programs: Harmful and Ineffective." May 2021. https://www.guttmacher.org/fact-sheet/abstinence-only-programs.

———. "Federally Funded Sex Education: Strengthening and Expanding Evidence-Based Programs." June 2021. https://www.guttmacher.org/fact-sheet/sex-education.

———. "Sex and HIV Education." July 1, 2021. https://www.guttmacher.org/state-policy/explore/sex-and-hiv-education.

Hains, Rebecca C. "An Afternoon of Productive Play with Problematic Dolls: The Importance of Foregrounding Children's Voices in Research." *Girlhood Studies* 5, no. 1 (Summer 2012): 121–40.

Halberstam, Jack. *In a Queer Time and Place: Transgender Bodies, Subcultural Lives*. New York: New York University Press, 2005.

———. "It Gets Worse . . ." *Social Text: Periscope,* November 20, 2010. https://journals.cdrs.columbia.edu/periscope/2010/11/it-gets-worse.php.

Hall, Ashley R. "Slippin' in and out of Frame: An Afrafuturist Feminist Orientation to Black Women and American Citizenship." *Quarterly Journal of Speech* 106, no. 3 (2020): 341–51.

Hamill, Sean D. "Students Sue Prosecutor in Cellphone Photos Case." *New York Times*, March 26, 2009. https://www.nytimes.com/2009/03/26/us/26sextext.html.

Harris, Anne, and David Farrington. "'It Gets Narrower': Creative Strategies for Re-broadening Queer Peer Education." *Sex Education* 14, no. 2 (2014): 144–58.

Harris, Leslie J. "'Whores' and 'Hottentots': Protection of (White) Women and White Supremacy in Anti-suffrage Rhetoric." *Quarterly Journal of Speech* 106, no. 3 (2020): 253–57.

Hartman, Saidiya. "The Belly of the World: A Note on Black Women's Labors." *Souls* 18, no. 1 (2016): 166–73.

Hasian, Marouf, Jr., Celeste Michelle Condit, and John Louis Lucaites. "The Rhetorical Boundaries of 'the Law': A Consideration of the Rhetorical Culture of Legal Practice and the Case of the 'Separate but Equal' Doctrine." *Quarterly Journal of Speech* 82, no. 4 (November 1996): 323–42.

Hasinoff, Amy Adele. *Sexting Panic: Rethinking Criminalization, Privacy, and Consent*. Urbana: University of Illinois Press, 2015.

Hector, Alley. "Oregon Sex Crime Laws Call a Young Queer a 'Child Pornographer.'" qPDX.com, December 2, 2010. https://archive.qpdx.com/2010/12/oregon-sex-crimes-laws-call-a-young-queer-a-child-pornographers/.

Henning, Kristin. *The Rage of Innocence: How America Criminalizes Black Youth*. New York: Vintage Books, 2021.

Hesford, Wendy S. *Violent Exceptions: Children's Human Rights and Humanitarian Rhetorics*. Columbus: The Ohio State University Press, 2021.

Hesse, Monica. "Cuties on Netflix Is an Unflinching Look at What It Means to Be a Preteen Girl." *Washington Post*, September 17, 2020. https://www.washingtonpost.com/lifestyle/style/cuties-is-an-unflinching-look-at-what-it-means-to-be-a-preteen-girl-no-wonder-people-cant-handle-it/2020/09/16/42fa1bc2-f783-11ea-a275-1a2c2d36e1f1_story.html.

Hester, Scarlett L., and Catherine R. Squires. "Who Are We Working For? Recentering Black Feminism." *Communication and Critical/Cultural Studies* 15, no. 4 (2018): 343–48.

Hill, Annie. "Producing the Crisis: Human Trafficking and Humanitarian Interventions." *Women's Studies in Communication* 41, no. 4 (2018): 315–19.

Hill Collins, Patricia. *Black Feminist Thought: Knowledge, Consciousness, and the Politics of Empowerment*. New York: Routledge, 1990.

Hohmann, James. "Please, Go On." *Washington Post*, July 2, 2021. https://www.washingtonpost.com/podcasts/please-go-on/gavin-grimm-on-a-watershed-moment-in-the-fight-for-transgender-rights/.

Holmes, Laura Graham, and Gabrielle Doyle. "Comprehensive Sex Education for Youth with Disabilities: A Call to Action." *SIECUS: Sex Ed for Social Change* (2021). https://siecus.org/resources/comprehensive-sex-education-for-youth-with-disabilities/.

Holmes, Linda. "'Bully' Problems: The MPAA Gives a Scarlet 'R' to a Thoughtful Documentary." NPR, February 24, 2012. https://www.npr.org/2012/02/24/147347673/bully-problems-the-mpaa-gives-a-scarlet-r-to-a-thoughtful-documentary.

Honig, Bonnie. *Democracy and the Foreigner*. Princeton, NJ: Princeton University Press, 2001.

hooks, bell. *Talking Back: Thinking Feminist, Thinking Black*. Boston: South End Press, 1989.

Horak, Laura. "Trans on YouTube: Intimacy, Visibility, Temporality." *TSQ: Transgender Studies Quarterly* 1, no. 4 (November 2014): 572–85.

"How the G.O.P. Picked Trans Kids as a Rallying Cry." *The Daily*, June 1, 2023. https://www.nytimes.com/2023/06/01/podcasts/the-daily/anti-trans-bills.html.

Howorth, Claire. "Raymond Chase Becomes Fifth Suicide Victim." *Daily Beast*, October 2, 2010. https://www.thedailybeast.com/raymond-chase-becomes-fifth-suicide-victim.

Hsu, V. Jo. *Constellating Home: Trans and Queer Asian American Rhetorics*. Columbus: The Ohio State University Press, 2022.

———. "Irreducible Damage: The Affective Drift of Race, Gender, and Disability in Anti-Trans Rhetorics." *Rhetoric Society Quarterly* 52, no. 1 (2022): 62–77.

Hubbard, Jeremy. "Fifth Gay Teen Suicide in Three Weeks Sparks Debate." *ABC News,* October 3, 2010. https://abcnews.go.com/US/gay-teen-suicide-sparks-debate/story?id=11788128.

Humbach, John A. "'Sexting' and the First Amendment." *Hastings Constitutional Law Quarterly* 37 (2010): 433–86.

It Gets Better Project. "How It All Got Started." https://itgetsbetter.org/how-it-all-got-started-2/.

Jarratt, Susan C. "Editor's Message." *Rhetoric Society Quarterly* 47, no. 1 (2017): 1–2.

Jaworski, Katrina. *The Gender of Suicide: Knowledge Production, Theory and Suicidology.* New York: Routledge, 2014.

Jensen, Robin E. *Dirty Words: The Rhetoric of Public Sex Education, 1870–1924.* Urbana: University of Illinois Press, 2010.

Johnson, Amber L., and Lore/tta LeMaster, *Gender Futurity, Intersectional Autoethnography: Embodied Theorizing from the Margins.* New York: Routledge, 2020.

Johnson, E. Patrick. "Put a Little Honey in My Sweet Tea: Oral History as Quare Performance." *Women's Studies Quarterly* 44, no. 3/4 (Fall/Winter 2016): 51–67.

Johnson, Paul Elliott. "The Art of Masculine Victimhood: Donald Trump's Demagoguery." *Women's Studies in Communication* 40, no. 3 (2017): 229–50.

———. "Walter White(ness) Lashes Out: Breaking Bad and Male Victimage." *Critical Studies in Media Communication* 34, no. 1 (2017): 14–28.

Jones, Alexis. "'Black Women Deserve Great Sex' Is the Motto That Keeps This Wellness Platform Running." *Popsugar,* August 10, 2022. https://www.popsugar.com/fitness/kimbritive-sex-positive-company-interview-48859051.

Jones, Nikki. *Between Good and Ghetto: African American Girls and Inner City Violence.* New Brunswick, NJ: Rutgers University Press, 2009.

Kaiser Family Foundation (KFF). "Abstinence Education Programs: Definition, Funding, and Impact on Teen Sexual Behavior." June 1, 2018. https://www.kff.org/womens-health-policy/fact-sheet/abstinence-education-programs-definition-funding-and-impact-on-teen-sexual-behavior/.

Kanjere, Anastasia. "Defending Race Privilege on the Internet: How Whiteness Uses Innocence Discourse Online." *Information, Communication & Society* 22, no. 14 (2019): 2156–70.

Karaian, Lara. "Policing 'Sexting': Responsibilization, Respectability and Sexual Subjectivity in Child Protection/Crime Prevention Responses to Teenagers' Digital Sexual Expression." *Theoretical Criminology* 18, no. 3 (2014): 282–99.

Katz, Jackson, and Sut Jhally. "The National Conversation in the Wake of Littleton Is Missing the Mark." *Boston Globe,* May 2, 1999. http://www.sutjhally.com/articles/missingthemark/.

Katz, Jennifer, Christine Merrilees, Jill C. Hoxmeier, and Marisa Motisi. "White Female Bystanders' Responses to a Black Woman at Risk for Incapacitated Sexual Assault." *Psychology of Women Quarterly* 41, no. 2 (2017): 273–85.

Kaufman, Gil. "Laverne Cox Called Out Gavin Grimm during the Grammy Awards: Who Is He?" *Billboard,* February 13, 2017. https://www.billboard.com/articles/news/grammys/7686420/laverne-cox-called-out-gavin-grimm-grammy-awards-who-is-he.

Keeling, Kara. *Queer Times, Black Futures.* New York: New York University Press, 2019.

Kelly, Casey Ryan. "Chastity for Democracy: Surplus Repression and the Rhetoric of Sex Education." *Quarterly Journal of Speech* 102, no. 4 (2016): 353–75.

———. "The Wounded Man: Foxcatcher and the Incoherence of White Masculine Victimhood." *Communication and Critical/Cultural Studies* 15, no. 2 (2018): 161–78.

Kessler, David. "The Grief of Bullycide." CNN, October 4, 2010. https://www.cnn.com/2010/LIVING/10/04/0.grief.of.bullycide/index.html.

Kim, Richard. "Against 'Bullying' or On Loving Queer Kids." *The Nation*, October 6, 2010. https://www.thenation.com/article/archive/against-bullying-or-loving-queer-kids/.

KIMBRITIVE. "About." https://www.kimbritive.com/about.

———. "How to Prep for Your Annual Wellness Visit." https://www.kimbritive.com/the-blog/annual-wellness-visit.

——— (@kimbritive). "I trust my embodied wisdom." Instagram post, March 24, 2023. https://www.instagram.com/p/CqLlxuvuAOB/?igsh=Z2FtMG01aXR6MnRu.

———. "What's Your Sexual Wellness Regimen?" https://www.kimbritive.com/the-blog/whats-your-sexual-wellness-regimen.

———. "Work with Us." https://www.kimbritive.com/work-with-us.

———. "Workshops + Events for Every Body." https://www.kimbritive.com/work-with-us.

———. "Your Sexual Wellness Regimen." https://www.kimbritive.com/opt-in.

Knibbs, Kate. "How Cuties Got Caught in a Gamergate-Style Internet Clash." *Wired*, September 15, 2020. https://www.wired.com/story/cuties-netflix-internet-clash/.

Koivunen, Anu, Katariina Kyrölä, and Ingrid Ryberg, *The Power of Vulnerability: Mobilising Affect in Feminist, Queer and Anti-Racist Media Cultures*. Manchester: Manchester University Press, 2018.

Kralik, Joellen. "'Bathroom Bill' Legislative Tracking." National Conference of State Legislatures (NCSL), October 24, 2019. https://www.ncsl.org/research/education/-bathroom-bill-legislative-tracking635951130.aspx#3.

Krutzsch, Brett. *Dying to Be Normal: Gay Martyrs and the Transformation of American Sexual Politics*. New York: Oxford University Press, 2019.

———. "A History of the 'It Gets Better' Campaign." *Oxford Academic*, June 28, 2019. https://medium.com/humanities-unveiled/it-gets-better-campaign-history-e3c5500cobba.

Kunstman, J. W., and E. A. Plant. "Racing to Help: Racial Bias in High Emergency Helping Situations." *Journal of Personality and Social Psychology* 95, no. 6 (2008): 1499–510.

Lacy, Michael G. "White Innocence Myths in Citizen Discourse, the Progressive Era (1974–1988)." *Howard Journal of Communications* 21 (2010): 20–39.

LaFerla, Ruth. "Underdressed and Hot: Dolls Moms Don't Love." *New York Times*, October 26, 2003. https://www.nytimes.com/2003/10/26/style/noticed-underdressed-and-hot-dolls-moms-don-t-love.html.

Lakshmin, Pooja. *Real Self-Care: A Transformative Program for Redefining Wellness (Crystals, Cleanses, and Bubble Baths Not Included)*. New York: Penguin Random House, 2023.

Lamb, Sharon, and Lyn Mikel Brown. *Packaging Girlhood: Rescuing Our Daughters from Marketers' Schemes*. New York: St. Martin's, 2006.

Lang, Nico. "2022 Was the Worst Year Ever for Anti-Trans Bills. How Did We Get Here?" *them*, December 29, 2022. https://www.them.us/story/2022-anti-trans-bills-history-explained.

Levin, Diane E., and Jean Kilbourne. *So Sexy So Soon: The New Sexualized Childhood and What Parents Can Do to Protect Their Kids*. New York: Ballantine Books, 2009.

Levin, Sam. "'A Talented, Goofy Kid': Family of Ryan Gainer, Autistic Teen Killed by Police, Speak Out." *The Guardian*, March 21, 2024. https://www.theguardian.com/us-news/2024/mar/21/ryan-gainer-autistic-teen-police-killing-california.

Levine, Judith. *Harmful to Minors: The Perils of Protecting Children from Sex.* Minneapolis: University of Minnesota Press, 2002.

Library of Congress. "A Century of Lawmaking for a New Nation: U.S. Congressional Documents and Debates, 1774–1875." https://memory.loc.gov/cgi-bin/ampage?collId=llsl&fileName=014/llsl014.db&recNum=058.

Lippman, Julia R., and Scott W. Campbell. "Damned If You Do, Damned If You Don't . . . If You're a Girl: Relational and Normative Contexts of Adolescent Sexting in the United States." *Journal of Children and Media* 8, no. 4 (2014): 371–86.

Lorang, Melissa R., Dale E. McNiel, and Renée L. Binder. "Minors and Sexting: Legal Implications." *Journal of the American Academy of Psychiatry and the Law* 44, no. 1 (2016): 73–81.

Lorde, Audre. *A Burst of Light: Essays.* Garden City, NY: Ixia Press, 2017 [1988].

———. *Sister Outsider.* Trumansburg, NY: Crossing Press, 1984.

Lu, Jessica H., and Catherine Knight Steele. "'Joy Is Resistance': Cross-Platform Resilience and (Re)invention of Black Oral Culture Online." *Information, Communication & Society* 22, no. 6 (2019): 823–37.

Lydon, Jason, with Kamaria Carrington, Hana Low, Reed Miller, and Mahsa Yazdy. "Coming Out of Concrete Closets: A Report on Black & Pink's National LGBTQ Prisoner Survey." Black & Pink, October 2015. https://www.blackandpink.org/.

Maher, Michelle. "Unlawful Justice: The Story of Antjuanece Brown and Jolene Jenkins." YouTube, January 20, 2012. https://www.youtube.com/watch?v=ig9Y5wcdry8.

Malatino, Hil. "Future Fatigue: Trans Intimacies and Trans Presents (or How to Survive the Interregnum)." *TSQ: Transgender Studies Quarterly* 6, no. 4 (November 2019): 635–58.

MAP: Movement Advancement Project. "Healthcare Laws and Policies: Bans on Best Practice Medical Care for Transgender Youth." October 12, 2023. https://www.lgbtmap.org/equality-maps/healthcare/youth_medical_care_bans.

Marshall, D. "Popular Culture, the 'Victim' Trope and Queer Youth Analytics." *International Journal of Qualitative Studies in Education* 23, no. 1 (2010): 65–85.

Mason, Carol. "Opposing Abortion to Protect Women: Transnational Strategy since the 1990s." *Signs: Journal of Women in Culture and Society* 44, no. 3 (2019): 665–92.

Mason, Myles W. "Embracing a 'Big, Black Ass' at a 'Tiny, Tiny Ass Desk': Lizzo's Affective Performance of Choric Self-Love." *WSQ: Women's Studies Quarterly* 50, nos. 1–2 (Spring/Summer 2022): 267–82.

McCann, Bryan J. "Lonely Young American: Queer Terrorist Recruitment and the Trope of the Child." *QED: A Journal in GLBTQ Worldmaking* 7, no. 2 (2020): 25–47.

McCann, Hannah. "Beyond the Visible: Rethinking Femininity through the Femme Assemblage." *European Journal of Women's Studies* 25, no. 3 (2018): 278–92.

McClelland, Sara I., and Michelle Fine. "Over-Sexed and Under Surveillance: Adolescent Sexualities, Cultural Anxieties, and Thick Desire." In *The Politics of Pleasure in Sexuality Education,* edited by Louisa Allen, Mary Lou Rasmussen, and Kathleen Quinlivan, 12–34. New York: Routledge, 2014.

McCormick, Samuel. "Arguments from Analogy and Beyond: The Persuasive Artistry of Local American Civic Life." *Quarterly Journal of Speech* 100, no. 2 (2014): 186–212.

McCune, Jeffrey Q., Jr. *Sexual Discretion: Black Masculinity and the Politics of Passing.* Chicago: University of Chicago Press, 2014.

McKinley, Jesse. "Suicides Put Light on Pressures of Gay Teenagers." *New York Times,* October 4, 2010. https://www.nytimes.com/2010/10/04/us/04suicide.html.

McNeal, Stephanie. "The Netflix Movie 'Cuties' Has Become the Latest Target of #SaveTheChildren Conspiracy Theorists." *BuzzFeed News,* September 11, 2020. https://www.buzzfeednews.com/article/stephaniemcneal/netflix-cuties-qanon-target.

Meiners, Erica R. *For the Children?: Protecting Innocence in a Carceral State.* Minneapolis: University of Minnesota Press, 2016.

———. "The Problem Child: Provocations toward Dismantling the Carceral State." *Harvard Educational Review* 87, no. 1 (Spring 2017): 122–56.

Merriam-Webster.com Dictionary. S.v. "figuration." Accessed July 29, 2021. https://www.merriam-webster.com/dictionary/figuration.

———. S.v. "figure." Accessed July 29, 2021. https://www.merriam-webster.com/dictionary/figure.

Michaels, Samantha. "We Tracked Down the Lawyers Behind the Recent Wave of Anti-Trans Bathroom Bills." *Mother Jones,* April 25, 2016. https://www.motherjones.com/politics/2016/04/alliance-defending-freedom-lobbies-anti-lgbt-bathroom-bills/.

Mills, Robert Elliot. "The Pirate and the Sovereign: Negative Identification and the Constitutive Rhetoric of the Nation-State." *Rhetoric & Public Affairs* 17, no. 1 (Spring 2014): 105–35.

Mitchell, Mary Niall. *Raising Freedom's Child: Black Children and Visions of the Future after Slavery.* New York: New York University Press, 2008.

Mittleman, Joel. "Sexual Orientation and School Discipline: New Evidence from a Population-Based Sample." *Educational Researcher* 47, no. 3 (2018): 181–90.

Mock, Janet. "Gavin Grimm." *Time,* April 20, 2017. https://time.com/collection-post/4742687/gavin-grimm/.

Mogul, Joey L., Andrea J. Ritchie, and Kay Whitlock. *Queer (In)Justice: The Criminalization of LGBT People in the United States.* Boston: Beacon Press, 2011.

Montgomery, James. "Rise Against's 'Make It Stop' Tackles Bullying, Suicide." *MTV News,* June 20, 2011. http://www.mtv.com/news/1666112/rise-against-make-it-stop-video/.

Moody, Erin. "Mother on Mission to Stop Bullying." *Citizens' Voice* (Wilkes-Barre, Pennsylvania), January 10, 2011. https://www.citizensvoice.com/news/mother-on-mission-to-stop-bullying/article_571e71e3-ea07-579c-97cf-83785c455678.html.

Moon, Dreama G., and Michelle A. Holling. "'White Supremacy in Heels': (White) Feminism, White Supremacy, and Discursive Violence." *Communication and Critical/Cultural Studies* 17, no. 2 (2020): 253–60.

Moore, Allison, and Paul Reynolds. *Childhood and Sexuality: Contemporary Issues and Debates.* London: Palgrave Macmillan, 2018.

Moran, Jeffrey P. *Teaching Sex: The Shaping of Adolescence in the 20th Century.* Cambridge, MA: Harvard University Press, 2000.

Morris, Edward W., and Brea L. Perry. "Girls Behaving Badly? Race, Gender and Subjective Evaluation in the Discipline of African American Girls." *Sociology of Education* 90, no. 2 (2017): 127–48.

Morris, Monique W. *Pushout: The Criminalization of Black Girls in Schools.* New York: The New Press, 2016.

———. "Race, Gender, and the School-to-Prison Pipeline: Expanding Our Discussion to Include Black Girls." New York: African American Policy Forum, 2012. https://schottfoundation.org/wp-content/uploads/Morris-Race-Gender-and-the-School-to-Prison-Pipeline.pdf.

Muñoz, José Esteban. *Cruising Utopia: The Then and There of Queer Futurity.* New York: New York University Press, 2009.

Murib, Zein. "Administering Biology: How 'Bathroom Bills' Criminalize and Stigmatize Trans and Gender Nonconforming People in Public Space." *Administrative Theory & Praxis* 42, no. 2 (2020): 153–71.

Musser, Amber Jamilla. *Sensual Excess: Queer Femininity and Brown Jouissance.* New York: New York University Press, 2018.

Nash, Jennifer C. "Practicing Love: Black Feminism, Love-Politics, and Post-Intersectionality." *Meridians: feminism, race, transnationalism* 11, no. 2 (2013): 1–24.

The National Center on Violence against Women in the Black Community. "Black Women and Sexual Assault." October 2018. https://ujimacommunity.org/wp-content/uploads/2018/12/Ujima-Womens-Violence-Stats-v7.4-1.pdf.

"New Film Takes an Intimate Look at School Bullying." NPR, March 13, 2012. https://www.npr.org/2012/03/13/148540633/new-film-takes-an-intimate-look-at-school-bullying.

Newman, Louise Michele. *White Women's Rights: The Racial Origins of Feminism in the United States.* New York: Oxford University Press, 1999.

Nirta, Caterina. *Marginal Bodies, Trans Utopias.* London: Routledge, 2017.

Nuyen, A. T. "The Role of Rhetorical Devices in Postmodernist Discourse." *Philosophy and Rhetoric* 25, no. 2 (1992): 183–94.

Nyong'o, Tavia. "Have You Seen His Childhood? Song, Screen, and the Queer Culture of the Child in Michael Jackson's Music." *Journal of Popular Music Studies* 23, no. 1 (2011): 40–57.

Ohi, Kevin. "Molestation 101: Child Abuse, Homophobia and the Boys of St. Vincent." *GLQ: A Journal of Lesbian and Gay Studies* 6, no. 2 (2000): 195–248.

Oliviero, Katie. *Vulnerability Politics: The Uses and Abuses of Precarity in Political Debate.* New York: New York University Press, 2018.

"On Anniversary of Billy Lucas' Suicide, Family Files Wrongful Death Lawsuit." *LGBTQ Nation*, September 9, 2012. https://www.lgbtqnation.com/2012/09/on-anniversary-of-billy-lucas-suicide-family-files-wrongful-death-lawsuit/.

Ore, Ersula J. *Lynching: Violence, Rhetoric, and American Identity.* Jackson: University Press of Mississippi, 2019.

Ore, Ersula, and Matthew Houdek. "Lynching in Times of Suffocation: Toward a Spatiotemporal Politics of Breathing." *Women's Studies in Communication* 43, no. 4 (2020): 443–58.

Oregonlaws.org. https://oregon.public.law/statutes/ors_chapter_163.

Orr, Lisa. "'Difference That Is Actually Sameness Mass-Reproduced': Barbie Joins the Princess Convergence." *Jeunesse: Young People, Texts, Cultures* 1, no. 1 (2009): 9–30.

Ott, Brian L., and Eric Aoki. "The Politics of Negotiating Public Tragedy: Media Framing of the Matthew Shepard Murder." *Rhetoric and Public Affairs* 5, no. 3 (Fall 2002): 483–505.

"Outlawing Trans Youth: State Legislatures and the Battle over Gender-Affirming Healthcare for Minors." *Harvard Law Review* 134, April 12, 2021.

Oxford English Dictionary. S.v. "figuration." Accessed August 2, 2021.

PACER. "Bullying Statistics." PACER.org. https://www.pacer.org/bullying/info/stats.asp.

Page, Morgan M. "One from the Vaults: Gossip, Access, and Trans History-Telling." In *Trap Door: Trans Cultural Production and the Politics of Visibility,* edited by Reina Gossett, Eric A. Stanley, and Johanna Burton, 135–46. Cambridge: MIT Press, 2017.

Pascoe, C. J. *Dude, You're a Fag: Masculinity and Sexuality in High School.* Berkeley: University of California Press, 2007.

Patchin, Justin W. "The Status of Sexting Laws across the United States." Cyberbullying Research Center, August 18, 2022. https://cyberbullying.org/the-status-of-sexting-laws-across-the-united-states.

Patchin, Justin W., and Sameer Hinduja. "It Is Time to Teach Safe Sexting." *Journal of Adolescent Health* 66 (2020): 140–43.

Patterson, GPat, and Leland G. Spencer. "Toward Trans Rhetorical Agency: A Critical Analysis of Trans Topics in Rhetoric and Composition and Communication Scholarship." *Peitho* 22, no. 4 (Summer 2020). https://cfshrc.org/article/toward-trans-rhetorical-agency-a-critical-analysis-of-trans-topics-in-rhetoric-composition-and-communication-scholarship/.

Paul, Pamela. *Pornified: How Pornography Is Transforming Our Lives, Our Relationships, and Our Families.* New York: Times Books, 2005.

Pearce, Ruth. *Understanding Trans Health: Discourse, Power and Possibility.* Bristol, UK: Bristol University Press, 2018.

Peskin, Melissa Fleschler, Christine M. Markham, Robert C. Addy, Ross Shegog, Melanie Thiel, and Susan R. Tortolero. "Prevalence and Patterns of Sexting among Ethnic Minority Urban High School Students." *Cyberpsychology, Behavior, and Social Networking* 16, no. 6 (2013): 454–59.

Philips, Rosemary R. "The Battle over Bathrooms: Schools, Courts, and Transgender Rights." *Theory in Action* 10, no. 4 (October 2017): 100–117.

Pierce, Charles P. "A Dangerous Law and the New Formula of Conservatism." *Esquire*, November 4, 2011. https://www.esquire.com/news-politics/politics/a11529/michigan-bullying-law-6542330/.

Pirius, Rebecca. "Oregon Statutory Rape Laws." *Criminal Defense Lawyer.* https://www.criminaldefenselawyer.com/resources/oregon-statutory-rape-laws.htm.

Planned Parenthood. "Our History." https://www.plannedparenthood.org/about-us/who-we-are/our-history.

Podlas, Kimberlianne. "The 'Legal Epidemiology' of the Teen Sexting Epidemic: How the Media Influenced a Legislative Outbreak." *Pittsburgh Journal of Technology Law & Policy* 12 (2012): 1–48.

Poster, Carol. "Being, Time, and Definition: Toward a Semiotics of Figural Rhetoric." *Philosophy & Rhetoric* 33, no. 2 (April 2000): 116–36.

Primack, Alvin J. "Youth Sexting and the First Amendment: Rhetoric and Child Pornography Doctrine in the Age of Translation." *New Media & Society* 20, no. 8 (2018): 2917–33.

Pryor, Jaclyn I. *Time Slips: Queer Temporalities, Contemporary Performance, and the Hole of History.* Evanston, IL: Northwestern University Press, 2017.

Puar, Jasbir K. "In the Wake of It Gets Better." *The Guardian*, November 16, 2010. https://www.theguardian.com/commentisfree/cifamerica/2010/nov/16/wake-it-gets-better-campaign.

———. *Terrorist Assemblages: Homonationalism in Queer Times.* Durham, NC: Duke University Press, 2007.

Rand, Erin J. "'Gay Boys Kill Themselves': The Queer Figuration of the Suicidal Gay Teen." In *Sexual Rhetorics: Methods, Identities, Publics*, edited by Jacqueline Rhodes and Jonathan Alexander, 175–87. New York: Routledge, 2016.

———. "PROTECTing the Figure of Innocence: Child Pornography Legislation and the Queerness of Childhood." *Quarterly Journal of Speech*, 105, no. 3 (2019): 251–72.

———. *Reclaiming Queer: Activist and Academic Rhetorics of Resistance.* Tuscaloosa: University of Alabama Press, 2014.

Randall, Liam. "Irreversible Damage: Trans Masculine Affectability and the White Family." In *The Routledge Handbook of Queer Rhetoric*, edited by Jacqueline Rhodes and Jonathan Alexander, 273–80. New York: Routledge, 2022.

Rattan, Aneeta, Cynthia S. Levine, Carol S. Dweck, and Jennifer L. Eberhardt. "Race and the Fragility of the Legal Distinction between Juveniles and Adults." *PLOS One* 7, no. 5 (2012): 1–5.

"Raymond Chase Commits Suicide, Fifth Gay Youth to Take Life in Three Weeks." *HuffPost*, October 1, 2010. https://www.huffpost.com/entry/raymond-chase-suicide_n_746989.

"Recent Youth Suicides Raise Concerns." *Los Angeles Daily News*, October 2, 2010. https://www.dailynews.com/2010/10/02/recent-youth-suicides-raise-concerns/.

Reed, Alison. "The Whiter the Bread, the Quicker You're Dead: Spectacular Absence and Post-Racialized Blackness in (White) Queer Theory." In *No Tea, No Shade: New Writings in Black Queer Studies*, edited by E. Patrick Johnson, 48–64. Durham, NC: Duke University Press, 2016.

Reed, Gabrielle. "How Black Women Are Empowering One Another to Talk Sexual Health." NBC News, August 12, 2021. https://www.nbcnews.com/news/nbcblk/black-women-are-empowering-one-another-talk-sexual-health-rcna1665.

Riedel, Samantha. "A Florida School's Transphobic Bathroom Policy Was Upheld by a Federal Appeals Court." *them*, January 4, 2023. https://www.them.us/story/drew-adams-florida-school-transphobic-bathroom-ban-upheld.

———. "Why Are Republicans So Obsessed With 'Grooming?'" *them*, April 7, 2022. https://www.them.us/story/republicans-conservatives-grooming-lgbtq-bills-dont-say-gay.

Rigney, Lester-Irabinna. "Aboriginal Child as Knowledge Producer: Bringing into Dialogue Indigenist Epistemologies and Culturally Responsive Pedagogies for Schooling." In *Routledge Handbook of Critical Indigenous Studies*, edited by Brendan Hokowhitu, Aileen Moreton-Robinson, Linda Tuhiwai-Smith, Chris Andersen, and Steve Larkin, 578–90. London: Routledge, 2020.

Riley, John. "Gavin's Story: Gavin Grimm Is the New Face of the Transgender Movement." *Metro Weekly*, May 12, 2016. https://www.metroweekly.com/2016/05/gavin-grimm-story/.

Ritchie, Andrea J. "#SayHerName: Racial Profiling and Police Violence against Black Women." *The Harbinger* 41 (August 11, 2016): 187–200.

Roberts, Dorothy. *Killing the Black Body: Race, Reproduction, and the Meaning of Liberty*. New York: Vintage Books, 1997.

———. *Torn Apart: How the Child Welfare System Destroys Black Families—and How Abolition Can Build a Safer World*. New York: Basic Books, 2022.

Robertson, Mary. *Growing Up Queer: Kids and the Remaking of LGBTQ Identity*. New York: New York University Press, 2019.

Robinson, Brandon Andrew, and Rachel M. Schmitz. "Beyond Resilience: Resistance in the Lives of LGBTQ Youth." *Sociology Compass* 15, no. 12 (2021): 1–15.

Robinson, Kerry H., and Cristyn Davies. "A History of Constructions of Child and Youth Sexualities: Innocence, Vulnerability, and the Construction of the Normative Citizen Subject." In *Youth Sexualities: Public Feelings and Contemporary Cultural Politics*, vol. 1, edited by Susan Talburt, 3–29. Santa Barbara, CA: Praeger, 2018.

Rodríguez, Juana María. *Sexual Futures, Queer Gestures, and Other Latina Longings*. New York: New York University Press, 2014.

Rofes, Eric. "Martyr-Target-Victim: Interrogating Narratives of Persecution and Suffering among Queer Youth." In *Youth and Sexualities: Pleasure, Subversion, and Insubordination in and out of Schools*, edited by Mary Louise Rasmussen, Eric Rofes, and Susan Talburt, 41–62. New York: Palgrave Macmillan, 2004.

Rolf, Jon E., and Meyer D. Glantz. "Resilience: An Interview with Norman Garmezy." In *Resilience and Development: Positive Life Adaptations*, edited by Glantz and Jeannette L. Johnson, 5–14. New York: Kluwer Academic/Plenum Publishers, 1999.

Rollo, Toby. "The Color of Childhood: The Role of the Child/Human Binary in the Production of Anti-Black Racism." *Journal of Black Studies* 49, no. 4 (2018): 307–29.

Ronan, Wyatt. "BREAKING: 2021 Becomes Record Year for Anti-Transgender Legislation." *Human Rights Campaign*, March 13, 2021. https://www.hrc.org/press-releases/breaking-2021-becomes-record-year-for-anti-transgender-legislation.

Rummler, Orion. "State Laws Restricting Rights of LGBTQ+ Youth Are Hurting Their Mental Health, Poll Shows." *The 19th*, January 19, 2023. https://19thnews.org/2023/01/lgbtq-mental-health-youth-laws/.

Russell, Stephen T. "Beyond Risk: Resilience in the Lives of Sexual Minority Youth." *Journal of Gay and Lesbian Issues in Education* 2, no. 3 (2005): 5–18.

"S.1689—Real Education and Access for Healthy Youth Act of 2021." Congress.gov. https://www.congress.gov/bill/117th-congress/senate-bill/1689/text.

Salamon, Gayle. *The Life and Death of Latisha King: A Critical Phenomenology of Transphobia*. New York: New York University Press, 2018.

Salas-SantaCruz, Omi. "Decoloniality & Trans* of Color Educational Criticism." *Theory, Research, and Action in Urban Education* 8, no. 1 (Spring 2023). https://traue.commons.gc.cuny.edu/decoloniality-trans-of-color-educational-criticism/.

Salazar, Philippe-Joseph. "Figures of the Republic." *Advances in the History of Rhetoric* 9, no. 1 (November 2006): 243–56.

Sánchez-Eppler, Karen. *Dependent States: The Child's Part in Nineteenth-Century American Culture*. Chicago: University of Chicago Press, 2005.

Santelli, John S., Leslie M. Kantor, Stephanie A. Grilo, Ilene S. Speizer, Laura D. Lindberg, Jennifer Heitel, Amy T. Schalet, Maureen E. Lyon, Amanda J. Mason-Jones, Terry McGovern, Craig J. Heck, Jennifer Rogers, and Mary A. Ott. "Abstinence-Only-Until-Marriage: An Updated Review of U.S. Policies and Programs and Their Impact." *Journal of Adolescent Health* 61 (2017): 273–80.

Sasse, Ryan. "The Case for Intersectionality: Supporting LGBTQ Youth amidst COVID-19." UNICEF USA, June 25, 2020. https://www.unicefusa.org/stories/case-intersectionality-supporting-lgbtq-youth-amidst-covid-19/37418.

Savage, Dan. "Bullied Gay Teenager Commits Suicide—Will His Tormentors Face Charges?" *The Stranger*, September 14, 2010. https://www.thestranger.com/news/2010/09/14/4880826/bullied-gay-teenager-commits-suicidewill-his-tormentors-face-charges.

Savin-Williams, Ritch C. *The New Gay Teenager*. Cambridge, MA: Harvard University Press, 2006.

"A School Board Will Pay $1.3M Over a Trans Student's Lawsuit against Its Bathroom Ban." NPR, August 27, 2021. https://www.npr.org/2021/08/27/1031640545/school-board-transgender-bathroom-policy-gavin-grimm.

Sedgwick, Eve Kosofsky. *Tendencies*. Durham, NC: Duke University Press, 1993.

———. *Touching Feeling: Affect, Pedagogy, Performativity*. Durham, NC: Duke University Press, 2003.

Setty, Emily. "A Rights-Based Approach to Youth Sexting: Challenging Risk, Shame, and the Denial of Rights to Bodily and Sexual Expression within Youth Digital Sexual Culture." *International Journal of Bullying Prevention* 1 (2019): 298–311.

"Sex and Tech: Results from a Survey of Teens and Young Adults." The National Campaign to Prevent Teen and Unplanned Pregnancy, 2008. https://apo.org.au/node/17127.

Sharpe, Christina. *In the Wake: On Blackness and Being.* Durham, NC: Duke University Press, 2016.

SIECUS: Sex Ed for Social Change. "2023 State of Sex Education Legislative Look-Ahead." January 2023. https://siecus.org/wp-content/uploads/2023/01/2023-State-of-Sex-Education-Legislative-Look-Ahead.pdf.

———. "A Call to Action: LGBTQ+ Youth Need Inclusive Sex Education." May 2021. https://siecus.org/a-call-to-action-lgbtq-youth-need-inclusive-sex-education/.

———. "History of Sex Education." https://siecus.org/resources/history-of-sex-ed/.

———. "The Real Education and Access for Healthy Youth Act of 2021." https://siecus.org/resources/reahya-fact-sheet/.

Singh, Anneliese A. "Transgender Youth of Color and Resilience: Negotiating Oppression and Finding Support." *Sex Roles* 68, no. 11/12 (2013): 690–702.

Slater, Jenny, Charlotte Jones, and Lisa Procter. "School Toilets: Queer, Disabled Bodies and Gendered Lessons of Embodiment." *Gender and Education* 30, no. 8 (2018): 951–65.

Slovic, Beth. "Sext Crimes." *Willamette Week,* November 30, 2010. http://www.wweek.com/portland/article-16544-sext-crimes.html.

Smith, Tracy. "Bullying: Words Can Kill." CBS News, September 16, 2011. https://www.cbsnews.com/news/bullying-words-can-kill/.

Snorton, C. Riley, and Jin Haritaworn. "Trans Necropolitics: A Transnational Reflection on Violence, Death, and the Trans of Color Afterlife." In *The Transgender Studies Reader,* edited by Susan Stryker and Aren Aizura, 66–76. 2nd ed. New York: Routledge, 2013.

Snorton, C. Riley. *Black on Both Sides: A Racial History of Trans Identity.* Minneapolis: University of Minnesota Press, 2017.

———. *Nobody Is Supposed to Know: Black Sexuality on the Down Low.* Minneapolis: University of Minnesota Press, 2014.

Sobande, Francesca, and Krys Osei. "An African City: Black Women's Creativity, Pleasure, Diasporic (Dis)Connections and Resistance through Aesthetic and Media Practices and Scholarship." *Communication, Culture & Critique* 13 (2020): 204–21.

Somerville, Siobhan B. "Queer Loving." *GLQ: A Journal of Lesbian and Gay Studies* 11, no. 3 (2005): 335–70.

Southern Poverty Law Center. "Alliance Defending Freedom." https://www.splcenter.org/fighting-hate/extremist-files/group/alliance-defending-freedom.

Spade, Dean, Kai Lumumba Barrow, Yve Laris Cohen, and Kalaniopua Young. "Models of Futurity." In *Trap Door: Trans Cultural Production and the Politics of Visibility,* edited by Reina Gossett, Eric A. Stanley, and Johanna Burton, 321–37. Cambridge: MIT Press, 2017.

Spangler, Todd. "'Cuties' Controversy: Surge in Netflix Cancellations Was Short-Lived, Data Shows." *Variety,* September 25, 2020. https://variety.com/2020/digital/news/cuties-cancel-netflix-account-surge-data-1234783460/.

Spieldenner, Andrew R., and Cerise L. Glenn. "Scripting Hate Crimes: Victim, Space and Perpetrator Defining Hate." *Continuum: Journal of Media & Cultural Studies* 28, no. 1 (2014): 123–35.

Spillers, Hortense. "Mama's Baby, Papa's Maybe: An American Grammar Book." *Diacritics* 17, no. 2 (1987): 65–81.

Stanger-Hall, Kathrin F., and David W. Hall. "Abstinence-Only Education and Teen Pregnancy Rates: Why We Need Comprehensive Sex Education in the U.S." *PLOS One* 6, no. 10 (2011): e24658.

Staver, Sari. "Pride 2018: Grimm Recalls 'Isolating' Experience in Trans Bathroom Fight." *Bay Area Reporter*, June 21, 2018. https://www.ebar.com/news/news//261542.

Stempel, Jonathan. "U.S. Appeals Court Upholds Florida High School's Transgender Bathroom Ban." *Reuters*, December 30, 2022. https://www.reuters.com/world/us/us-appeals-court-upholds-florida-high-schools-transgender-bathroom-policy-2022-12-30/.

Stockton, Kathryn Bond. "The Queer Child Now and Its Paradoxical Global Effects." *GLQ* 22, no. 4 (2016): 505–39.

———. *The Queer Child, or Growing Sideways in the Twentieth Century*. Durham, NC: Duke University Press, 2009.

Students v. United States Department of Education. United States Department of Education Office of Civil Rights, No. 05-14-1055 (2015).

"Support Antjuanece Brown." December 8, 2010. https://antjuanecebrown.wordpress.com/.

Swed, Mark. "Gay Bullying Inspires Composer David Del Tredici's 'Bullycide.'" *Los Angeles Times*, August 15, 2013. https://www.latimes.com/entertainment/arts/culture/la-et-cm-david-del-tredici-bullycide-20130814-story.html.

Talbott, Margaret. "Department of Marketing: Little Hotties." *New Yorker*, December 4, 2006. http://www.newyorker.com/archive/2006/12/04/061204fa_fact_talbot.

Talburt, Susan. "Intelligibility and Narrating Queer Youth." In *Youth and Sexualities: Pleasure, Subversion, and Insubordination in and out of Schools*, edited by Mary Louise Rasmussen, Eric Rofes, and Susan Talburt, 17–39. New York: Palgrave Macmillan, 2004.

Talburt, Susan, and Mary Louise Rasmussen. "'After-Queer' Tendencies in Queer Research." *International Journal of Qualitative Studies in Education* 23, no. 1 (2010): 1–14.

Temkin, Deborah. "All 50 States Now Have a Bullying Law. Now What." *HuffPost*, April 27, 2015. https://www.huffpost.com/entry/all-50-states-now-have-a_b_7153114.

———. "Why Criminalizing Bullying Is the Wrong Approach." *HuffPost*, June 6, 2014. https://www.huffpost.com/entry/criminalizing-bullying-is-wrong_b_5460074.

Tinubu, Aramide. "'Cuties' Director Maïmouna Doucouré Speaks Out on the #CancelNetflix Controversy." *Zora*, September 10, 2020. https://zora.medium.com/the-director-in-the-middle-of-the-cancelnetflix-backlash-speaks-out-90b58f5afc64.

Tracy, Karen. *Challenges of Ordinary Democracy: A Case Study in Deliberation and Dissent*. University Park: Pennsylvania State University Press, 2010.

Trans Legislation Tracker. https://translegislation.com/. Accessed March 26, 2024.

The Trevor Project. "2022 National Survey on LGBTQ Youth Mental Health." https://www.thetrevorproject.org/survey-2022/#intro.

———. "Black LGBTQ Youth Mental Health." February 13, 2020. https://www.thetrevorproject.org/2020/02/13/research-brief-black-lgbtq-youth-mental-health/.

———. "Implications of COVID-19 for LGBTQ Youth Mental Health and Suicide Prevention." April 20, 2020. https://www.thetrevorproject.org/2020/04/03/implications-of-covid-19-for-lgbtq-youth-mental-health-and-suicide-prevention/.

———. "National Survey on LGBTQ Youth Mental Health 2021." https://www.thetrevorproject.org/survey-2021/.

Tristano, Michael, Jr. "Performing Queer of Color Joy through Collective Crisis: Resistance, Social Science, and How I Learned to Dance Again." *Cultural Studies ↔ Critical Methodologies* 22, no. 3 (2022): 276–81.

"Two More Gay Teen Suicide Victims—Raymond Chase, Cody Barker Mark 6 Deaths in September." *LGBTQ Nation,* October 1, 2010. https://www.lgbtqnation.com/2010/10/two-more-gay-teen-suicide-victims-raymond-chase-cody-barker-mark-6-deaths-in-september/.

United States Department of Education. "Analysis of State Bullying Laws and Policies." 2011. https://www2.ed.gov/rschstat/eval/bullying/state-bullying-laws/state-bullying-laws.pdf.

———. "Guidance Targeting Harassment Outlines Local and Federal Responsibility." October 26, 2010. https://web.archive.org/web/20101206081537/http://www.ed.gov/news/press-releases/guidance-targeting-harassment-outlines-local-and-federal-responsibility.

———. "Key Policy Letters from the Education Secretary and Deputy Secretary." December 16, 2010. https://www2.ed.gov/policy/gen/guid/secletter/101215.html.

———. "Statement by U.S. Secretary of Education Arne Duncan on the Recent Deaths of Two Young Men." October 1, 2010. https://web.archive.org/web/20101003103158/https://www.ed.gov/news/press-releases/statement-us-secretary-education-arne-duncan-recent-deaths-two-young-men.

———. "Student Reports of Bullying: Results From the 2017 School Crime Supplement to the National Crime Victimization Survey." NCES 2019-054, July 2019. https://nces.ed.gov/pubs2019/2019054.pdf.

United States Department of Justice. "Citizen's Guide to U.S. Federal Law on Child Pornography." https://www.justice.gov/criminal-ceos/citizens-guide-us-federal-law-child-pornography.

———. "Statement by Attorney General Jeff Sessions on the Withdrawal of Title IX Guidance." Office of Public Affairs, February 22, 2017. https://www.justice.gov/opa/pr/statement-attorney-general-jeff-sessions-withdrawal-title-ix-guidance.

"Unjust: How the Broken Juvenile and Criminal Justice Systems Fail LGBTQ Youth." Center for American Progress and Movement Advancement Project, August 2016. http://www.lgbtmap.org/policy-and-issue-analysis/criminal-justice-youth.

Valdivia, Angharad N. "This Tween Bridge over My Latina Girl Back: The U.S. Mainstream Negotiates Ethnicity." In *Mediated Girlhoods: New Explorations of Girls' Media Culture,* edited by Mary Celeste Kearney, 93–112. New York: Peter Lang, 2011.

Van Asselt, Bess Collins. "Imagining Otherwise: Transgender and Queer Youth of Color Who Contest Standardized Futures in Secondary Schools." *TSQ: Transgender Studies Quarterly* 6, no. 4 (2019): 608–19.

Van Ouytsel, Joris, Ellen Van Gool, Michel Walrave, Koen Ponnet, and Emilie Peeters. "Sexting: Adolescents' Perceptions of the Applications Used for, Motives for, and Consequences of Sexting." *Journal of Youth Studies* 20, no. 4 (2017): 446–70.

Vandello, Joseph A., and Jennifer K. Bosson. "Hard Won and Easily Lost: A Review and Synthesis of Theory and Research on Precarious Manhood." *Psychology of Men & Masculinity* 14, no. 2 (2013): 101–13.

Vargas, João Costa, and Joy A. James. "Refusing Blackness-as-Victimization: Trayvon Martin and the Black Cyborgs." In *Pursuing Trayvon Martin: Historical Contexts and Contemporary Manifestations of Racial Dynamics,* edited by George Yancy and Janine Jones, 193–204. London: Lexington Books, 2013.

Velasco, Gina K. *Queering the Global Filipina Body: Contested Nationalisms in the Filipina/o Diaspora.* Urbana: University of Illinois Press, 2020.

Vianna, Natasha, and Christine Soyong Harley. "Long Overdue: A Call to Action for Shame-Free Sex Education." *SIECUS: Sex Ed for Social Change.* https://siecus.org/long-overdue-a-call-to-action-for-shame-free-sex-education/.

Vuong, Ocean. "All the Ways to Be with Bryan Washington and Ocean Vuong." *A24* podcast, December 21, 2020. https://a24films.com/notes/2020/12/all-the-ways-to-be-with-bryan-washington-ocean-vuong.

Waidzunas, Tom. "Young, Gay, and Suicidal: Dynamic Nominalism and the Process of Defining a Social Problem with Statistics." *Science, Technology, & Human Values* 37, no. 2 (2012): 199–225.

Walker, Lisa M. "How to Recognize a Lesbian: The Cultural Politics of Looking Like What You Are." *Signs* 18, no. 4 (1993): 866–90.

Wanzer-Serrano, Darrel. "Rhetoric's Rac(e/ist) Problems." *Quarterly Journal of Speech* 105, no. 4 (2019): 465–76.

"The War over Gender." *The Problem with Jon Stewart,* October 6, 2022. https://tv.apple.com/us/episode/the-war-over-gender/umc.cmc.1jj39s607lehulo4koiscsarp.

West, Isaac. "PISSAR's Critically Queer and Disabled Politics." *Communication and Critical/Cultural Studies* 7, no. 2 (2010): 157–75.

West, Isaac, Michaela Frischherz, Allison Panther, and Richard Brophy. "Queer Worldmaking in the 'It Gets Better' Campaign." *QED: A Journal in GLBTQ Worldmaking,* Inaugural Issue (Fall 2013): 49–86.

Whitaker v. Kenosha Unified School District. United States Court of Appeals for the Seventh Circuit, No. 16-3522 (2017).

The White House. "Executive Order on Preventing and Combating Discrimination on the Basis of Gender Identity or Sexual Orientation." January 20, 2021. https://www.whitehouse.gov/briefing-room/presidential-actions/2021/01/20/executive-order-preventing-and-combating-discrimination-on-basis-of-gender-identity-or-sexual-orientation/.

Wilson, Kirt H. "The Contested Space of Prudence in the 1874–1875 Civil Rights Debate." *Quarterly Journal of Speech* 84, no. 2 (1998): 131–49.

Womack, Sarah. "The Generation of 'Damaged' Girls." Telegraph.co.uk, February 21, 2007. https://web.archive.org/web/20070222061306/http://www.telegraph.co.uk/news/main.jhtml?xml=/news/2007/02/20/ngirls20.xml.

Wong, Brittany. "Worried about Grooming? Teaching Kids Comprehensive Sex Ed Could Help." *HuffPost,* July 18, 2022. https://www.huffpost.com/entry/children-groomer-fears-comprehensive-sex-ed_l_62cf1fdce4boeef119c19e88.

Wuest, Jo. "The Scientific Gaze in American Transgender Politics: Contesting the Meanings of Sex, Gender, and Gender Identity in the Bathroom Rights Cases." *Politics & Gender* 15 (2019): 336–60.

Zaborskis, Mary. "Eve Sedgwick's Queer Children." *GLQ* 25, no. 1 (2019): 29–32.

INDEX

abortion, 70, 77

Adams, Andrew, 152

Adkins, Brendan, 34–35

Adolescent Family Life Act (AFLA), 161, 162, 168

Advocates for Youth, 173–74

Affordable Care Act, 162n24

Afrosexology, 178n70

age of consent laws, 37, 38, 54; in Oregon, 37; in Washington, 37

agency: abundance and, 157, 159, 183, 190–92, 197; gendered, 47; instrumentalizing childhood, 17–23; legal rights and, 21; race and, 36, 47, 49–50, 69; and right of dependency, 21–22; sexual, 3, 36, 38, 40, 90–91, 93–94, 132, 173; sexual, female, 35–36, 40, 43, 61, 65, 69, 153–92, 194–95; vulnerability and, 20, 21, 32; youth innovations in, 193–207

Aguilera, Christina, 45

Ahmed, Sara, 16, 80, 187–88

Albury, Kath, 201–2

Alexander, Bryant Keith, 28

Alexander, Elizabeth, 10

"All the Ways" (Vuong), 193

Alliance Defending Freedom, 112

Amar, Paul, 21

American Academy of Pediatrics, 160

American Association of Pediatrics, 1

American Civil Liberties Union (ACLU), 107, 114

American College of Obstetricians and Gynecologists, 160

American Medical Association, 1

American Psychological Association (APA), Task Force on the Sexualization of Girls, 44–45

Amin, Kadji, 120

Annamma, Subini, 57

Anti-Bullying Bill of Rights, 83

Arkansas ban on gender-affirming medical care, 1–3

Asakura, Kenta, 97

Asen, Robert, 25, 109, 117

athletics/school sports, 152

Attwood, Feona, 43

Barbie, 46, 47
Barker, Cody J., 71, 72
Barnard, Ian, 4
bathroom bills, 5, 30–31, 77, 106–53
Benjamin, Harry, 123–24
Bernstein, Robin, 11–12
Bey, Marquis, 134
Beyond Bullying Project, 32, 198–201
Biden, Joseph, 73, 112–13
Billboard Hot Rock Songs chart, 74
Black and Pink, 58
Black Girl's Guide to Surviving Menopause, 178n70
"Black Girls Matter" report, 57
Blackness: adultification of Black boys, 50–51; adultification of Black girls, 36, 48–53; agency of Black girls, 49–50; ambivalent, 9–14; anxiety and Black youth, 10–11; Black masculinity, 50, 51; Black motherhood, 49; caricatures of Black womanhood, 30, 36, 48–53, 56, 145, 148, 162, 169, 180; childhood and, 6, 8–14, 17; and coerced sexual contact, 155; criminalization of Black youth, 10, 36, 51, 53–57, 60–61; deferral of, 109, 143–50; dehumanizing figurations of Black girlhood, 36, 61; disciplining Black youth, 55–57, 59–60; erotics of Black women, 186–87; and excess, 106–53; exclusion of, 34–35, 48–53, 61, 65, 114, 125–26, 156, 197; and female sexuality, 65, 69, 154–59, 162, 190; and feminism, 186–87; gender-nonconforming Black girls, 57–61, 64–65; hypersexualization of Black girls, 30, 36, 48–53, 56, 148, 155, 184; and joy as survival mechanism, 159, 192; materiality of, 17; maternal mortality rate, 155; perpetual presence of, 133–36; queer relations and, 32, 36, 57–61; racial segregation and, 138–41; and safeties of childhood, 18–19, 26; sexting and queer Black girls, 33–66; stereotypes of sexuality, 30, 36, 48–53, 56, 145, 148, 169; and STIs, 155, 164; and suicide attempts, 82; surveilling of Black youth, 56, 59, 61; temporality of, 13, 18–19, 30, 110, 125–26, 148, 149–53; transitivity of, 137, 150; transness and, 133–36, 144–50; ungendering of, 135; violence and, 12–14, 185
Board of Education of the Highland Local School District v. United States Department of Education, 111n15

"Born This Way" (Lady Gaga), 75
Bosson, Jennifer K., 80, 102, 104
Bostock v. Clayton County, 113, 141
Brathwaite, Brittany, 154–56, 164, 173, 176–78, 180, 181 fig. 1, 187
Bratz dolls, 45–48; marketing of, 46–47
"broken windows" policing, 58
Brophy, Richard, 74
Brouwer, Daniel C., 28
brown, adrienne maree, 180
Brown, Antjuanece, 27n76, 30, 69; arrest, 33–34, 62, 63; conviction, 34–35, 38, 54–55, 64–66; conviction consequences, 36, 38, 62–63; gender presentation, 59–60, 65; sexting case, 33–66
Brown, Asher, 71
Brown, Harrison Chase, 72, 79
Bruhm, Steven, 15, 16
Bryan, Audrey, 94–95, 104, 198
Bryant, Anita, 92
Bucholtz, Mary, 78, 80
Bully, 75
bullycide, 75–76
"Bullycide" (Del Tredici), 75
Bullycide: Death at Playtime (Marr and Field), 75
Bullycide in America (Highs), 75
Bullycide Project, The, 75
bullying, 30, 32, 147, 203; of cisgender gay boys, 5, 31, 66–105; defining the problem of, 81–82; effects of, 87–88; federal guidance on, 83–86; policies, 68, 73, 83–86, 101; popularization of federal guidance on, 86–91; prevention programs, 83–87, 95; risk factors, 82, 86–90, 101–3, 127; suicide and, 68, 71–76, 85–86, 101–5; three key characteristics of, 85; verbal, 81
"Bullying Surveillance Among Youth" (CDC/HRSA), 84–87
bullying.gov, 82
Byron, Paul, 201–2

Calafell, Bernadette Marie, 28
California Healthy Youth Act, 162
Callen, Maude, 180
Calvente, Lisa B. Y., 28
Campbell, Scott W., 39

#CancelNetflix, 193
Cárdenas, Micha, 120, 122, 132
Cardi B., 180
Carey, Tamika L., 185
Carter, Julian, 79, 165, 167, 170
Cassils, 108
Castañeda, Claudia, 18, 20, 25
Center for American Progress and the Movement Advancement Project, "Unjust," 57
Center for Disease Control (CDC), 84–85, 94, 102; Youth Risk Behavior Survey, 94, 101–2
César Awards, 193
Chase, Raymond, 71
Chávez, Karma R., 28
Chen, Jian Neo, 120, 122, 132
child beauty pageants, 195
child pornography laws, 34–35, 37, 62; federal, 37; ineffectiveness of, 38; teen sexting and, 40–41, 64; temporality of, 109
Child Trends, 84
child/childhood: as barometers of social unrest, 39; becoming/incompleteness of, 20; Blackness and, 10–11, 18–19, 26, 33–66, 148, 155, 184; controversies in sexuality, 27–32; cultural ideas of, 5, 8; definition, 21; exiled from, 9–14; fantasy of, 7, 22; figure of The Child, 7–8, 22, 26, 204; hetero(non)sexuality of, 15–17, 22–23, 69; infantilization of, 21, 28; lived experiences, 27–28; malleability of, 18–19, 23, 26, 157, 196; mobilization of, 4; normative expectations of, 35, 76, 118, 152; purity/innocence/sanctity of, 4, 6–7, 9–11, 17, 19, 22–23, 29, 36, 45, 196–98; queerness of, 6–9, 14–17, 23, 68, 69, 76, 195–96; racial figurations of, 5, 6–14, 19–20, 22–23, 26, 30, 36, 48, 61, 68–69, 118, 151–52, 157, 159, 190, 196–98, 206; rhetorical figuration of, 3, 5, 9, 22–27, 32, 76, 198; right of dependency, 21–22; safeties of, 18–19, 126–27; sexualization of, 29, 44–45; subhuman, idea of, 12; temporality, 118, 132; vulnerability, 14, 17–23, 36, 47, 61, 198; welfare system, 10; whiteness of figural, 5, 6–9, 12, 14, 23, 152
"child-in-peril" figure, 20
Chow, Rey, 79
chrononormativity, 119–20, 150, 157, 172–73, 198; disruption of, 121, 130–31; reinforcing, 133; temporal containment of, 119; whiteness, 132–33
cisgender privacy, 142, 149, 153
civil rights, 138–44, 149–50
Civil Rights Act of 1866, 141
Civil Rights Act of 1964, 141
Civil War, 141
Clementi, Tyler, 71, 83
Clinton, Bill, 161
Clinton, Hillary, 74
Cohen, Yve Laris, 115
Colebrook, Claire, 134–35
collective imagining, 25
collective symbols, 25
colonialism/colonization, 9, 13, 28, 55, 77, 116, 132–34, 158
Columbine school shooting, 83
Combahee River Collective, 185–86, 188
Cooper, Brittany, 180, 186–87
Cottom, Tressie McMillan, 52
Cover, Rob, 91–92, 94
COVID-19, 67, 71
Cox, Laverne, 108
Cram, Emerson, 18
critical race theory, 4
critical reflexivity, 28
cultural capital of victimhood, 79
cultural responsiveness, 173–74
Cuties, 193–95, 203; critics of, 194–95; queerness of childhood in, 195–96; sexual agency depicted in, 194–96
cyberbullying, 40, 81, 87

Da Costa, Jade Crimson Rose, 119
Daughters of the Diaspora, 175
DeChaine, D. Robert, 24
Decolonizing Contraception, 178n70
Dehnert, Marco, 28
Del Tredici, David, 75
DiAngelo, Robin, 78
Dixon, Travis L., 78
Dobbs decision, 182
Doucouré, Maïmouna, 193–94, 196

drag performances, 114; panics, 19; story hour, 4
Duncan, Arne, 73
Durham, M. Gigi, 43, 47
Dyer, Hannah, 6
Dyer, Richard, 92

Edelman, Lee, 7–8, 14, 26, 204–5
Egan, R. Danielle, 44, 60
Elders, Jocelyn, 180
11th Circuit Court of Appeals, 151–52
Elliott, Sinikka, 126
Ellison, Treva, 135
Endocrine Society, 1
Eng, David, 140
enslavement/slavery, 77; Black youth and, 10–12; chattel slavery, 12; gender-segregated bathrooms and, 133–34; histories of, 141, 156; legacy of, 9, 191–92; slave economy, 52
"Equality House," 108

Facebook, 106
"fag discourse," 102–3
"Family Life Education" programs, 172
Fanon, Franz, 13
Federal Partners in Bullying Prevention Steering Committee, 84, 86
Federal Partners in Bullying Prevention Summit, 84
female sexual desire, 42–43, 53, 65; queer, 59
female sexual expression, 40–43
femmephobia, 102–3
Ferguson, Roderick A., 115
Field, Tim, 75
Fields, Jessica, 95, 199–200
figure of the foreigner, 24
Fine, Michelle, 163, 171, 201
Fischer, Mia, 111
Fitzpatrick, Katie, 202
Flores, Lisa, 26, 206
48 Hours, 75
Fourth Circuit Court of Appeals, 106, 113, 114n29, 150

Frischherz, Michaela, 74

Gainer, Ryan, 51
Galarte, Francisco J., 24
Garmezy, Norman, 96–97
gay-straight alliances (GSAs), 67, 71
gender dysphoria, 2
gender expression: sexual threat of, 109–10, 118–22, 127–29, 132–33, 146, 150–51; white performances of, 133
gender nonconformity, 3, 5, 9, 101, 125, 129–30, 133, 144–51, 157, 200; Black girls and, 57–61, 64–65; disjunct time of, 120, 128; identity construction and, 28–29, 123, 143, 147–50, 152; legislation against, 114; mental health challenges and, 68; policing of, 55; suicide and, 69; survival as endurance and, 204–5; vulnerability and, 67–105
gender passing, 114, 116
gender performativity, 48
gender-affirming care: hormone blockers, 122; restrictions on, 1–3, 152; social and legal benefits of, 2, 152
gender-segregated bathrooms, 106–53; legacy of slavery and, 133–34
Georgetown Law Center, "Girlhood Interrupted," 51
Gilbert, Jen, 95, 199, 200
Gill-Peterson, Jules, 21, 123–24, 132, 153
Gloucester County Public Schools, 123
Gloucester County School Board (GCSB), 31, 107–9, 113, 122, 128, 136, 146, 149, 151; December 2014 meeting, 126, 136, 150; invocation of Blackness at meetings, 110, 133–40, 142; November 2014 meeting, 131, 136, 150; resolution for gender-segregated facilities, 116–18, 123–25, 133, 136, 141–43; Student Advisory Committee, 138
Gloucester High School, 117
GLQ, 6
Goff, Phillip Atiba, 50
Gomez, Logan Rae, 119
Gossett, Che, 133–34
Grammy Awards, 108
Green, Marshall (Kai M.), 135–36, 146
Grimm, David, 131

Grimm, Deidre, 131
Grimm, Gavin, 31, 106–44; "aging up," 130–32; gender presentation and identity, 115–16, 122, 124–25, 128, 130–33, 144–46, 149; lawsuit, 143, 146, 150; misgendering, 124–25, 131; parents, 117; restroom options, 107, 115, 125, 151; rights, 118, 137–38, 140–42, 151
Grimm v. Gloucester County School Board, 106, 150–51
"groomers," 19, 92, 164
Guerrero, Lisa, 46
Gumbs, Alexis Pauline, 189, 192
Gun Free Schools Act (GFSA), 56
Gutierrez-Maldonado, Ricky, 15, 110, 145–49

Hains, Rebecca C., 46
Halberstam, Jack, 120
Hall, Ashley R., 185
Haritaworn, Jim, 116, 146
Harris, Eric, 83
Hartman, Saidiya, 11
Hasinoff, Amy Adele, 35, 40, 41–43
hate crimes, 148
Health Resources and Services Administration (HRSA), 84
Heart, 175
Hector, Alley, 34
Henning, Kristen, 10, 53
Hensley, Kim, 142–43
Hesford, Wendy S., 20, 120
Hesse, Monica, 195
Hester, Scarlett L., 157
Highs, Brenda, 75
Hill Collins, Patricia, 185, 189
Hinduja, Sameer, 64
HIV/AIDS, 154–55, 174, 177, 204; prevention programs, 172
Holling, Michelle, 77
homophobia, 34, 68, 69–71, 76, 89–90, 95, 204; bullying and, 102–3
Honig, Bonnie, 24
Hook, Carla, 127–28, 142
hooks, bell, 184–85

Horak, Laura, 120, 121
hormone time, 121
Houdek, Matthew, 119, 185
House Bill 2, 112
Hsu, V. Jo, 111–12, 158–59, 192
Huggins, Kimberly, 154, 156, 164, 173, 176–78, 181, 181 fig. 1, 187; death of uncle, 154–55
Humbach, John, 38
Hurley, Natasha, 15–16

IFundWomen, 176
immigration discourse, 24
InStyle, 108
It Gets Better Project, 68, 73–74, 199

Jackson, Aaron, 108
Jarratt, Susan, 4
Jaworski, Katrina, 103–4
Jenkins, Jolene, 30, 33, 69; gender presentations, 59; mother, 33–34, 42; sexting case, 33–66
Jensen, Robin E., 165–66
Johnson, Amber L., 133
Johnson, E. Patrick, 28, 176
Johnson, Marsha P., 180
Johnson, Paul, 80
Jones, Nikki, 49
Jordan, June, 185

Kanjere, Anastasia, 78
Karaian, Lara, 42
Keeling, Kara, 204
Kelly, Casey Ryan, 80, 168
Kendall, Kate, 35, 62
Kilbourne, Jean, 43, 45
KIMBRITIVE, 27n76, 31, 156, 165, 181 fig. 1, 201; affirming abundance, 183, 185, 190–92, 197; Black feminist love-politics, 32, 157–58, 177, 184–91, 197, 198; breast/chest self-exam infographic, 182–83, 183 fig. 2, 183 fig. 3; child-rearing practices and, 188–90; goals, 177, 178; guide to contraception, 182; Instagram feed, 180; reproductive justice, 156–57, 160, 182–83; self-care practices, 179–80, 182–83, 187–

88; sexual wellness platform, 156–58, 160, 173–90, 192, 197; sexuality education for youth, 178–79; slogan, 181–82; talk backs, 32, 156, 160, 184–90; website, 179–80; workshops, 179–80, 182; "Your Sexual Wellness Regimen," 179–80

King, Larry/Latisha, 29, 110–11, 144–51; Black femininity of, 147–49; bullying, 147; gender presentation, 144, 147–49; murder, 146–48; temporality of, 146–48, 151; "too muchness," 116, 144–50, 152

Klebold, Dylan, 83

Koivunen, Anu, 206

Krutzsch, Brett, 74

Kyrölä, Katarlina, 206

Lady Gaga, 75

Lakshmin, Pooja, 187

Lamda Legal, 152

LeMaster, Lore/tta, 28, 133

Lesko, Nancy, 95, 199, 200

Levin, Diane E., 43, 45

Levine, Judith, 164

Lewis and Clark College, 35

LGBTQ+ youth, criminalization of, 57–61

Lippman, Julia R., 39

Lolita Effect (Durham), 43

Lorde, Audre, 10, 180, 185–87

Lucas, Billy, 72, 79

Maher, Michelle, 35, 61–63

Mainstreaming Sex (Attwood), 43

"Make It Stop (September's Children)" (Rise Against), 74–75

Malatino, Hill, 121

Mamo, Laura, 95, 199–200

Marr, Neil, 75

Marshall, Daniel, 92

Martin, Tayvon, 51

Martyr-Target-Victim model, 93

Mason, Carol, 77

McClelland, Sara I., 163, 201

McGlashan, Hayley, 202

McIlrath, Tim, 74

McInerney, Brandon, 144, 147–49

media: influence on girls, 45, 52; panics, 39, 40, 44, 63; racial bias in, 78; suicides in, 72, 92, 100–105; trans people in, 108, 144, 146

Megan Thee Stallion, 180

Meiners, Erica R., 27

#MeToo, 77

Mignonnes, 193

Miller, Terry, 73–74

Mitchell, Mary Niall, 12, 51

Mittelman, Joel, 59

Mock, Janet, 108, 114

Mogul, Joey L., 55

Moon, Dreama, 77

Moran, Jeffrey, 170

Morgan, Joan, 185

Morris, Monique, 50, 52, 55–56, 59

Motion Picture Association of America (MPAA), 75

MTV Video Music Awards, 75

Muñoz, José Esteban, 8, 17, 118, 203

Nash, Jennifer C., 157, 185

National Campaign to Prevent Teen and Unplanned Pregnancy, "Sex and Tech" survey, 39–40

National Center for Lesbian Rights, 35, 62

Netflix, 193–95; cancellations, 193–94

neurasthenia, 79

New York Times, 56; "Suicides Put Light on Pressures of Gay Teenagers," 71

Newsweek, 144

Nolt, Caleb, 72

Nyong'o, Tavia, 8

Obama, Barack, 73, 112–13, 162n24

Office of Civil Rights (OCR), 112–13, 143; Data Collection, 57

Office of Human Research Protections (OHRP), 27n76

Oliviero, Katie, 22, 70, 104

ordinary democracy, 109, 117

Ore, Ersula, 61, 119, 185

Orr, Lisa, 47
"othermothering," 189

Panther, Allison, 74
Parks, Rosa, 114, 136, 143–44, 150
Pascoe, C. J., 102–3
Patchin, Justin W., 64
Patterson, GPat, 111n1
Paul, Pamela, 43
Pearce, Ruth, 121
People in Search of Safe and Accessible Restrooms (PISSAR), 129–30
Perry, Brea L., 59
Personal Responsibility and Work Opportunity Act, 161
Personal Responsibility Education Program (PREP), 162
PISSED (Cassils), 108
police brutality, 61
Pornified (Paul), 43
Pough, Gwendolyn, 185
Powers, Leigh, 72
privilege: class, 8–9; gender, 80, 146; race, 8–9, 19, 26, 61, 70, 111–17, 143, 146, 198; and racial figurations of masculine vulnerability, 77–81, 102
Problem with Jon Stewart, The, 1–2, 4
Pryor, Jaclyn I., 119
Pushout (Morris), 55

QAnon, 194
Queer Endeavor, A, 175
queer time, 120
Queer Youth Suicide, Culture and Identity (Cover), 91
queer/queerness: advocacy symbols, 114; ambivalence toward, 204; bullying, 5, 31, 66–105; childhood and, 14–17, 19, 23; color and, 7–8, 29, 30, 48, 50, 56–61, 110, 144; community building, 74; criminalization of queer youth of color, 53–61; desire and, 35, 59; destruction of social order, 7; developmental narrative of, 22; as form of unintelligibility, 15; "gender ideology," 63; incarceration of, 36, 57–61; inequalities for, 34; lived experiences, 27; materiality of, 17; mental health challenges, 68; "one-dimensional," 115–16; politics, 115–16; racial figuration of, 68–69, 91–92, 103, 143; "real strategic value" of, 7; resilience model, 91, 96–100, 105; rhetorical figurations of, 23, 76; rights, 140; risk as resource, 198–203; risk-based/deficit models of, 95–98; safeties of childhood, 18–19; scapegoating of racialized, 36, 48, 61, 65; scholarly narratives of, 91–96; sexting panic, 61–66, 202; sexual awareness of, 53; stereotypes, 92–96; strength-based perspective of, 97; suicide, 69, 66–105, 203; survival as endurance, 204–5; temporality of, 18–19, 120; too muchness, 15–16, 31, 60, 110; troublemakers, 27–32, 36; vulnerability, 67–105; white masculinity and, 101–5, 143
qPDX.com, 34

racial capitalism, 135
racial hierarchy, 13
racial segregation, 138–41, 152
racism, 68; archetypes of, 49; cultural discourses of, 35; education on systemic, 4; systemic, 25
Ransby, Barbara, 186
Rattan, Aneeta, 50
Real Education and Access for Healthy Youth Act (REAHYA), 174–75
Reed, Alison, 139, 143, 145
reproductive futurism, 7, 204; definition, 7; white, 8
Reproductive Justice Initiative, 178n70
resilience, 91, 96–100, 105; neoliberal foundations of, 98; as psychological trait, 96–97; script, 99; strategies, 98–99
"Respect Yourself" campaign, 42
RespectAbility, 175
rhetorical figurations: of childhood, 3, 5, 9, 22, 23–27, 32, 76, 198; definition, 25–26; of gay youth, 23, 76; process of, 25; purpose of, 25; racial, 5, 6–14, 19–20, 22–23, 26, 30
Rice, Tamir, 51
Richardson, Matt, 136
Rigney, Lester-Irabinna, 8
Rise Against, 74–75
Ritchie, Andrea J., 54, 58

238 • INDEX

Roberts, Dorothy, 10, 49
Robinson, Brandon Andrew, 97, 100
Rodríguez, Juana María, 6
Roe v. Wade, 155
Rofes, Eric, 93–94
Rollo, Toby, 12–13
Rutledge, Leslie, 1–4, 21
Ryberg, Ingrid, 206

Sacco, Felix, 72
Salamon, Gayle, 126, 147–48
Salas-SantaCruz, Omi, 134
Salazar, Philippe-Joseph, 24
same-sex marriage, 70
San Francisco Pride Parade, 108
Sánchez-Eppler, Karen, 20–22
Sanger, Margaret, 170–71
Santelli, John S., 163
Savage, Dan, 73–74
Save Our Children campaign, 92
#SaveTheChildren, 194
Savin-Williams, Ritch, 93
schizophrenia, 96–97
Schmitz, Rachel M., 97, 100
school-to-prison pipeline, 55, 84
Sedgwick, Eve Kosofsky, 6, 91, 158, 203–4
self-care, 184–91; "faux," 187; political force of, 187–88
sex education, 4–5, 30, 145, 153–92; abstinence-only, 156, 158–65, 168, 172, 174; American, 156, 158, 160, 164, 172; Black girls and, 155–59, 172, 190, 198; cis- and heteronormativity, 153, 156, 158–61, 164–65, 169, 172, 174, 181, 184, 191; comprehensive approach to, 160–62, 171, 174, 184; consent and, 154–55, 164, 191; contraception and, 160–62, 171; controversies, 161; decision-making, 154; disability inclusive, 174–75; discourse of desire in, 171, 173; eugenicist goal of, 167–68, 171; female sexuality as vulnerability in, 171–73, 190; gender roles according to, 169–70; language used in, 165–66; LGBTQ+-inclusive, 174; in military, 166, 169; mission of, 158; pleasure and, 154, 157, 159, 165, 168, 171–73, 180–81, 184–90; public school, 164; purpose of, 159, 190; racist discourses in, 157, 159–60, 169–70, 180; relationality, 184–90; religion and, 160–61, 164; reticence of sexual expression and, 165–66, 181; self-care, 184–90; sex-negativity in, 153, 158, 164, 180–81, 190; STIs and, 155, 163, 173, 191; teen pregnancy and, 155, 163, 173–74, 191; venereal contagion model of, 166, 169–70; white supremacy in, 153, 156–59, 161, 164–69, 184, 184, 190–91, 197; zoological model of, 166–67, 170
Sex S.Y.M.B.A.L.S. (Sexually conscious, Youthful, Mature, Black And Latino Students), 177
sexting, 30, 129; benefits, 64; campaigns against, 42–43; child pornography and, 34; criminalization of black girls over, 33–66; definition, 40; gendered contours of, 35–36, 41–42; media and, 39–40, 63; nonconsensual, 63–64; panic, 5, 33–66, 172, 202; prevalence of teen, 40; public conversation about, 39; queering, 61–66; racial figuration of, 35–36, 40, 48; racialized contours of, 37–43, 47; rhetorical effects of, 38–39; as sexual expression, 40–43
Sexuality Information and Education Council of the United States (SIECUS), 160, 161, 174
sexualization: of culture, 36, 43–48, 52; discourse of, 44, 47–48; racialized, 45–47
Shange, Ntozake, 185
Sharpe, Christina, 191–92
Shepard, Matthew, 114
Singh, Anneliese A., 98–99
Slovic, Beth, 34, 59
Snorton, C. Riley, 116, 134–36, 146, 150
So Sexy So Soon (Levin and Kilbourne), 43
Somerville, Siobhan B., 139
Southern Democrats, 141
Southern Policy Law Center, 112
Spears, Britney, 45
Spencer, Leland G., 1n1
Spillers, Hortense, 11
Squires, Catherine R., 157
#StandWithGavin, 108
Stewart, Jon, 1–2, 4

Stockton, Kathryn Bond, 8, 15, 132

stopbullying.gov, 86–90

"straight time," 118

Students v. United States Department of Education, 111n15

suicide(s), 32, 203; attempted, 103–4; bullying and, 85–86, 101–5; of cisgender gay boys, 5, 31, 66–105; consensus, 95; gender and, 103–4; interventions, 69; media coverage of, 75–76; of nonbinary youth, 67, 69; normalizing, 85–86; popular culture response to, 74–76; prevention programs, 67, 95; risk factors for, 82, 89–91, 93–96, 101–5; September 2010, 71–76, 83, 91, 100, 105; of transgender youth, 67, 69

Suicide Prevention Resource Center, Information Center, 72

Sundance Film Festival, 193

Syracuse University, 177; Institutional Review Board, 27n76

Talburt, Susan, 22

Teen Pregnancy Prevention Program (TPPP), 162

Temkin, Deborah, 84

temporality: acceleration, 122, 125–33; self-naturalizing, 118; time of anticipation, 121; trans time versus cis time, 122

Tendencies (Sedgwick), 91

Time, 108, 111

Title V Abstinence Only Until Marriage (AOUM) Program, 161–63, 174

Title VII, 113

Title IX, 83–84, 106–7, 112–13, 143

Toddlers & Tiaras, 195

Tracy, Karen, 109, 117

transgender/trans youth, 9, 17, 21; agency of, 132, 197; analytic, 135–36; anti-trans legislation and, 114; bans on gender-affirming care and, 1–3; bullying of, 81–82; of color, 3, 7–8, 24, 27, 98–99, 110–11, 136, 144–51; community understanding of, 117–18; figuration of, 109; genealogy of, 135, 144; identity as threat, 109–10, 118–22, 127–29, 132–33, 146, 150–51; identity construction and, 28–29, 31, 123–24, 132, 143; materiality of, 17, 136; media visibility of, 108; mental health challenges of, 68; racialization of, 31, 109, 133–45, 149–51;

resilience strategies, 98–99; rights, 111–17, 135–44, 151, 197, 203; suicide, 67, 69; survival as endurance, 204–5; temporal acceleration and, 125–33, 146–48; temporality, 106–53, 197; too muchness, 15–16, 31, 60, 106–53

transitivity, 134–35, 137

transmisogyny, 145–46

transphobic panics, 68, 129

Trayvon Generation, 10, 11

Trevor Project, 67, 102; National Survey on LGBTQ+ Youth Mental Health, 81–82

Triple Cripples, The, 178n70

Tristano, Michael, Jr., 158, 192

"troublemakers," 16–17; queer, 27–32, 36

Trump, Donald, 80, 112–13

Tuck, Eve, 158

Twitter, 193

UNICEF USA, 67

"Unlawful Justice," 61–62

US Constitution, Fourteenth Amendment, 107

US Department of Education, 56, 73, 83–84, 112, 143

US Department of Health and Human Services, 86, 91

US Department of Justice, 83

US Supreme Court, 113–14, 116, 141, 145, 150–52, 155

Valdivia, Angharad N., 46

Van Asselt, Bess Collins, 132

Vandello, Joseph A., 80, 102, 104

virginity pledges, 163, 164

vulnerability, 3; adult investment in childhood, 22; agency and, 20, 21, 32, 39; assumed, 97; conferring, 70, 81; corporeal, 70; exclusion from, 34–35, 48–53, 61, 65, 114, 125–26, 156, 197; manipulation of, 77; masculine, 69, 76–81, 100–105, 110, 126–27, 148–49; material, 156, 190–91; naturalizing, 22, 94; queer, 67–105; racialization of, 14, 30, 36, 39, 43–48, 61, 65, 68–69, 76–81, 91–92, 100; rhetorical ascription of, 155, 190; universal, 206; white fragility and, 78–80, 93,

100–105, 110, 148–49; white women and, 77–78, 171–73, 190; youth innovations in, 193–207

Vuong, Ocean, 193, 207

Waidzunas, Tom, 76, 96

"wake work," 191–92

Walker, Alice, 185

Walsh, Seth, 71

"WAP" (Cardi B. and Megan Thee Stallion), 180

Washington Post, 195

West, Isaac, 74

Westboro Baptist Church, 108

Whitaker v. Kenosha Unified School District, 111n15

white restorative agenda, 96–100

white supremacy, 49, 53, 55, 61, 77–78, 119, 132, 148, 153, 158, 197, 205; childhood and, 9, 14; religion and, 167; self-discipline of, 165–68; sex education and, 153, 156–59, 161, 164–69, 184, 190–91, 197; white family and, 164–69

Willamette Week, 34, 59, 63

Willard, Frances, 167, 171

Wilson, Kirt H., 141

WitnessLA, 71

Women's Christian Temperance Union (WCTU) White Cross Campaign, 167

World War I, 166, 169

Youssouf, Fathia, 193

YouTube, 62, 73

Zaborskis, Mary, 6

www.ingramcontent.com/pod-product-compliance
Lightning Source LLC
Chambersburg PA
CBHW020649230426
43665CB00008B/360